Transforming the Internal World and Attachment

Transforming the Internal World and Attachment

Volume II: Clinical Applications

Geoff Goodman

JASON ARONSON
Lanham • Boulder • New York • Toronto • Plymouth, UK

Published by Jason Aronson
An imprint of Rowman & Littlefield Publishers, Inc.
A wholly owned subsidiary of The Rowman & Littlefield Publishing Group, Inc.
4501 Forbes Boulevard, Suite 200, Lanham, Maryland 20706
http://www.rowmanlittlefield.com

Estover Road, Plymouth PL6 7PY, United Kingdom

British Library Cataloguing in Publication Information Available

Library of Congress Cataloging-in-Publication Data

Goodman, Geoff.
Transforming the internal world and attachment / Geoff Goodman.
p. cm.
Includes bibliographical references and index.
ISBN 978-0-7657-0709-3 (cloth : alk. paper) — ISBN 978-0-7657-0711-6 (electronic)
1. Psychotherapy. 2. Attachment behavior. I. Title.
RC480.G659 2010
616.89'14—dc22 2009034588

∞™ The paper used in this publication meets the minimum requirements of American National Standard for Information Sciences—Permanence of Paper for Printed Library Materials, ANSI/NISO Z39.48-1992.

Printed in the United States of America

In memory of
George David Goodman
1928–1991
My pursuit of self-discovery in psychoanalysis has always been a simultaneous pursuit to discover you in me

Contents

Figures and Tables

FIGURES

TABLES

Acknowledgments

No one ever told me the second book would be immeasurably harder to write. I never imagined that the entire process would actually yield three books (see also Goodman, *Therapeutic Attachment Relationships*). That was not my intention. Part of the difficulty had to do with the fact that I chose a topic that fell just outside my zone of proximal development. I have established a career writing about the intergenerational transmission and development of psychopathology from an attachment perspective, so turning my attention to the implications of attachment theory for psychotherapy process proved challenging. I overcompensated for my lack of expertise by reading everything I could on the subject matter, reflecting on this accumulated body of knowledge, and writing about it from an outsider's point of view. What helped me most was the treatment of two adult control cases to fulfill the training requirement for my psychoanalytic certificate. I have received outstanding supervision on these two cases from three persons—Phyllis Sloate, John Rosegrant, and William Greenstadt. The learning curve was steep, and the lessons I learned at their feet will stay with me for a lifetime.

The other part of the difficulty had to do with all the other things simultaneously going on in my life: preparing to graduate from my psychoanalytic training program, applying for grants from the International Psychoanalytical Association and the American Psychoanalytic Association, applying for board certification from the American Board of Professional Psychology (ABPP), preparing from scratch a new doctoral-level course on object relations theories, leaving my group practice to fly solo, and planning my wedding. I have two pieces of advice to those of you planning to write a book: (1) be sure you have time to write it, and (2) be sure to check the word count in your book contract *before* you start writing.

I need to make several additional general acknowledgments related to the realization of this book. Valeda Dent, associate university librarian for research and instructional services at Rutgers University, reproduced in Microsoft Word and PowerPoint all the tables and figures presented in this book (unless otherwise noted); read the entire manuscript for comprehension as well as grammar, spelling, and punctuation; located and obtained reference materials; and obtained the copyright for the painting she selected for the book cover (which she also designed). Other than me, no one was more dedicated to the realization of this book than she was. Valeda's fingerprints are all over this document. Now we can turn our attention to writing our wedding vows! I hope that process will not take quite as long. Marcia Miller, chief librarian at Weill Cornell Medical College, is simply the best librarian in psychiatry and psychology I have ever worked with. Long ago, I lost count of how many times Marcia went out of her way to locate a reference, suggest other references that she thought might be helpful to me, or simply show an interest in what I was writing about. I wish all of you had a librarian of this caliber at your disposal, because you would understand the depth of my gratitude if you did. Dustin Kahoud, my faithful research assistant, alphabetized the entire reference section, a massive undertaking that he accomplished with a smile. Ian Rugg undertook the arduous task of creating two separate reference sections for volumes I and II and checking the text citations against the reference sections. Sushma Meka alphabetized all the journal articles and book chapters I cited and neatly placed them into folders. The Psychodynamic Research Listserve cofounded by Mark Hilsenroth and Andrew Gerber has educated me about many of the issues tackled in this book. I thank Mark and Andrew for inviting me to join. Darryl Voorhees produced the high-resolution digital image of the painting for the book cover. Cristin O'Keefe Aptowicz of the Artists Rights Society assisted with the use of copyrighted art. Julie Kirsch and Jessica Bradfield provided steady editorial leadership at Jason Aronson. Patricia Stevenson, production editor, does Jason Aronson proud with her meticulous work, which makes me sound almost like a professional writer. Leonard Rosenbaum, who also worked with me on my first book in 2002, provided the skill and precision necessary to compile the author and subject indexes.

I will acknowledge the other persons to whom I am indebted chapter by chapter. For chapters 2 and 3, I want to thank Sharon Clark (my transcriber), the anonymous interviewer, and the anonymous researcher who coded my Adult Attachment Interview (AAI). Mary Main personally trained this researcher to reliability on AAI classification. The two patients presented in chapters 2 and 3 deserve my deepest appreciation for everything they have taught me about psychotherapy process and about myself. Other patients mentioned in other chapters also served as incidental clinical illustrations for which I am grateful. The late Kurt Cobain's lyrics inspired the title of chapter 4. I want to thank Cheryl Goldberg-Berkowitz and several anonymous reviewers for comments on a previous version of chapter 4. I also want to thank Tom Lopez for the outstanding supervision I received on my child control case. For chapter 5, my supervisees and all the students in my doctoral course were generous to me in their completion of many Q-sorts. I also acknowledge Tai Katzenstein's meticulous comments on a previous version of chapter 5. Stuart Ablon and Celeste Schneider graciously shared with me their Psychotherapy Process Q-Set (PQS) and Child Psychotherapy Process Q-Set (CPQ) prototype data, respectively. For chapter 6, I want to express appreciation to my group coleader, Amy Manierre, M.Div., to the nursing staff of Otto Kernberg's inpatient unit, and to the group participants who graciously shared their beliefs and feelings. Neil Madero and Dolores Burns graciously assisted with the preparation of the patient illustrations, figure 6.1 and figure 6.2. Clovia Ng (www.cngraphics.com), a talented graphic designer, reproduced figure 7.1 in Adobe Illustrator. For chapter 8, I want to thank the staff at Doctors of the World (www.dowusa.org) for giving me the opportunity to volunteer on behalf of their clients seeking political asylum. I participated in specialized training provided by Doctors of the World in the assessment of psychological sequelae of torture.

On a personal note, I wish to thank Marshall Silverstein, my esteemed colleague and friend at Long Island University, for offering constant encouragement and support in all my academic endeavors. Marshall is a true friend. Celeste Schneider has recently become a collaborator on various research projects. I am grateful to have her in my corner as an astute researcher, therapist, and friend. Dr. Marvin Markowitz, my psychoanalyst for the past thirteen years, has helped me to transform my own internal world and attachment. A simple "thank you" is not enough for showing me how to carry my emotional burden. My dear Uncle Ed and Aunt Fran urged me to include them in my acknowledgments, and why not? Throughout the entire process, they supported me with regular e-mail messages asking me about the book's progress. Finally, I want to acknowledge my mother, Carol Steele Goodman, and my late father, George David Goodman, for making me who I am. Everything begins and ends with them.

Chapter One

Introduction

> Come to me, all you who are weary and burdened, and I will give you rest.
>
> Matthew 11:28

> Carry each other's burdens.
>
> Galatians 6:2

The year was 1987, and I was a twenty-six-year-old doctoral student at Northwestern University. I wanted to find out for myself what psychoanalysis was all about. I had read about it and studied it in school, and found it gently pulling me toward it, like the moon's gravitational pull on the ocean tides. I had heard that psychoanalytic institutes offered low-fee psychoanalysis to persons who agreed to work with their candidates, and thought this might be the most economical way of experiencing psychoanalysis for myself.

I contacted an institute near my university dormitory on Chicago's North Lake Shore Drive and scheduled an appointment with one of their candidates. I have no memory of this call. I do remember the initial appointment. The analyst's office was located in a red brick office building just a couple of blocks away. I took the elevator to the office and took a seat in the waiting area. A short, slender, white-haired, middle-aged woman with an accent I could not place opened the office door at the appointed time. I tentatively walked into her office as she motioned that I take a seat on the black leather couch. She sat down in a chair across from where I was seated and asked me why I was coming for treatment. I explained that I was a doctoral student in clinical psychology and had an interest in learning more about psychoanalysis. I then launched into some pervasive family problems that were making me feel depressed at the time. The analyst listened intently as I shared with this stranger some hidden details of my life—details I had never shared with anyone else before. I began to share with her some childhood experiences that bore directly on the family problems and noticed that the theme of feeling depressed kept emerging in my narrative.

At some point, the analyst stopped me and asked, "Are you in pain?" No one had ever asked me that question before. I thought, what a strange yet compassionate question to ask! This person actually cared about whether I was in pain. I had never thought that I was in pain—only that I felt sad about some things in my life that I had always kept to myself. That question has haunted me ever since. It has helped me to frame what it is that patients come to see me for: relief from pain. Of course, patients come to see me for many reasons, but I believe that this is the chief reason. Why else would people spend all that time and money and risk the shame of exposure to talk to someone they have never met?

Thus began my first four-times-per-week psychoanalysis, my experiential introduction to the world of Freud. More important, though, it was my experiential introduction to the world of caring—the experience of someone listening to my emotional burdens and, during a forty-five-minute session, taking them on herself. For me, psychotherapy is the daily carrying of another person's burdens. Only when the person is ready to carry his or her own load do we give them back. This idea about psychotherapy resonates with the work of Bion (1962, 1967), who compared the therapist to a temporary container of the patient's unbearable emotional states. The therapist is responsible for detoxifying these states—making them easier to carry—and then returning them to the patient, who is now ready to carry them with the help of loved ones in his or her daily life. This is how the therapist transforms the internal world and attachment.

The idea to write this book series coalesced in 2005. I had been invited to contribute a chapter to an edited book on attachment interventions for children. Simultaneously, a colleague of mine invited me to consult with her on an early intervention project in which she was giving videotaped feedback to biological mothers of children in foster care. In June of 2005, I attended a presentation by Tai Katzenstein (2005) at the ninety-fourth annual meeting of the American Psychoanalytic Association in Seattle titled, "Validating Change: Empirical Methods and Clinical Work." Tai presented her work with Stuart Ablon at Harvard Medial School. She had used the Psychotherapy Process Q-Set (PQS; Jones, 2000) to examine therapist adherence to cognitive-behavioral, interpersonal, and psychodynamic process in seventeen treatments of patients diagnosed with panic disorder. She found that cognitive-behavioral process was most characteristic of these treatments, but psychodynamic and interpersonal process was significantly correlated with outcome.

The PQS grabbed hold of my fascination. I had been aware of Q-sort methodology since the publication of Waters and Deane's (1985) attachment Q-set. I loved its idiographic properties—the fact that Q-sort methodology could yield a profile of a single person independent of normative data. It seemed ideally suited for characterizing the uniqueness of the therapeutic relationship. I had also had my own personal experience with Q-sort methodology, having developed my own Q-sort to measure the quality of the caregiver's mental representations of his or her child (Goodman, 2005a). Thus, I was familiar with this clever methodology and wanted to learn more about how Enrico Jones had applied it to the assessment of psychotherapy process.

The fact that I had just begun work in the fall of 2004 on two control cases to fulfill the training requirement for my psychoanalytic certificate also stimulated my interest in psychotherapy process. Both patients fell in the spectrum of borderline psychopathology but had different personality features. I chose two supervisors who advocated different approaches to these patients' treatment but who both helped me navigate an effective psychoanalytic process with both patients (see chapters 2 and 3). All these experiences coalesced into a decision to write about psychotherapy from the perspective of someone who has spent his entire professional career writing about the intergenerational transmission and development of psychopathology from an attachment perspective. Initially, I questioned mounting such an ambitious project because psychotherapy process and outcome research represented a shift away from the familiar area of psychopathology, my comfort zone. Did I want to risk writing a book series outside this comfort zone? When I stopped to think about it, however, I realized that I had entered the field of clinical psychology to help people. I studied psychopathology so that others could use this knowledge to help people. Thus, it made sense to apply my knowledge of psychopathology to psychotherapy.

This two-volume book, therefore, is a sequel to my first book, *The Internal World and Attachment.* Unfortunately, so little actual research has been conducted on psychotherapy process and outcome from an attachment perspective that this sparse literature has left me to speculate about what the application of attachment theory to psychotherapy research would look like. The theoretical treatise published several years ago by Peter Fonagy and his colleagues (Fonagy, Gergely, Jurist, and Target, 2002) represents a giant leap in this direction because it laid the foundation for a psychotherapeutic approach to psychopathology grounded in contemporary attachment research. Bateman and Fonagy's (2004) treatment manual explicating an attachment-informed psychotherapy for patients diagnosed with borderline personality disorder represents one application of this theoretical work. Yet we still know so little about the mysteries of the consulting room.

In this two-volume work I offer some tentative ideas about these mysteries. Specifically, I review and discuss three theories about what makes psychotherapy effective across forms of treatment, treatment settings, and diagnostic categories: mindfulness, mentalization, and psychological mindedness. In a third book, *Therapeutic Attachment Relationships: Interaction Structures and the Processes of Therapeutic Change* (Goodman, in press), I review and discuss a fourth theory—the therapeutic attachment relationship.

In volume I of this two-volume work (*Transforming the Internal World and Attachment: Theoretical and Empirical Perspectives*), I offer some provisional hypotheses about therapeutic effectiveness and suggest some ways of testing these hypotheses empirically. In advocating an empirical approach to understanding the mysteries of psychotherapy, I share Seligman's (1991) concern that "the quantification of complex theoretical systems [in empirical research] here threatens to confine a critical topic that has emerged from a very rich clinical and theoretical soil to a relatively narrow arena" (p. 128). I believe, however, that this empirical work is a risk worth taking. With sophisticated assessment instruments such as the PQS that measures psychotherapy process, the Social Cognition and Object Relations Scale–Global (SCORS-G; Westen, 1995) that measures quality of object relations, the Adult Attachment Interview (AAI; George, Kaplan, and Main, 1996) that measures attachment organization, and the Reflective Functioning Scale (RFS; Fonagy, Target, Steele, and Steele, 1998) that measures reflective functioning, researchers can approach psychotherapy process and outcome research with a level of complexity and nuance not available to psychotherapy researchers of previous generations.

Without this research, the entire field of psychotherapy is in crisis. Managed-care companies are withholding reimbursements for treatments not considered "empirically supported." From 1995 to 2005, psychiatric hospital referrals to outpatient treatment after discharge dropped from 90 percent to 80 percent. In that same period, referrals from primary care physicians to psychotherapy dropped between 40 percent and 50 percent as physicians increasingly prefer the putative benefits of psychopharmacotherapy. This diminishing demand for the services of mental health professionals has produced a 15 percent decrease in reimbursement fees from managed-care companies and the federal government, while inflation has exceeded 15 percent in the same period (Cummings, 2008). Those of us who care about the survival of all forms of psychotherapy, and particularly those treatments with a smaller evidence base such as psychodynamic therapy, need to support efforts to test the therapeutic effectiveness of these treatments. Otherwise, to paraphrase Rosenzweig (1936), we might all go the way of the dodo bird, even as we fight among ourselves about which form of treatment is superior. It reminds me of the black-on-black violence of apartheid-era South Africa: we end up displacing our frustrations onto each other as the pharmaceutical companies and managed-care companies laugh all the way to the bank.

Instead of engaging in horse races with randomized controlled trials (RCTs), we need to establish an empirical basis for the therapeutic effectiveness of all forms of treatment. I am suggesting moving beyond examining common factors such as the therapeutic alliance (Wampold, 2001) and turning our collective attention to common factors that psychotherapy researchers often erroneously promote as specific factors. Perhaps these so-called specific factors produce therapeutic change regardless of the brand-name treatment packages through which they are typically delivered. These specific factors might also work better for particular groups of patients with specific problem areas such as affect dysregulation and impulsivity. Clinical practice guidelines need to promote empirically informed change processes rather than horse-race winning treatment packages. If we as a community of therapists want our craft to survive, we must submit it to empirical scrutiny before the pharmaceutical drug lords strip it away from us.

Volume I is divided into two broad sections. In part I, "Processes of Therapeutic Change in the Context of Psychoanalytic and Attachment Theories," I discuss the need to turn away from brand-name treatments and a treatment outcome mentality and turn our collective attention instead to the processes of therapeutic change that promote both symptomatic and structural change. In part II, "Specific Factors Related to Common Processes of Therapeutic Change," I discuss three specific factors that might be effective across forms of treatment: mindfulness, mentalization, and psychological mindedness. I consider part II to contain the central message of volume I: to direct the reader to the effective ingredients in therapeutic processes rather than to treatment outcomes such as symptom reduction, which often proves fleeting in follow-up studies (Westen, Novotny, and Thompson-Brenner, 2004).

In volume II (*Transforming the Internal World and Attachment: Clinical Applications*), I discuss the application of processes of therapeutic change from both psychodynamic and attachment perspectives. I close volume II with a most unusual application of therapeutic processes to four clinical interviews I conducted with two political refugees.

I will now provide an overview of the chapters contained in volume II. In chapters 2 and 3, I discuss the psychotherapy process of two control cases from my psychoanalytic training. Conceptualized by attachment research (Fonagy et al., 1996) as the casualties of preoccupied attachment relationships, these two patients who occupy the spectrum of borderline psychopathology serve as the canvass on which I illustrate psychotherapy process informed by my understanding of two-person psychoanalytic and attachment theories. I have seen both patients in four-times-per-week psychoanalysis. Structurally, I diagnosed both patients with borderline personality organization (Kernberg, 1986a) because both of them experienced identity diffusion manifested in split-off self- and object representations, poor anxiety tolerance, shifts toward primary-process thinking, and inconsistently available sublimatory channels. I diagnosed one patient with borderline personality disorder (BPD), the other with narcissistic personality disorder (NPD) with borderline features. Both patients expressed their profound attachment insecurity in different ways. The BPD patient found security in her attachment to external substances—food, drugs, alcohol, flirting—while the NPD patient found security in her attachment to an internal fantasy world that enveloped her like a protective bubble (Modell, 1975). Their respective attachment organizations could both be classified as "cannot classify" (Hesse, 1996). In spite of the similarities in personality and attachment organization between these two patients, my countertransference reactions and therapeutic interventions differed between them. Notably, the interaction structures that developed in both treatments contained sadomasochistic elements. Their mentalization skills have gradually developed over time.

Chapters 4 and 5 form a medley on the theme of transforming clinical training. In these chapters, I discuss how I have used my experiences as a clinical supervisor in my doctoral program to transform clinical training. In chapter 4, I use the concept of projective identification to account for the feelings of helplessness and demoralization I often observe in fledgling supervisees who are treating patients who have negative therapeutic reactions. Misinterpreted by these supervisees as their own incompetence, these feelings are actually communicating something profoundly important about the internal worlds of these patients. In a two-person supervision, the clinical supervisor can serve the function of an attachment figure, who can contain these feelings, sort them out, and metabolize them for the supervisee on behalf of the patient, who in turn can receive these communications back from the therapist in a tolerable form.

In chapter 6, I apply the PQS and the Child Psychotherapy Process Q-Set (CPQ; Schneider, 2004; Schneider and Jones, 2004; Schneider, Pruetzel-Thomas, and Midgley, in press)—two Q-sort measures of psychotherapy process—to the supervision experience. Over the past two years, I have documented my doctoral supervisees' increase in the knowledge of psychodynamic process using this instrument. I correlated their prototypical psychodynamic Q-sort with the prototypical psychodynamic Q-sort established by expert raters (see volume I, chapter 4) at three times during the academic year—September (starting point), January (midpoint), and July (endpoint). At each point, we discuss areas of psychodynamic process where the supervisees disagree with the prototypical psychodynamic process. I educate them about aspects of psychodynamic technique that they did not fully comprehend. Second, my supervisees and I also discuss their weekly PQS or CPQ Q-sorts of their psychotherapy sessions and the discrepancies between these Q-sorts and the PQS or CPQ psychodynamic prototypes. Using the PQS and CPQ, therefore, I can help my supervisees improve not only their knowledge of psychodynamic process but also their execution of it.

Third, I coteach a required doctoral-level course that assists our third-year clinical psychology students in their preparation to present a psychotherapy case from their externship training to a review panel of expert therapists. Over the past two years, all students enrolled in this course have completed prototypical Q-sorts from their preferred theoretical orientation (i.e., psychodynamic or CBT). These students have discovered how much they actually know about the psychotherapy process of their preferred theoretical orientation. Fourth, they must Q-sort an actual session from the psychotherapy case they will be presenting to determine how closely they adhered to their preferred prototype during that session. Low correlations have shocked some students into selecting a different session or even a different case altogether to present because low correlations suggest unacceptably low adherence to their preferred theoretical orientation. Of course, students can use case material to argue why they strayed from the psychotherapy process most characteristic of their preferred theoretical orientation. This quantitative approach to learning psychotherapy process has been helpful to our students and welcomed by the American Psychological Association reaccreditation site visitors as they evaluate our program on our methods for assessing clinical competence among our students.

In chapter 6, I present the processes of therapeutic change in a psychodynamically oriented, exploratory spirituality group for nine female psychiatric inpatients diagnosed with BPD (none of these participants was part of the study presented in chapter 4 of volume I). Through drawings and group process, the patients uncovered and elaborated on their representations of God. Two patterns of representations were identified: (1) representations of a punitive, judgmental, rigid God that seemed to reflect directly and correspond with parental representations, and (2) representations of a depersonified, inanimate, abstract God reflecting aspects of idealization that seemed to compensate for inadequate parental representations. Interestingly, the second pattern was associated with comorbid narcissistic features in the patients. Those patients who presented punitive God representations were able to begin the process of re-creating these representations toward more benign or benevolent images in the context of this group, while those participants who presented depersonified God representations seemed unable to do so. I believe that the secure base that the group leaders provided for the participants facilitated the openness to the group experience observed in the patients without narcissistic features.

In chapter 7, I discuss the need for attachment-based intervention programs for children beyond the preschool years. Although attachment-based interventions with mothers and infants are beginning to flourish, guidelines for developing attachment-based intervention with prepubertal children are lacking. I attempt to remedy this lack by discussing two areas: (1) potential intervention points of entry with prepubertal children based on attachment theory, and (2) the impact of parent, child, and therapist characteristics, notably mental representations (also known as internal working models), on the potential intervention points of entry being targeted. In contrast to attachment-based early intervention, in which parental characteristics are targeted, attachment-based intervention with prepubertal children must include the child as well as the parents. Therapists attempting an attachment-based intervention with prepubertal children must take into account the quality of the child's and the parent's mental representations as well as their own quality of mental representations to provide an effective clinical experience. The processes of therapeutic change critically depend on the reciprocal influence of these characteristics.

Finally, in chapter 8, I share my personal experiences interviewing two persons on the fringes of our society—victims of political torture living on the streets of New York City. Entering the minds of these two adolescent boys contradicted my expectations at every turn and left me wondering how I could help them. I weave an attachment perspective into my understanding of these experiences and conclude, ultimately, that the concealment of human misery is sometimes so absolute that current therapeutic methods might be incapable of challenging it.

Transforming the Internal World and Attachment: Clinical Applications (volume II) comes at a time when psychodynamically oriented therapists are becoming acquainted with attachment theory and the ambitious project to ground psychoanalytic theory and practice in empirical research and neuroscience findings. These ideas are just beginning to find publication in the psychoanalytic journals. No book has formally introduced the psychoanalytic audience to empirically derived processes of therapeutic change (e.g., interaction structures, mentalization) within a theoretical framework grounded in psychoanalytic and attachment theories. The twofold shift to a two-person psychology and an empirical assessment of clinical evidence has created fertile ground for the psychoanalytic community to examine the compelling evidence provided by attachment research to support key aspects not only of its theories of development and psychopathology (Goodman, 2002) but also of its processes of therapeutic change.

It has been twenty-one years since I walked into my first psychoanalyst's office for the first time and heard the words, "Are you in pain?" To understand the pain of another person, we must be open to experiencing that pain—in all its sadness, rage, desperation, and ultimately helplessness. This book attempts to understand the process of bearing the burden of pain in our patients and in ourselves in the therapeutic encounter.

Chapter Two

The Protective Bubble: Processes of Therapeutic Change Observed in an Analysand with Narcissistic Personality Disorder

I want to tell the tale of two analysands—Mei Ling and Carly. I have treated Mei Ling and Carly in four-times-per-week psychoanalysis over a period of over three years to fulfill the requirements of my psychoanalytic training. I am using these two clinical cases to illustrate some of the points I made in volume I of this two-volume book series. In volume I, I articulated and discussed the theories related to the processes of therapeutic change. One might ask, however, what do these processes of therapeutic change actually look like? These two clinical cases document some of these processes and the therapeutic changes that these processes appeared to facilitate.

In chapters 2 and 3, I will argue that these two patients had formed what I will call an "alternate attachment"—not to a primary caregiver but to a nonhuman entity—that served numerous functions for them. Critically, this alternate attachment provides a false sense of protection and the temporary restoration of affect regulation, especially when the attachment system is activated during moments such as loss, separation, fear, stress, injury, fatigue, illness, and punishment (Bowlby, 1973; Main, Kaplan, and Cassidy, 1985). The hallmarks of attachment to a primary caregiver—proximity-seeking and contact maintenance (Ainsworth, Blehar, Waters, and Wall, 1978)—are similarly present in the alternate attachment but perhaps not as obvious.

The ultimate goal of the alternate attachment is to protect the person from the awareness of psychological separation from the primary caregiver. The alternate attachment produces the illusion that no separation between the person and the primary caregiver has occurred. When conditions that threaten separation awareness emerge, particularly when the attachment system is activated (see above), the person seeks protection from the alternate attachment by seeking proximity to and maintaining contact with the substitute attachment figure. The alternate attachment therefore preserves the denial of the awareness of psychological separation from the primary caregiver.

A false sense of protection is so vital to the person's survival because a personality organized at a borderline level is fragmented by virtue of pervasive splitting processes. Affects associated with gratification and comfort are split off from affects associated with intrusion and deprivation (Kernberg, 1975), which produce frantic attempts to manufacture feelings of security in the face of these negative affects. Modell (1975) has highlighted the "narcissistic defense against affects" that protects the person from "a fear of closeness to the object" (p. 275).

I would add that, although the defense against affects can encompass all affects in extreme cases, I have observed this defense mobilized primarily around the threatening awareness of separation anxiety, when the attachment system has been activated and the person does not expect the primary caregiver to terminate this system (see also Solomon and George, 1999c). In an earlier paper, Modell (1961) also associated this form of denial to a failure to accept the separateness of objects. Similarly, Fintzy (1971) and Volkan (1973) have suggested that the substitution of nonhuman entities for human contact represents "the magical undoing of separation from the mother" (Volkan, 1973, p. 373). In this state of denial, the person can imagine a world of supreme security and protection from split-off negative affects, whether perceived internally or externally. Interestingly, one of the hallmarks of anxious-avoidant (A) attachment in preschool and school-aged children assessed using the Attachment Story-Completion Task (Bretherton, Ridgeway, and Cassidy, 1990) is the attempt to undo the separation from the mother that characterizes story 4 (Solomon, George, and De Jong, 1995).

In the two patients whose treatments I will be presenting, the alternate attachment appeared in two different forms. Winnicott's (1953) concept of transitional phenomena is helpful in understanding the alternate attachment because the alternate attachment, like transitional phenomena, exists neither inside the person's subjective experience nor outside in external reality, but somewhere in between—under the person's complete control. Paradoxically, the person both creates and discovers the alternate attachment out of materials in the intermediate area of his or her internal and external experience. This intermediate area, "unchallenged in respect of its belonging to inner or external (shared) reality, constitutes the greater part of the infant's experience, and throughout life is retained in the intense experiencing that belongs to the arts and to religion" (Winnicott, 1971, p. 14). For these two patients with borderline personality organization, however, the alternate attachment assumed the role of a compensatory structure (Kohut, 1977) that serves critical self-regulatory functions rather than life-enhancing functions.

The first patient, Mei Ling (see below), created an elaborate series of fantasies that she depended on during critical moments of activation of the attachment system that helped her to regulate negative affects and block separation awareness. In her psychoanalysis, she came to call her retreat into this elaborate fantasy world her "bubble," where she felt completely secure and immune to debilitating affects such as loneliness and inadequacy. This manufactured security offered by the bubble protected her from having to rely on anyone in the real world. In this state of mind, she could deny the awareness of her physical separation from her mother and continue the illusion of absolute dependence on her mother that resembled a state of primitive fusion. The bubble effectively compensated for the reality that Mei Ling is an adult whose mother is physically and psychologically separate from her.

Volkan (1973) referred to these phenomena as "transitional fantasies," which he defined as "intangible representations of transitional objects" (p. 351). Like transitional objects, the person regards these fantasies as though "they had lives of their own and behaving as though he were addicted to them, although they were at the same time subject to his absolute control, whereby he could maintain the illusion that he had similar control over the real environment" (p. 352). Modell (1975) noted that such persons "describe themselves as encased in a 'plastic bubble' or feel that they are really not 'in the world'—they are in a cocoon" (p. 276). Typically, Mei Ling's transitional fantasies, which constituted her self-described bubble, revolved around unconsummated romantic encounters and affairs with unavailable men. These fantasies sometimes took the form of enactments in her "real" life.

In stark contrast to Mei Ling, the second patient, Carly (see chapter 3), created an elaborate array of transitional objects that she similarly depended on during critical moments of activation of the attachment system that helped her to regulate negative affects and block separation awareness. These transitional objects preserved the illusion of self-sufficiency amid absolute dependence on her lesbian partner and masochistic submission to her antisocial mother. In rare moments when her alternate attachment yielded to an awareness of her absolute dependence, she would characterize herself as a "jellyfish"—a fat blob with no definitive identity, purpose, or structure for her life in the absence of a defining object.

The principal difference between these two patients' transitional phenomena is that, whereas addiction to never-ending fantasies comprised Mei Ling's bubble, addiction to limitless external substances comprised Carly's bubble (these substances included food, alcohol, drugs, and surreptitious flirting with females in her and her partner's circle of lesbian friends). Whereas Mei Ling formed her alternate attachment to internal fantasies, Carly formed her alternate attachment to external substances. In spite of the different targets chosen, these two alternate attachments to transitional fantasies (Mei Ling) and transitional objects (Carly) both served to deny the awareness of physical and psychological separation from the primary caregiver and the terrifying dependence on the primary object that such separation implies.

Of course, the protective bubble constructed by these two patients, using different "raw materials" culled from internal or external experiences, served other purposes as well. The protective bubble helped to restore affect regulation, provided a false sense of protection from and control over the unpredictability and unreliability inherent in interpersonal relationships, and virtually abolished the experience of loneliness. In his clinical vignette of a man who fantasized about living inside an iron ball, Volkan (1973) observed that the man actually provoked rejection from others "to prove that loneliness and fantasy offered superior safety" (p. 362) to the vulnerability inherent in depending on others. Because the alternate attachment, regardless of its assumed form, serves many different psychic functions, the person experiences it as virtually impossible to relinquish—an addiction. He or she instead prefers a peculiar intrapsychic isolation at the cost of the vicissitudes of full emotional participation in the community of fellow human beings.

Although these two patients share a borderline personality organization, the difference I am highlighting between them—the nature of the alternate attachment—might also be related to different structural variations within this organization. Both patients experienced identity diffusion manifested in split-off self- and object representations, poor anxiety tolerance, shifts toward primary-process thinking, and inconsistently available sublimatory channels (Kernberg, 1986a). I diagnosed Carly with borderline personality disorder (BPD) and Mei Ling with narcissistic personality disorder (NPD) with borderline features. In narcissistic personalities organized at a borderline level, a condensation of idealized object and self-representations and real self-representations constitutes the pathological grandiose self (Kernberg, 1986b). This pathological structure protects the person from anticipated persecution and attack from projected superego precursors through "widespread, devastating devaluation of external objects and their representations" (Kernberg, 1986b, p. 262). I am suggesting that the pathological grandiose self—in whatever form it takes—serves as an alternate attachment figure to compensate for profound attachment insecurity.

Kernberg (1986b) distinguished between narcissistic personalities organized at a borderline level and typical borderline personalities: "The absence of the capacity to depend upon others on the part of narcissistic personalities, in contrast to the clinging dependency and persistent capacity for a broad spectrum of object relations in borderline patients, contributes fundamentally to the differential diagnosis of narcissistic personalities functioning on an overt borderline level from usual borderline patients" (pp. 255, 256). I am suggesting that Mei Ling's alternate attachment to her elaborate fantasy world and escape to her bubble reflect the narcissistic personality's absence of the capacity to depend on others, while Carly's alternate attachment to external substances and flirtation with other women reflect the typical borderline personality's clinging, jellyfish-like dependency. Nevertheless, Carly's substance abuse and flirtation with other women created a euphoria that produced in her a sense of self-sufficiency and invincibility that resembles Mei Ling's experience of her bubble. As I mentioned earlier, when Carly's awareness of psychological separateness and absolute dependence on her partner would occasionally break through, however, she would refer to herself as a "jellyfish"—a metaphor for her feelings of vulnerability and undifferentiation in the absence of a defining object.

Given the profound attachment insecurity and reliance on an alternate attachment observed in these two patients with borderline personality organization, information about their respective attachment patterns might further illuminate their diagnostic differences and different targets chosen for their alternate attachments. I did not want to assume the role of an evaluator during the analytic treatment in the event that it could introduce iatrogenic effects; furthermore, my supervisors forbade any formal assessment procedures conducted by others. Thus, I did not administer the Adult Attachment Interview (AAI; George et al., 1996). Instead, I used two new instruments that assess attachment quality using the therapist as the informant. The Attachment Prototype Questionnaire (APQ; Westen, Nakash, Thomas, and Bradley, 2006) yields an attachment category assigned by the therapist based on four detailed prototypical descriptions of the four attachment patterns: secure, dismissing, preoccupied, and incoherent/disorganized (unresolved). The therapist rates the strength of the patient's match to each prototype on a five-point Likert-type scale and designates one of the four prototypes as best fitting. The Attachment Questionnaire (AQ; Westen et al., 2006) yields four factors that correspond to the four attachment patterns. The therapist rates the accuracy of thirty-seven attachment-relevant items on a seven-point Likert-type scale. Items that load onto each factor are summed and averaged to provide four dimensional attachment ratings that supplement the best-fitting prototype classification.

I completed the APQ and AQ on both my patients and obtained completed APQs and AQs from my clinical supervisors (two supervisors completed questionnaires on Mei Ling because my first supervisor moved out of state after the first two and a half years of treatment but agreed to participate). On the APQ, my first supervisor and I both classified Mei Ling as having a dismissing attachment pattern, while my second supervisor indicated an incoherent/disorganized attachment pattern. On the APQ, I classified Carly as having a dismissing attachment pattern, while my supervisor indicated an incoherent/disorganized attachment pattern.

On the AQ, my attachment ratings for Mei Ling were positively correlated with the attachment ratings of both my first supervisor, Cronbach's alpha = .51, $p < .05$, and my second supervisor, Cronbach's alpha = .41, $p < .10$. Considering the four AQ mean factor scores, the mean preoccupied (PRE) factor score for Mei Ling was higher than the other three mean factor scores (secure [SEC], dismissing [DIS], incoherent/disorganized [INC/DIS]). This finding was true for both supervisors and me. The ordinal rankings of these four factors, however, were moderately homogeneous:

Geoff: PRE > DIS > SEC > INC/DIS

Super1: PRE > DIS > SEC > INC/DIS

Super2: PRE > DIS > INC/DIS > SEC

These equations illustrate some basic agreement among the three informants regarding the relative influence of each of the four attachment patterns in Mei Ling's overall attachment organization.

On the AQ, my attachment ratings for Carly were nonsignificantly correlated with the attachment ratings of my supervisor, Cronbach's alpha = .36, n.s. Considering the four AQ mean factor scores, the mean DIS factor score for Carly was higher than the other three mean factor scores for me, while the mean PRE factor score for Carly was higher than the other three mean factor scores for my supervisor. The ordinal rankings of these four factors were moderately heterogeneous:

Geoff: DIS > PRE > SEC > INC/DIS

Super: PRE > DIS > INC/DIS > SEC

This illustrates only modest agreement between the two informants regarding the relative influence of each of the four attachment patterns in Carly's overall attachment organization.

Visual inspection of these four mean factor scores across all informants yields addition information about the attachment organization of these two patients. Compared to the four mean factor scores derived from a large national sample provided by Westen and his colleagues (Westen et al., 2006, p. 1077), the mean PRE, DIS, and INC/DIS factor scores of Mei Ling and Carly were almost one standard deviation higher, and the mean SEC factor scores almost one standard deviation lower, than Westen et al.'s outpatient participants. This information suggests that Mei Ling and Carly's attachment insecurity is more profound than the average outpatient's is. Furthermore, the high scores on all three insecure factors (PRE, DIS, INC/DIS) suggest that multiple internal working models are operational in both Mei Ling and Carly. Visual inspection of the two diagrams above, as well as the APQ classifications, suggest that preoccupied and dismissing internal working models predominate over secure and incoherent/disorganized internal working models in Mei Ling and Carly's respective overall attachment organizations. The fact that one pattern does not appear to be predominant could account for the disagreements among the four informants on these two patients' attachment classifications and ratings. I speculate that on the AAI, both patients would receive cannot classify (CC) classifications typically found in high-risk populations. Hesse (1996) reported an incidence rate of 7–10 percent in low-risk samples.

In my first book (Goodman, 2002), I argued that patients with multiple internal working models can shift between deactivating and hyperactivating attachment strategies characteristic of the dismissing and preoccupied internal working models, respectively (see Goodman, in press, chapter 6). These shifts occur when attachment-based anxieties overwhelm the frontline strategy of deactivation: "The underlying defensive structure of self-sufficiency and denial of attachment needs weakens," which leaves the person "feeling painfully helpless and vulnerable" (Goodman, 2002, p. 139). Another possible outcome is that the therapist's interpretation—for example, that a patient is beginning to feel emotionally close to the therapist because the patient feels that the therapist understands him or her—causes an overreliance on a deactivating strategy and a resulting attempt to block all feelings of closeness from awareness.

Both Mei Ling and Carly demonstrate oscillations between dismissing and preoccupied internal working models characteristic of persons categorized by the AAI as cannot classify. Therapists working with such patients need to be acutely aware of the moment-to-moment shifts in the patient's affect states and direct their interventions to identifying these shifts and uncovering the underlying thoughts and perceptions that accompany them. This painstaking work serves the objective of personality integration with a subjective sense of wholeness. I have found that attachment-based anxieties usually stimulate such shifts. These anxieties can originate in the recall of specific memories (or fantasies) of a particular category of attachment-relevant situations (e.g., bodily injury, fear, loss of a caregiver) or interactions with a caregiver (e.g., mother, father).

For example, these shifts in attachment strategy can occur when the patient shifts in a therapy session from a maternal to a paternal transference. We know that infants can demonstrate different attachment patterns with different parents in the Strange Situation paradigm (Main and Weston, 1981). These different attachment patterns reflect different underlying attachment strategies used to manage anxieties stimulated by different patterns of parental responsiveness. That different internal working models are formed to accommodate these different patterns of parental responsiveness could account for the presence of the "cannot classify attachment" category in at least some persons so identified.

In chapter 6 of Goodman (in press), I discuss the formation of interaction structures in the therapeutic relationship. Interaction structures consist of reciprocally influencing behaviors between the therapist and the patient at every moment in every session (Jones, 2000). These behaviors often go unnoticed in the background of the treatment. In chapter 4 of volume I, I identified four interaction structures present, to varying degrees, in five treatments of patients with borderline personality disorder: (1) Collaborative Relationship with Supportive, Reassuring Therapist, (2) Therapist Attunement/Sensitivity/Affective Involvement, (3) Erotized Transference, and (4) Controlling Therapist with Compliant Patient. In chapter 6 of Goodman (in press), I propose that therapist-patient interaction structures are defined by each member's pattern of affect regulation and dysregulation. In figure 6.1 of Goodman (in press), I define four prototypical interaction structures based on the different combinations of preoccupied/hyperactivating and dismissing/deactivating attachment strategies between the therapist and patient: sterile, expressive, containing, and chaotic. In a patient who has encased her emotional life in a protective bubble, the resulting interaction structures would reflect the bubble's varying permeability and the patient's wishes and fears surrounding this permeability. The therapist's characteristic attachment strategy would also contribute to the quality of the resulting interaction structures.

On the AAI, I was classified as having a secure attachment organization with an F4 subclassification, which is consistent with "strong valuing of relationships, with some accompanying preoccupation with attachment figures" (Main and Goldwyn, 1994, p. 137). According to the principle of noncomplementarity (e.g., Bernier and Dozier, 2002), therapists are optimally effective with patients whose secondary attachment strategy differs from their own (see Goodman, in press, chapter 6). Thus, I would be most effective with Mei Ling and Carly when they are using a dismissing/deactivating attachment strategy in our interactions. Because both patients seemed to use both preoccupied/hyperactivating and dismissing/deactivating attachment strategies intermittently (suggesting the "cannot classify attachment" category), my therapeutic effectiveness might have also been intermittent. I have tried to be aware of any underregulated affects I might be experiencing during sessions that could interfere with the containment of my patients' own underregulated affects. Paying close attention to the therapeutic process between my patients and me has helped facilitate my awareness of my own affects and their potential impact on my interactions with these patients.

In Mei Ling's and Carly's respective treatments (described below and in chapter 3), my interventions (whether they were clarifications, confrontations, or interpretations) or lack of interventions were meaningful events, not necessarily because of their content but rather because of their symbolic significance vis-à-vis the bubble. These patients could experience my interventions as attempts to puncture the bubble and attack the vulnerable self concealed inside or take away the life-sustaining alternate attachment. In contrast to Volkan's (1973) patient's "iron ball" (p. 351), a bubble does not offer much protection from external impingements. Conversely, the absence of interventions also represented meaningful events. These patients could experience my silence as deprivation, neglect, and withholding of love and nurturance.

Thus, the bubble places the therapist in a double bind: too many poorly timed interventions could place the patient's defensive system on high alert, while too few interventions could overly frustrate the patient, make them precociously aware of their dependence on the therapist, and cause the patient to abandon the therapist to reassure themselves of their self-sufficiency. In Mei Ling's treatment, the establishment of an interaction structure in which she experienced my interventions as impingements was inevitable. Whenever Mei Ling retreated into her bubble of transitional fantasies, her mother would sneak up behind her and poke her in the back with her stiff, bony fingers. My interpretation of her maternal transference onto me only reinforced the experience of her mother's stiff, bony finger poking her in the back (I also sit behind her).

In Carly's treatment, the establishment of an interaction structure in which she experienced my silence as a deprivation was also inevitable. Whenever Carly paraded her self-destructive behavior in front of me, such as smoking marijuana while driving at high speeds without wearing a seat belt, she seemed to be experiencing the abstinence of psychoanalysis as a massive deprivation and wished to startle me into action. I fed her bland, technically neutral interpretations that lacked the delicious, active interventions she craved, such as pleas to stop hurting herself or after-hours telephone calls to confirm that she had made it safely through another day. She experienced silence as a deprivation, which she responded to with provocative behavior, which I in turn responded to with interpretation, which she experienced as more neglect, thus reinforcing the familiar experience of her mother's routine obliviousness to her emotional needs.

These anticipated interaction structures led my supervisors and I to formulate two unique treatment approaches that would help me avoid potential pitfalls. In Mei Ling's treatment, I needed to avoid the "poking" interpretations that could arouse persecutory anxiety and pose a threat to the treatment's survival.

Mei Ling's narcissistic vulnerability demanded a holding environment that minimized the impingements associated with her mother. In Carly's treatment, I needed to avoid a conventional abstinent stance and make more interventions than I usually would to limit her rationalization for self-destructive behavior. Carly's neediness—in evidence when her transitional objects failed to make her feel self-sufficient—demanded a highly interactive approach in which I bathed Carly in interventions that minimized the deprivation associated with her mother. My goal was to continue to apply these two different treatment approaches until each patient could tolerate a more conventional approach without the presence of these parameters.

In both treatments, I was careful to pay attention to the meaning of the therapeutic process—the affective moments that passed between us—and to help my patients similarly pay attention, rather than simply pay attention to the content of the patient's clinical material. In this sense, my treatment strategy owes a debt of gratitude to the mindfulness literature, which suggests that paying attention to one's thoughts and feelings without acting on them or ruminating about them produces therapeutic benefits (see volume I, chapter 5).

I agree with Volkan (1973) and Kohut (1971), who suggested that the interpretation of fantasy content ignores the functions these fantasies serve: "Illusions for the protection of [the patient's] narcissism and omnipotence, and bridges between me and not-me" (Volkan, 1973, p. 372). As I conducted psychoanalysis with these two patients, I asked myself three questions that organized my thinking about their respective treatments: (1) What is the current interaction structure we are enacting together? (2) Is the patient currently functioning in a dismissing or preoccupied mode of relating? (3) How can I move the patient into a secure mode of relating in the therapeutic relationship? I am defining "a secure mode of relating" as the capacity to depend on me for the containment of unbearable longings and anxieties associated with both individuation and fusion rather than (1) depend on the alternate attachment (i.e., transitional fantasies or objects) to avoid dependence on me (dismissing mode of relating) or (2) force me to join them in the bubble in a state of fusion (preoccupied mode of relating).

Given this broad theoretical framework, I speculated that Mei Ling would be inclined to depend on her transitional fantasies, while Carly would be inclined to depend on her transitional objects. Yet I also monitored the therapeutic process for shifts that indicated that these patients wanted me to collude with them in condoning what Mei Ling came to refer to as her "bubble behavior." For example, Mei Ling would try to convince me why an available man who showed an interest in her was hopelessly flawed. Similarly, Carly would try to convince me that smoking marijuana was therapeutic because it soothed her and facilitated her sobriety.

In their own unique ways, both patients oscillated between the poles of isolation and fusion, spending most of the time in a state of isolation with occasional forays into a state of fusion. I wanted to help them to reflect on these insecure modes of relating and, through the resulting experience of containment, shift them into a secure mode of relating. To accomplish this task, I emphasized the timing and titration of interventions more than their content. In these treatments, the meaning of making an intervention superceded the meaning of its content. I wanted to help them to reflect on their mode of relating to me as well as give them an opportunity to experience a secure mode of relating in the therapeutic relationship.

I want to make a final comment about the facilitation of mentalizing processes in these two patients. I wanted to help both my patients to become aware of and use their underlying mental states to interpret the accurate meaning of their behaviors in interaction with others (for a full treatment of mentalization, see volume I, chapter 6). Each patient, in her own way, posed specific challenges to this objective. Carly relied on an alternate attachment to transitional objects in her environment. This exclusive focus on substances external to herself interfered with the self-reflective and empathic processes necessary to identify underlying mental states located within herself and other persons, which she could use to interpret her own and others' behaviors and interactions.

Over time, I learned that Carly's alternate attachment to transitional objects seemed to predispose Carly to concrete thinking—what Fonagy and his colleagues (Fonagy et al., 2002) have referred to as "psychic equivalence mode" (for a full discussion, see volume I, chapter 6). For example, Carly's sitting up from the couch before the end of one session gave her time to fix her hair, even though she had never complained about her flattened hair in any previous session. My effort to connect the sitting-up behavior to her discomfort with talking about her sexuality while lying down in my presence, only a minute before she sat up, just fell on deaf ears. She looked at me, mystified, and remarked, "I don't know where in the world you come up with those things."

Mei Ling, on the other hand, relied on an alternate attachment to transitional fantasies located in her mind. This exclusive focus on romantic scenarios in which men and women interacted with each other seemed to facilitate the self-reflective and empathic processes necessary to identify underlying mental states located within herself and other persons, which she could use to interpret her own and others' behaviors and interactions in reality.

Over time, I learned that Mei Ling's alternate attachment to transitional fantasies in the bubble seemed to predispose Mei Ling to more abstract thinking. Mei Ling's transitional fantasies reflected a capacity to symbolize her thoughts and feelings and reflect on them as transitory conditions and not as actions. In contrast, Carly refused to talk about her worries about her mother's or partner's health problems because merely thinking about their death was equivalent to killing them herself. This difference in cognitive style alone could account for the different pace of progress I observed in their respective treatments.

In both treatments, I attempted to adjust my level of mentalizing to my patients' level of mentalizing. Diamond and her colleagues (Diamond, Stovall-McClough, Clarkin, and Levy, 2003) have suggested that a therapist's level of mentalizing must be neither too discrepant nor too parallel to their patient's level of mentalizing for changes in mentalization to occur. In other words, the patient's development of the capacity to understand the mental states of self and others depends on the therapist's ability to titrate the patient's understanding by mentalizing at a level just above that of the patient—a concept similar to Vygotsky's (1978) zone of proximal development (for a full treatment of this theory, see Goodman, in press, chapter 5).

Because I have a tendency to intellectualize, adjusting my level of mentalizing sometimes proved difficult. With the assistance of my clinical supervisors, however, I was able to understand under what conditions I intellectualized my interpretations and use this information as a form of communication from my patients. I tended to intellectualize whenever Mei Ling, and especially Carly, would repeatedly ask me to elaborate on an interpretation. Out of frustration, I would present the interpretation in increasingly intellectualized ways in an effort to stop them from badgering me. In supervision, I learned that my patients were torturing me! I did not want to see this dynamic. Mei Ling wanted me to feel what she had experienced with her intrusive mother, so she would play the maternal role while I would unwittingly play her as a frustrated, helpless child. Carly, on the other hand, wanted to engage me in a sadomasochistic interaction reminiscent of her relationship with her mother; such interactions would forestall an overwhelming sense of deprivation from her mother during childhood. Similarly, she wanted to pull me out of what she perceived as my deprivation of her, expressed through my analytic attitude (Schafer, 1983).

In the treatment summaries that follow (described below and in chapter 3), I do not explicitly refer to the theoretical framework I have developed here because I want the clinical material to speak for itself, independent of excessive editorializing. The reader should keep in mind, however, that, as is the case with all case histories (Michels, 2000), this theoretical framework was operating in the background of my mind as I interacted with these patients and made my interventions. At the time of this writing, both patients have made significant progress in the almost four years I have been treating them—preliminary clinical evidence to support this theoretical framework. Indices of progress include these patients' level of self-reflectiveness, awareness of characteristic defensive processes and patterns of interaction with others and me, tendencies to sabotage themselves, and the motivations behind these actions. The substitution of the alternate attachment for secure attachments with real people, however, remains incomplete. Continued intensive work with both patients is indicated to help them overcome their addiction to a protective bubble that offers only isolation, aloneness, and self-deception.

MEI LING

Chief Complaint at Initial Consultation

"I feel unsuccessful in every aspect of my life. I don't have my own family at thirty-four, and I'm unsuccessful in my career."

Brief Personal History

Mei Ling is a thirty-eight-year-old secretary and struggling artist of Chinese descent who initially presented with symptoms of depression, hopelessness, low self-esteem, and anhedonia. Her chief complaints included a sense of failure in her art career and uncertainty about whether to continue in an unfulfilling romantic relationship that held little hope of producing a stable marriage and children. Mei Ling's parents moved the family to the United States from Taiwan when she was eighteen months old to seek enhanced educational opportunities for Mei Ling and her older sister Jade, who is now forty years old. Sometime after her graduation from Williams College, Mei Ling's parents moved back to Taiwan while retaining property in the United States. Mei Ling experienced this move as a traumatic abandonment—perhaps a repetition of traumatic threats of abandonment made by her mother throughout childhood. These feelings were exacerbated in December 2003, when her midtown Manhattan apartment was burglarized, with many family heirlooms and some of her sketches saved on her computer hard drive stolen. Prior to her beginning psychoanalysis, Mei Ling was engaged in psychodynamically oriented, once-weekly psychotherapy with two different therapists over a five-year period that made her function better but produced no lasting change. Her boyfriend had recommended psychoanalysis, which he had experienced as helpful to him.

As Mei Ling now recalls it, her relationship with her mother was marked by profound ambivalence. She described her mother as extremely controlling, paranoid, and demanding. As early as she can remember, Mei Ling decided to become her mother's "minion," which meant obeying her mother's every whim to earn her mother's recognition, approval, and love. In exchange for Mei Ling's unquestioning obedience, Mei Ling developed a pervasive feeling that she had a gold star on the back of her head—"that I live a charmed life." The extent to which Mei Ling's mother controlled her and her sister included allowing them to take only several bites of a dessert and leaving the rest, forbidding them from lying on their beds except to go to sleep at night, and forcing them to pursue interests that did not interest them. For example, the mother forced Mei Ling's sister to take piano lessons even though it was Mei Ling who had requested them, while she forced Mei Ling to take dance lessons even though it was her sister who had requested them. Mei Ling remembered an incident that took place during her elementary school years that encapsulates a mother-child relationship filled with underlying maternal disappointment and even disdain: Mei Ling's mother is sitting behind her while her mother callously removes lice eggs from Mei Ling's hair and squashes them on a piece of paper next to her without any words of compassion or solace. Mei Ling felt that getting lice at school was her own fault. To avoid such experiences, Mei Ling pledged her unwavering loyalty to her mother. Early in the treatment, Mei Ling defended her mother from any attempts by me to portray her mother as anything other than idealized. In the early sessions, Mei Ling described her mother as having an impeccable fashion sense, exhibiting a creative frugality with clothing and food purchases, maintaining a beautiful and clean home, and serving delicious, healthy, and well-prepared meals. Mei Ling depicted her as a paragon of domestic virtue. As the treatment has progressed, Mei Ling has begun to appreciate the fact that her mother probably has an untreated mental illness with prominent paranoid and obsessive-compulsive features, which Mei Ling can now anticipate and, to some extent, manage. This idealization supported other defensive attitudes that protected Mei Ling from underlying feelings of rage toward her mother.

Mei Ling's perceived relationship with her father has only recently become a theme of treatment as we have explored her resistances to talking about him. Because Mei Ling's father moved to the United States while her mother was pregnant with Mei Ling to make preparations to move the entire family, Mei Ling did not meet her father until she was eighteen months of age, which she believes accounts for her awkwardness with men. She described her father during childhood as "checked out," working long hours as a laundromat owner and leaving most household management decisions to his wife. According to Mei Ling, the only substantial contact Mei Ling had with him was over Sunday breakfast, when he gave her lectures based on platitudes. She also sensed that her father often made up or exaggerated stories of his childhood, such as walking seven miles each day to school and back. Her father told these stories with the expectation that Mei Ling and her sister would believe them. Mei Ling also shared memories of her father walking around the house in his boxer shorts and feeling repulsed by the sight. The only positive memory of her father from childhood was an excursion they took together to the convenience store when he bought her some candy normally forbidden by the mother.

Case Formulation

Mei Ling presented with tremendous narcissistic vulnerability and suspicion of potential helpers that reflects a primal fear that she could be abandoned at any time. Indeed, her mother frequently packed her bags and threatened to leave the house if compliance was not swift and unwavering. In response to this abandonment anxiety, Mei Ling identified with the mother's ideals and values to please her mother and thus insure her mother's presence. She idealized her mother's sterile codes of neatness and cleanliness and devalued her own vulnerable feelings. In one session, Mei Ling ridiculed herself as a five-year-old child because she remembered having tripped in the leg braces her mother had made her wear to straighten her gait. Mei Ling valorized and idealized these sterile, unemotional elements of the mother's personality, and split off the sinister, sadistic aspects that sometimes emerged in childhood nightmares of the mother's approaching her with a sword raised over her head. In her relationships with her mother and with school peers, Mei Ling identified with the masochistic, beleaguered representation of this mother-daughter tandem. She remembered doing everything her mother told her to do to keep her mother from abandoning her. In spite of her efforts, Mei Ling's mother found ways of torturing her, thus establishing a sadomasochistic relationship with her daughter. As mentioned earlier, Mei Ling's mother gave her what she did not want and did not give her what she did want. Shopping for clothes in the department store, Mei Ling's mother would whisk Mei Ling away from the clothes she liked and took her to the back of the store to try on the discounted items. Mei Ling experienced the mother's behavior as a dismissal of her needs and a confirmation that she deserved only second best—that she was also discounted. Mei Ling still identifies with this masochistic position by entertaining the idea of a suitable job, a suitable career, a suitable place to live, a suitable man to date—only to sabotage these aspirations by taking ersatz substitutes. I tended to treat this issue primarily as a conflict over separation and individuation from the mother and only secondarily as a regression from oedipal wishes and fears because, until recently, Mei Ling seldom mentioned her father or manifested a paternal transference.

The assumption of a masochistic position permitted Mei Ling to stay connected to her mother and served to defend against her fear of abandonment. If she did her mother's bidding, her mother would not leave her. Recently, Mei Ling has begun the anxiety-provoking process of separating from her mother. She moved out of a condominium in midtown Manhattan co-owned by her mother and her. We have come to view this condominium as a symbolic womb, which Mei Ling has had difficulty leaving. She has often talked about her living space as belonging to her mother and containing her mother's possessions. Mei Ling bid on a beautiful condominium of her own in Staten Island at the end of last year. When the bidding went above what she had originally prepared to spend, she impulsively pulled out of the bidding. She recently purchased a more reasonably priced condominium in the same neighborhood but berated herself for not having purchased the original condominium. She experienced exquisite difficulty preparing to move in: "If only I had taken the other place. This new apartment has no place at the door for me to leave my shoes when I come in. It is very important in Asian culture to take your shoes off at the door." The masochistic wish—wanting only what she deserves, which is the second best of everything—and the wish never to leave her mother's womb—are simultaneously evident. After developing delusional symptoms in this new apartment (see below), Mei Ling decided to move out and rent an apartment in lower Manhattan.

Finally, Mei Ling has described her mother as depriving her of her most prized possession—her mental space. Whenever Mei Ling was lost in reverie, her mother disturbed her peace of mind, often by poking her in the side or back with her finger. In a sense, Mei Ling feels that her mother still owns her interior mental space. This feeling manifests itself in her occasional inability to let her thoughts wander and in her reluctance to display her thoughts to the public in a gallery showing. Success as an artist (her career aspiration) would signify a betrayal of her mother's ownership over her mental products and risk her mother's abandonment.

During her childhood school years, Mei Ling also assumed a masochistic position vis-à-vis her peers. She remembered that she did not tell a female peer that she was stepping on Mei Ling's hand because Mei Ling did not want to make the peer feel uncomfortable. Similarly, Mei Ling responded to male peers' racist remarks by verbally taunting them, which only increased their insults. Mei Ling felt deeply hurt and victimized by these experiences, and only recently began to acknowledge the role she had played in the maintenance of these sadomasochistic interactions. Daydreams of interrupted romantic scenarios consumed Mei Ling's mental life during class at school.

The boy and girl would meet and begin talking to each other about mundane topics, but they would never become romantically involved. The daydream would suddenly break off, and she would start a new daydream that recycled these same themes. The internalization of a punitive superego, formed in the shape of her mother's role as interrupter of her thoughts and wishes, resulted in excessive self-monitoring and abrupt endings to her fantasies when they entered forbidden territory. According to Mei Ling, her mother often displayed her disgust whenever sexually charged scenes were featured on television. Mei Ling ultimately drew the conclusion that her mother's minion should not be thinking those thoughts.

Regarding her father, Mei Ling stated that she seldom saw him and had little relationship with him. She remembered long-winded lectures from him on Sunday mornings in which he instructed her to be "number one best" academically. She also remembered feeling disgust whenever she saw him walking around the house in only his boxer shorts. Mei Ling has been unresponsive to oedipal interpretations of this material at this stage of treatment. She has preferred to think of her father almost as a nonentity. Generally, her romantic relationships have consisted of men who were emotionally unavailable to her. She has felt rejected and victimized in all her romantic relationships, which recapitulates the masochistic position with which she is all too familiar. By selecting such men, Mei Ling seems to be submitting to the mother's implicit demand for absolute devotion to her.

Transference-Countertransference Paradigm

The pervasive transference-countertransference paradigm has been sadomasochistic. The paradigm usually operates at a low hum in the background, which occasionally makes a loud entrance into the foreground. The clinical material often consists of subtle devaluation of those around Mei Ling whom she perceives as substandard or second best. When I have interpreted the link to me and my uncertified status as a psychoanalyst in training, Mei Ling has dismissed the observation by citing a lack of experience with other psychoanalysts and a consequent inability to make comparisons. Early in the treatment, she also referred to the noises inside and outside the office (such as the clock ticking), the inconvenient appointment days and times, and the inconvenient office location. Last year, she unilaterally raised my fee $5 per week. She responded to my initial inquiry by saying that she felt I deserved more money (I had been charging her $135 per week) and that she was now able to pay an additional $5. I felt simultaneously gratified and devalued by the paltry increase. One week later, she asked whether we could begin meeting again in my former office in midtown Manhattan. I informed her that the former office was no longer available, and I wondered why she wanted to move. She responded that she was planning to move to Staten Island, and seeing me in midtown Manhattan would be more convenient for her. I quickly formed a hypothesis about this request and asked her whether her raising my fee had anything to do with her request. With some interpretive assistance, she acknowledged that she had raised my fee to manipulate me into doing her bidding—moving to midtown Manhattan to treat her. She identified with the sadistic, manipulative, conniving mother, while I identified with the guilty, vulnerable, humiliated child. Her insight into this paradigm is only partially developed.

At other times, she has placed me into the role of the mother, and she into the role of the child. Two years ago, Mei Ling fell in love with a man who lives in Virginia. He had a significant drinking problem and, perhaps more seriously, a profound fear of emotional commitment that Mei Ling expended mental energy trying to ignore. Mei Ling interpreted my comments to help her reflect on her avoidance of these issues as my desire to sabotage this relationship. At these moments, Mei Ling was unavailable for exploration. In this scenario of the paradigm, I was the sadistic, depriving, critical mother, while she was the victimized, deprived, misunderstood child relegated to desiring only what was hanging on the bargain rack. Reflecting on the demise of this relationship (he essentially vanished), Mei Ling chided me for not warning her about him so that she could have avoided the misery that followed. She placed me into the role of the uncaring, neglectful, unprotective mother, while she played the role of the uncared for, neglected, unprotected child who submits to her mother's perceived wishes for absolute devotion. In contrast to the childhood experience of her relationship with her mother, in which Mei Ling denied her feelings of rage, Mei Ling was able to express her resentment and dissatisfaction with me over the vulnerable feelings I had helped her to experience without avoidance. Mei Ling has begun to acknowledge the masochistic elements of her personality organization but has been less successful at acknowledging the sadistic elements.

The paternal transference, on the other hand, has not emerged as a consistent theme for investigation. I have made the interpretation that Mei Ling's "marriage" to her mother interferes with her aspirations to marry a man and have a family. Mei Ling responded that a part of her has often felt like a man in her relationship with her mother as well as in some nonfamilial contexts.

Description of Psychoanalytic Process

Having been referred by my psychoanalytic training institute, Mei Ling first met me in May 2004. While I was seeking a supervisor for this case, I decided that I would treat Mei Ling in once-per-week psychotherapy until September 2004, when I would convert the treatment into a four-times-per-week psychoanalysis. Mei Ling reacted with rage toward me for what she perceived to be my denying her the treatment she had been seeking. I also believed the rage to be, in part, a displacement of the rage she experienced toward another psychoanalytic institute for what she perceived as their abandonment of her for not accepting her as a control case and, genetically, toward her mother for her frequent threats of abandonment used as a control strategy. Other examples of Mei Ling's rage, accompanied by an inadequate capacity during these critical moments to reflect on the related unconscious dynamics, followed in subsequent sessions. This disagreement about the start date of the formal psychoanalysis did not get resolved, and the residual resentment continued to influence subsequent psychotherapy sessions until psychoanalysis formally began in September. Mei Ling also decided to continue seeing her other therapist simultaneously. The interpretation that Mei Ling had experienced my delay of the start of psychoanalysis until September as a rejection of her did little to change the acrimony that had developed in Mei Ling's relationship with me. In several sessions following the announcement of the delayed timetable, Mei Ling stated that she was feeling ambivalent about beginning psychoanalysis, citing financial concerns, the loudness of the office clock, and my asking a "stupid question" during the initial consultation. At this point, I began to wonder whether Mei Ling would stay in treatment, considering the lack of reflective capacity exhibited by Mei Ling during these moments of rage; however, Mei Ling's obvious intellectual gifts, coupled with my need for a control case, convinced me to continue with the plan to begin psychoanalysis in September. She probably stayed in treatment with me because, unlike her mother, I did not threaten abandonment when she acted unruly.

Complicating matters, Mei Ling became pregnant by her boyfriend just weeks after beginning psychotherapy. According to Mei Ling, her boyfriend, who was working on an art project in Italy, was not ready for fatherhood. She would keep the baby if he did not want any part of it. Later in the session, Mei Ling stated that she would terminate the pregnancy if her boyfriend wanted to participate as a father. When confronted by the apparent contradiction, Mei Ling accused me of making a sexist assumption that she would need to ask for a man's approval to give birth. Mei Ling also used this opportunity to express continued ambivalence about beginning psychoanalysis. When I pointed out that Mei Ling seemed to be on a roller coaster, she attributed her outburst to hormonal changes associated with the pregnancy.

Subsequent sessions consisted of Mei Ling's expression of anguish about whether to keep the baby or terminate the pregnancy, which seemed to parallel her unconscious worries about whether I was going to keep *her* in treatment or terminate *her*. I chose not to make this interpretation because Mei Ling did not yet experience the treatment as a holding environment. She sometimes perceived interpretations as attacks. In late June 2004, Mei Ling decided to terminate both her pregnancy and the therapy with the other therapist. I believe that holding onto the other therapist was like staying in a leaky boat until she could determine whether the other boat was seaworthy. Feeling secure in me and in the treatment, she could give up the other therapist and treatment. When I pointed out that Mei Ling was experiencing two losses—the loss of the pregnancy and the loss of her previous therapist—Mei Ling angrily responded that I spend too much time on "process" when all she wanted to do in the session was talk about her training for the New York City Marathon coming up in November. I was preventing her from talking about what she wanted to talk about.

Mei Ling's proneness to irritability with me continued into September 2004, when psychoanalysis, as well as weekly supervision, began. Early in the psychoanalysis, the supervisory advice seemed to consist of "weather the storms for now." As the reader will see from the case material, this advice was probably most helpful because it gave Mei Ling permission to express hostile feelings without the fear of perceived counterattack. As I continued to weather the storms, Mei Ling began to develop trust in me as a nonjudgmental, safe person who could tolerate her sense of badness without retaliation. Subsequent work revealed that Mei Ling experienced a profound sense of badness and related feelings of shame that she expended an enormous amount of mental energy trying to conceal from others. As this trust in my good will and nonjudgmental character continued to develop, a psychoanalytic process also began to develop in which Mei Ling was able to examine her angry reactions to me nondefensively. Mei Ling also began to realize that she was developing this latent reflective capacity, which has produced feelings of gratitude toward me for not giving up on her.

By the end of September 2004, I could comment on this profound sense of badness without an accompanying angry outburst. Mei Ling had been expressing a desire to break up with her boyfriend because she felt that her presumed failure as an artist made her an embarrassment to him at the artists' parties he invited her to attend with him. She had noticed that he never put his arm around her in public settings. I stated, "You feel you bring with you a sense of badness, which you feel hangs over him at these parties like a black cloud." The purpose of this interpretation was to increase her self-awareness of an unconscious self-perception while at the same time show her that this self-perception affects her perception of her boyfriend's respect and love for her. She did not respond defensively with an outburst, but neither did she respond reflectively to this comment. Rather, the comment seemed to grant Mei Ling permission to elaborate on this fantasy of contagion: "I fear that I could bring down his career because my friends reviewed his previous showing, and they could review his new showing and give him a bad review." Mei Ling seems to be saying that her friends, who are just as morally defective as she is, could easily turn on her and hurt her by hurting her boyfriend. She also seems to be conveying an unconscious sense of malevolent power, which could be contrasted with her conscious sense of herself as powerless. Finally, on a deeper level, her envy of her boyfriend's career success, and her resultant wish to destroy this success, are evident. I chose to point out the unconsciously perceived powerfulness of the malevolent self-perception rather than risk a deeper interpretation that could have created an outburst: "Pretty powerful." Mei Ling responded by demonstrating a nascent ability for self-reflectiveness: "Well, I know it's irrational, but I still think it's possible." I also noted the threshold of Mei Ling's tolerance for self-revelation, revealed in the slight tone of defensiveness contained in the phrase, "I still think it's possible."

Mei Ling's nascent ability to engage in self-reflectiveness, coupled with her reduction in angry outbursts, gradually made me realize that Mei Ling might actually stay in treatment. I allowed myself to be more hopeful about presenting this case someday to a panel of analysts in fulfillment of the final requirement for certification. The supervisor also noted the shift in Mei Ling's attitude toward me. In November 2004, Mei Ling completed the New York City Marathon, which filled her with pride. She had finally accomplished a difficult task without sabotaging it—a feat that she partly attributed to her progress in psychoanalysis. As I continued to point out the cruelty with which she often treated herself, thus analyzing the punitive aspects of her superego, Mei Ling's angry outbursts continued to diminish, and a theme of emotional depletion leading to self-destruction emerged. It seems as though this rage, often directed toward me but also toward significant others in her life, protected her from feelings of overwhelming despair and instead replaced them with feelings of self-sufficiency.

This sense of depletion was associated with childhood memories of her mother's seeming to look right through her, all the while producing "vitriolic spews of bile against humanity." Mei Ling disclosed that her mother often told her that her mother would someday have a heart attack because of her. Empathizing with the child in Mei Ling, I replied, "What a burden to carry." Then Mei Ling mentioned that she had gone shopping earlier in the day and "tried to see my body as belonging to me." When asked what she sees, Mei Ling replied that she "look[s] into the middle distance—seeing but not seeing. I can't see what I really look like. I lose a sense of my body, becoming detached. Eyes and brain floating in the world, detachment. For three years from the time I was twenty-four, I wore the same clothes every day." Making sense of this behavior for Mei Ling, I stated, "Wearing those clothes every day gave you a sense of continuity, a sense of stability about your body." She replied, "Yes, I still look fondly on those clothes as I think about them. . . . I sometimes feel my body floating away; I can't keep track of what's happening to me. I go shopping to find out whether I'm still the same by trying on a size that I know fits me. . . . I feel empty and can never feel full." She then disclosed a childhood memory of her mother's taking her shopping and repeatedly shouting her name to get her to see some clothes in the bargain section of the store. At these moments, I felt like a silent witness to a woman who at times felt that she was losing her mind, but who had clasped onto analysis like a lifesaver in the middle of the ocean.

This sense of depletion and fragmentation continues to emerge, particularly when Mei Ling experiences a narcissistic injury. In early February 2005, Mei Ling encountered an old boss on the street when she used to work as a graphic designer for an online movie magazine—a glamorous job she now regrets having given up ten years ago. As she tells it, Mei Ling's boss caught her up on all her former coworkers, who had gone on to become presidents of film companies, film directors, and film producers. And she was feeling left out, a lowly secretary at an accounting firm. Later in the session, Mei Ling stated that like her favorite authors and artists—Fitzgerald, Plath, van Gogh, Basquiat—she was going to burn out soon and die. She started crying softly. She feared that her boyfriend was going to die, that artists look awful. I interpreted the sense of depletion, the fantasy that creativity is distributed in limited amounts. This interpretation stimulated a memory of her parents turning gray before her eyes while running a laundromat business in Queens. She wondered whcther the same fate would befall her. Although not interpreted, it seems as though Mei Ling was communicating a sense of depletion she experienced in her parents, which resulted in a lack of recognition of her personhood. She grew up with a sense that she was not being held in her parents' minds, even in their presence. And now she was unable to hold a sense of her creativity, even a sense of her body, in her own mind. Entropy—the tendency for all matter in the universe to become disordered and random—seemed to be the dominant fantasy of her mental processes.

Although I did not interpret much of this material concerning depletion directly, the fact that I was listening to the sense of depletion, without looking through her, appeared therapeutic in itself. This deepening of the therapeutic relationship was beautifully illustrated in a session that took place just before my vacation in early June 2005. Mei Ling had begun painting again for the first time in almost two years and had just completed a first sketch of a painting. In this session, she announced that she had applied to an artist's colony. I asked how the colony might affect our work together. Mei Ling replied that the colony would not take place until 2006, "but I don't know how long this therapy is supposed to go. I guess it isn't even appropriate to talk about the end—I don't know." Sensing the connection between the artist's colony and my upcoming vacation, I replied, "But you've mentioned the end—I wonder whether your talking about the end has something to do with my going away." Mei Ling agreed that she had thought about that possibility, but an artist's colony would serve the purpose of fulfilling her ultimate dream of becoming an artist. Mei Ling defended against the awareness that she was moving away from me because of my impending loss through vacation by arguing that she was making a healthy career move. How could a therapist (or she) see anything pathological in that?

As I continued to inquire about her motives, Mei Ling finally stated, "Well, I don't want to depend on you. This [colony] gives me a glimmer of the end. I don't want to be in analysis forever." I decided first to interpret the anxiety surrounding the vacation and leave the accompanying anger for later: "Perhaps my going away has frightened you. This is the first time you've started talking about the end and attending an artist's colony." Getting slightly defensive, Mei Ling replied, "It scares me more that it seems to me that you want me to need you—like my mom. I'm afraid of losing objectivity and clarity and fighting. It was easy to fight with you at the beginning. Remember how many fights we had? I didn't want to know you; I didn't want to be here. I'm afraid of losing myself in the chaos. You usually remind me that you're trustworthy, that you're not going to judge me, so I don't think it would happen in here. This is the point in the relationship in which if you were my boyfriend, I would start getting fat." I analyzed the defense here: "Would that be distancing from me?" She confirms this interpretation: "Yeah, the relationship would end, but I'm in a different head space now. I think I would stop sharing everything because I'm so judgmental. I just think the judgmentalism, rejection, and wants—these are my core issues." Sensing that Mei Ling had just revealed her feelings behind the anxiety over my vacation, I made an interpretation: "I wonder whether my going away has stirred up these issues in a nonobvious way—that you want me to stay next week, but I'm leaving, and something about that feels like rejection and judgment to you."

Mei Ling's statement immediately following this interpretation confirms the progress she has made since the beginning of treatment:

> Yeah, I think I do depend on you, and my first inclination is to become self-sufficient. I feel like I'm taking on all the responsibility of carrying on this work. [My boyfriend] and I always had trouble depending on each other. It was hard

> to go to therapy just because I didn't think anyone else would help me. I think I am starting to learn how to elicit help, by being independent in one way. I trust you to help me. I think the natural reaction I have to your going away—I'm not feeling emotions to your going away, but my response is pragmatic. I'm going to be doing the work myself.

Analyzing the defense again, I responded, "Could that be a way of protecting yourself from feeling the emotions?" Mei Ling replied, "Yeah, that's opened up a whole area for me. If someone bumps into me or steps on my toe, I won't say anything for a long time because I feel I'm not allowed to complain or say 'ow!' As an adult, I've felt this fear that my protection would fail me when I would need it the most. I'm used to feeling the pain weeks later. I think a measure of success in here might be to be able to scream in pain when something painful is happening to me." Playfully, I replied, "Or to scream at me when I go away on vacation." Understanding my comment and recognizing her need for continued therapy, Mei Ling replied, "Yes, but I don't even have the emotional response for that yet."

The critical moment of this session takes place just following my interpretation of Mei Ling's feelings of rejection and judgment of her innate sense of badness, stimulated by my upcoming perceived abandonment of her. She first acknowledged her dependency on me, and then acknowledged her characteristic defense in such situations—self-sufficiency. Placed into the context of the early sessions, therefore, Mei Ling's angry outbursts might be understood as serving the purpose of making her feel more self-sufficient and less dependent on me. Emotional intimacy was too dangerous to risk because it makes the inevitable perceived abandonment that much more disorienting and fragmenting; self-sufficiency was equally dangerous because it was accompanied by emptiness and despair. These issues continued to emerge, and we continued to work through them as the analysis continued to deepen.

During the following years of analysis, Mei Ling seems to have changed in several ways. She seems better equipped to listen to and reflect on my comments nondefensively. I no longer feel as though I have to "walk on eggshells." Mei Ling can also articulate how she is feeling under challenging circumstances. Working empathically with Mei Ling's narcissistic vulnerabilities—particularly her neediness and defenses against it—seems to have facilitated these changes. Mei Ling has struggled with her art career and the twin fears of success and failure. She applied to an artist's colony in Vermont to hone her painting skills and bolster her self-esteem regarding her painting talents, but later devalued this colony for accepting her because "I wouldn't want to be a member of any club who accepts me." In one session, she complained of artist's block on a painting she had been working on. She also mentioned her fascination with a child who had been abducted in the 1970s, was raised by child molesters, and was finally returned to his original home, where he could not fit in. I said, "It's interesting if we look at the flow of this session. You began to talk about the inability to finish your painting. The implication is that if you finish it, you might get the recognition that is so terrifying to you. Then you mentioned the boy removed from his home and removed from all possible recognition, and then he is returned home and is never the same. It seems that in your mind, the lack of recognition can never be fixed." Mei Ling responded, "Yeah, and how his brother was so angry about what happened to the boy that he killed a family of women. He wasn't psychotic or psychopathic but was so angry about what had happened. I'm afraid that if I get recognition for this painting, it won't be enough." I said, "It's like you eating Cheetos in front of the TV and always wanting more Cheetos—never feeling fulfilled or filled with recognition." In a surprised tone of voice, Mei Ling replied, "Yes! That's what my painting is about. It's called 'Doritos'! With my family, there was always the next goal, always thinking about the future." I said, "It's hard for you to feel recognized when the focus is always on the future and goals rather than on you." Mei Ling then elaborated that her mother thinks about heaven as her ultimate goal in life and that Mei Ling feels guilty for not planning for her parents' retirement because the expectations are so high. Mei Ling also felt like a failure in school when her grades did not meet her parents' expectations. I remarked, "So what you were recognized for was only in certain areas. Recognition was dependent on success in these certain areas." Mei Ling replied, "I felt responsible for the money situation in my family, and I never got any gift I ever wanted in childhood." I reiterated, "Again, a lack of recognition for what *you* wanted and needed." Mei Ling said, "Yes, the threat of disowning me lasted until after I was out of the house—until there was nothing she [Mei Ling's mother] could disown me for." Because of Mei Ling's narcissistic vulnerability to feeling criticized and shamed, I was focusing on making empathic interpretations that would help Mei Ling feel understood rather than focusing on the rage implicit in her lack of recognition and embodied in the violent imagery surrounding the story of the abducted boy and his vengeful brother. More recent work has focused on Mei Ling's rage and the guilt and self-punishment it elicits (see below).

Mei Ling's feelings of recognition from others, in those rare moments when she does experience them, sometimes become sexualized. In one session, Mei Ling mentioned that a friend of hers in psychoanalysis quit because she thought that the male analyst was "after her sexually." She then associated to her previous therapist who had asked her whether she experienced sexual feelings toward him, which prompted an uncontrollable bout of giggling. She stated that she did not feel attracted to him because he was "from the '70s" and did not allow herself to feel sexual with him. She then spontaneously compared the previous therapist to me: "You seem more accessible, more familiar to me. You're more present to me." I asked, "Since you brought it up, do you have sexual feelings toward me?" Mei Ling replied, "I think I could if I thought about it, but I block out that whole part of you. I got a little dizzy saying that. I think it's hard to talk about sexuality when I'm trying to get help from you—nonsexual help." I responded, "You seem to feel that just talking about sexuality, even if it's between us, that something would actually happen." Mei Ling remarked, "I think I'm very impressionable. If the suggestion is out there, I just might take it. . . . Ashley's mother fell in love with her therapist. We thought how pathetic and lonely a person is for falling in love with your therapist. It's already a strange relationship—like you know more about me than anybody else."

In a later session, Mei Ling returned to this theme: "I tried hard not to give off sexual vibes in the last therapy so that I wouldn't have to deal with sexual countertransference—as if I could control that. . . . I think you see me as this petty and irritating person you have to come and treat. . . . This is the point [in the treatment] where I've had sexual relationships with men when they've found me irritating. . . . This weight gain could be about our relationship, so I wouldn't see you as having sexual feelings toward me." I responded, "So on a superficial level, you're afraid I might find you petty and irritating, but at a slightly lower level, you're afraid I might find you sexually attractive." Mei Ling responded, "Exactly. Actually, I'm glad you're a male so that I can work through this. I'm feeling like a preadolescent. I just started having a sexual relationship and pretended I wasn't too abnormal about it." Mei Ling then talked about previous boyfriends who have left her and how there are no second chances. I asked, "Does that include me?" Mei Ling replied, "Well, I'm afraid you're sick of me. . . . There's a possibility you could leave—not treat me anymore. I don't know how these things end, but there's more certainty that it will end professionally. Everyone else hasn't loved me enough to stay bound to me; they leave." I remarked, "On the one hand, you fear I might be sexually attracted to you. On the other hand, I might leave you. That sounds like opposite ends of the spectrum." She responded, "It's all about you, isn't it? [laughs] You're right; I either get no attention at all from guys, or they see me as a sexual object. My cynicism, though, actually made that true. I actually looked for the Asiaphiles at Williams [College]. I saw it happen with my sister—either nothing or sexual object." I responded, "So either I'm an Asiaphile and you're my prey, or I'm vaguely annoyed by you and will get rid of you." Mei Ling replied, "Yes, I feel I'm really not attractive to men. I combine the worst stereotypes of Asian and Jewish women. . . . I can't believe

I just admitted that to you. I can't believe it, but I don't know you socially. I've been admitting a lot more to you lately. I make myself into the worst possible personality." I said, "There's an assumption that if you were who you were at your core, you would be totally unlovable to another person." Mei Ling responded, "But I think it's based on experience. At my core I'm a fat feminist. [laughs]"

In this session, one notices the progression in reflective functioning that Mei Ling has made over the course of treatment. At the beginning of treatment, Mei Ling often accused me of focusing exclusively on "process"—by which she meant her perceptions of me—and ignoring her real daily concerns. In this session, however, we notice that her diminished narcissistic vulnerability allows for a shift toward a more open stance toward transferential material. Mei Ling still accuses me of focusing the treatment on myself, but now she can joke about it and even illustrate my point by discussing her self-constructed Asiaphile experiences at college. Mei Ling's ability to tolerate transference interpretations has thus increased.

Mei Ling attended the artist's colony in Vermont for one month. My supervisor and I decided along with Mei Ling that we would have phone analysis four times per week. To my surprise, Mei Ling did not follow through on phone analysis. In the first session following her return, Mei Ling stated that her cell phone did not work at the colony and that the public phones did not afford her the privacy necessary to participate in phone analysis. Mei Ling also acknowledged that she wanted to know whether she could exist without me during that month of separation. She shared her fears of dependency and her concern (and simultaneous wish) that the analysis would last forever. She also seemed to feel reassured that I was still here—that I had survived the separation and was ready to return to exploration with her. Soon after her experience at the artist's colony, Mei Ling met a man (Matthew) at the wedding of a friend in Tahiti. This man was attending the wedding with his girlfriend but made sexual advances toward Mei Ling, who readily accepted them. I interpreted that she might be attracted to him because of her awareness that he had a girlfriend in tow, but she rejected this interpretation. They sneaked around this girlfriend and had sex in Tahiti. Matthew explained that he had been planning to break up with her for some time and was trying to find the right words and the right time to do it. They had been together for six years. Eventually, Matthew did break up with his girlfriend, and for a while Mei Ling was relatively happy in this new long-distance relationship (he lives in Virginia). She described her discovery of feelings of emotional intimacy during sex with Matthew and her wish to "nest" with him and start a family.

Simultaneous with these feelings of exhilaration and hope were feelings of profound pessimism rooted in the expectation (perhaps a wish) that Matthew would ultimately abandon her because of some infraction or series of infractions. In one session, Mei Ling confided, "I'm at a point [in my treatment] where I can attract someone like Matthew, but I need to work on keeping him." I said, "You sound as though he could slip through your fingers at any time." Mei Ling responded, "But that's not surprising, is it? I like to paint about self-loathing." I said, "I wonder whether your self-loathing has a function of keeping you connected to your mother, so it's reassuring to you. If Matthew leaves, well, you'll still have the haunting presence of your mother to keep you company." Mei Ling replied,

> Yes, there's truth in that, because that's what I was rewarded for. There's a comfort zone in that—"I'm working really hard, but I'm not succeeding. People aren't recognizing what I'm doing." I used to rail against that as a child, but that characterizes my father and sister. . . . I was then proud of quitting [my prestigious job at a major magazine] and having no health insurance and living on $7,000 that year. First time I was ever alone—and a real purity and solitude about that—and I felt proud of that. But I realized it's impossible to live a life like that in black and white like my mother. But what I thought was rebelling against her was really getting closer to her. It's ironic, but I took on those traits—she's infiltrated every pore of my body—and I think I've begun to separate from her, but it's going to take a long time to get her critical thoughts out of my mind.

In contrast to Mei Ling's zeal in the early stages of treatment to protect her mother from any kind of implicit criticism, in this session, Mei Ling elaborated on my comment that her fear of losing Matthew through self-loathing disguises an underlying wish to lose Matthew and therefore remain loyally connected to her mother. This separation-individuation process continues as Mei Ling develops an awareness that both she and her mother will survive the psychic differentiation taking place within her.

An outgrowth of this evolving psychic differentiation is Mei Ling's increased potential for healthy self-assertion. She was becoming increasingly self-reflective about it: "I remember at the beginning of analysis, there was a point where we were discussing when I was treated badly, and you put it like—people said things to me and I just took it. I felt defensive when you said that because I thought I didn't take anything. I'd get angry, but it was a way of covering how destroyed I was. But I would confuse it with not taking it. I didn't understand that at the time, but I do now." Through this growth, Mei Ling was able to confront Matthew when he began to pull away from her and eventually stopped communication altogether. Matthew's reasons for pulling away and stopping communication were completely unsatisfactory to Mei Ling, sounding more like excuses. Matthew told her that he realized that he had not mourned the loss of his ex-girlfriend and that he needed to sort through his feelings on his own. He would rejoin her in a relationship when he was ready. Matthew never contacted her again. Matthew's abandonment prompted a long period of self-reproach that proved difficult for Mei Ling to observe and reflect on. She was convinced that she had driven him away—specifically, that her constant need for reassurance of his love drove him away. Interpretations seemed to have little impact on her need to reproach herself for this loss. At this point in the treatment, it was unclear whether Mei Ling would risk seeking another nonincestuous object or once again fall back on the comfort of the sadomasochistic relationship with her mother.

While grieving the loss of Matthew, Mei Ling was simultaneously making strides to move out of the condominium she co-owned with her mother and move into her own place, which suggests a significant move toward individuation and the possibility of oedipal love. In one session, Mei Ling stated, "I'm having difficulty moving out of my mother's place and into this new apartment [my broker found for me]." I said, "What it could mean is that you can't separate from your mother." Mei Ling responded:

> I'm very much her minion, or was, or continue to be a little bit. I think we're connected by the heart, and what you said reminds me of her saying I was going to give her a heart attack [throughout my childhood]. You're right that this apartment is symbolic of my mother. . . . My mother thinks everyone's against her, and maybe by giving up the apartment, she'll think I'm against her, and maybe she will die [crying]. I guess I've always taken my mother seriously. I felt we [she and her sister] couldn't do as much as we could.

I replied, "You were a child. What *could* you do?" Mei Ling said, "I know. [sobbing] It was like being raised in an attic. I wondered why I was so nervous and anxious and why I couldn't relax, and it just makes so much sense now." In this vignette, Mei Ling understands the symbolic nature of her living space and her fear of separating from it because of the damage it could do in fantasy to her mother. Mei Ling is now risking experiencing angry feelings toward her mother. She now appears poised to kill off her mother in fantasy to free herself from this symbiotic relationship. As the analysis continues to deepen, we will have many more opportunities to explore her aggressive urges toward her mother, her mother's survival of these fantasized attacks in reality, and the resultant effects on her autonomy.

In a later session, Mei Ling revisited the issue of her symbiotic relationship with her mother in connection with her career ambitions:

> I feel that when I'm successful, my mother will have a heart attack—that I'll suddenly have to support her and be at her side. That's been my job her whole life. She's still doing that: "Don't do your bidding; do *my* bidding." . . . My mother said I should be a medical assistant, and I think she's happy that I'm a

> secretary. . . . It's part of my family's tragedy because we were not allowed to do the things that came naturally to us. Our conversations were so absurd—her arguing [with me] that I should have plastic surgery. . . . But she didn't want my sister to have it when my sister really wanted it! [laughs]

I remarked, "It seems that you need to punish yourself for your success and autonomy by being in servitude to your mother, which is both a fear and a wish of yours." Mei Ling replied, "Yeah, I am hurting myself, I'm downwardly mobile. . . . Did my mother try to usurp the things I wanted?"

More recently, however, Mei Ling suggested that, at age thirty-eight, her failure to have a successful career and a family has brought shame on her parents, who belong to a Chinese community where children bring honor to their parents through career achievement and having grandchildren. I interpreted the underlying rage in this context by linking these perceived failures to her retaliation against her parents' unrealistic expectations and lack of recognition of her emotional needs. This passive-aggressive attack against them then produces guilt feelings, which only increase the need for self-punishment in the form of sabotaging her own goals for herself. Mei Ling has reached a stage in the treatment where she was able to acknowledge this dynamic and express her rage toward her parents, and especially toward her mother, in a more direct manner in sessions.

Over the course of an entire year, Mei Ling struggled with her feelings of loss in the wake of Matthew's abandonment, her wish to cling to him in a sadomasochistic relationship, and her questioning whether psychoanalysis is helping or hurting her—in other words, whether she and I are engaged in a sadomasochistic relationship. Considering the sacrifices I make to treat Mei Ling—in money, time, and travel—I have had some countertransferential difficulty allowing myself to be cast in a sadistic role. At times, Mei Ling has complained that I am making matters worse and on one occasion implied that I was responsible for the failure of her relationship with Matthew, and more broadly, for causing the misery of loneliness and longing outside her protective "bubble." Supervision and my own analysis have been helpful in working through my responses to her need to perceive me as unhelpful or sadistic. In one session, Mei Ling stated, "I think there's still something scary about psychoanalysis, and I want to overcome it." I said, "Maybe we could talk about it and figure it out together." She continued:

> Well, I guess I feel that part of the reason the relationship with Matthew failed—I want to hold onto the sadomasochism. Not that I want to be undignified, but I'm not sure I want to do the right thing. . . . This is all about self-esteem, and I want higher self-esteem in my art but not always in my relationships. I know you're right, but I don't want to be perfect. Maybe perfect in art but not in my

> relationships. . . . I guess I want to think that there is a promise of a relationship with Matthew.

I responded, "But it's become a cat-and-mouse game, and I think there is a certain measure of pleasure that you get out of it." She said, "I'm getting irritated, and I know that you're right whenever I get irritated. But I don't think I want to explore it. There are just so many other things to understand. These are moments of resistance. I'm not totally devastated, but I'm feeling bad." I replied, "So what might be going on is that you come in here, and I'm just picking at the scab that has formed on the open wound, so I can understand how you might not want to come in here and have me picking at your scab." Mei Ling remarked, "I think that's totally it. You see me for forty-five minutes, but for nine hours before, I feel as though I'm starting to feel better. . . . I can see what you're saying about Matthew because I'm like the loving puppy dog just waiting to serve Matthew, and that comes out of my relationship with my mother." In this passage, Mei Ling attacks psychoanalysis for upholding the value of self-esteem, which she views as a threat to her wish to hold onto Matthew, a man who has rejected her. Her irritation with me over her perception that I was depriving her of this relationship did not prevent her, however, from exploring her desire to reengage with Matthew sadomasochistically by groveling to get him back.

In a later session, I addressed her frustration with me: "You're frustrated this isn't helping, but you don't share that with me." She replied, "Why would I get angry at you? It's the process. It's me, you, the process, and Freud—not just you." I quipped, "It's suddenly become very crowded in here." She laughed and continued, "Why get angry at you? You're familiar, and it's hard for that to come out." I responded, "So perhaps you like me, and it's hard to show anger when you have liking feelings toward me. If you show them, then maybe you'll spoil our relationship, or I'll go away." Mei Ling replied, "Well, I do worry about how far you have to drive, and it makes me feel guilty." I asked, "Why do you take that on? . . . You're so invested in trying to guess what others are thinking and feeling so that you can adjust your thoughts and feelings accordingly. But what happens to *you*? You get obscured in all that, and it's all to forestall potential abandonment." Mei Ling agreed: "Yeah, I think that's it—a primary fear of abandonment." One notices Mei Ling's difficulty with tolerating her feelings of anger toward me because she fears that I will abandon her.

Mei Ling also sometimes longs for the days when she could be oblivious to her anger, her anxieties, and even time itself. She called her current state of mind "being out of the bubble—and there are feelings coming up." I said, "I think you're realizing that 'being out of the bubble' involves facing some harsh realities, which can be painful—looking at the flaws and weaknesses in yourself—painful stuff." She continued, "Yeah, I'm really feeling that, and you know what the biggest difference is? All the time I have now, and all the time I've squandered, [crying] especially the opportunities I've squandered to have a lasting relationship with people, because it's hard to do that at my age when everybody's on their second child. I'm just angry at myself and at all the forces that kept me in the bubble—all the time wasted. . . . I make choices that make my world like my mother's." Mei Ling has continued this mourning process for a past life lost in daydreaming and confusion as she also begins to actualize her capacity to live a present and future life filled with meaning and hope.

During the third year of psychoanalysis, three major external events occurred that have affected the treatment process and Mei Ling's state of mind: her purchase of a condominium in Staten Island, her interest in a male co-worker, and my shift of supervisor because my former supervisor moved out of state. These three events, taken together as a whole, created a version of "a perfect storm" that resulted in some breaches of empathy for the patient in some sessions. These breaches of empathy, I believe, have diminished as my new supervisor and I have begun to develop a common understanding of this patient.

In April 2007, Mei Ling purchased a condominium in Staten Island. She had been looking for condominiums in Staten Island since 2006, but inevitably she would look for and find "a fatal flaw" with each one and begin a new search. I painstakingly analyzed these "false starts" as attempts at staying connected, psychologically and physically, with her mother, who owned the condominium in midtown Manhattan where she had been living for many years. At the same time, these searches reflected what I believe was a healthy urge to individuate from her mother and begin a new life as an adult, not simply "a minion" of her mother, as she had perceived herself for so many years. This desire to find a new place to live—a place she could call her own—was stimulated by her mother's pronouncement that she would be moving to New York from Taiwan, where she has been living intermittently with Mei Ling's father. Mei Ling felt terrified that her mother would impose on her to move into the midtown condominium owned by her mother—a typical one-bedroom living space the size of some celebrities' walk-in closets. In March 2007, Mei Ling's mother made good on her pronouncement and moved in with Mei Ling. Initially, while still in Taiwan, Mei Ling's mother informed Mei Ling that the move would be only temporary but provided no reason for this move. After moving in, however, Mei Ling's mother said that she in fact had no plans on moving back to Taiwan. Mei Ling expressed rage toward her mother in sessions for lying about her intentions but refused to manifest it directly to her mother because she feared that it would make the living situation even more difficult to tolerate than it already was. This series of events accelerated Mei Ling's search for her own condominium in Staten Island—close enough to her job and analysis but far enough away from midtown Manhattan and her mother.

According to Mei Ling, her mother quietly accepted Mei Ling's new purchase at first. Mei Ling's mother and father visited the Staten Island condominium without making any comment on its appearance or location. The mother's true feelings about Mei Ling's departure from the mother became more apparent in the ensuing months, when she started threatening to throw away various items that Mei Ling had left in the midtown condominium. In sessions, Mei Ling used her mother's callous treatment of these items as evidence that she has no warmth. For example, she contrasted her mother's behavior to that of the parents of her friends, who have kept childhood possessions in their parents' homes with no threats of removal. These fears of removal paralleled Mei Ling's fears that I would remove her because she believed she was not making sufficient progress in the treatment. Conveying this insight to Mei Ling compelled her to recount all the successes she feels she has made in analysis—an attempt to protect me from any potential damage to my self-esteem brought about by her profound sense of badness, a theme sounded many times during the course of this treatment. Mei Ling seems poised to discover that her sense of badness originates in her murderous wishes toward her loved mother as well as in the internalization of the mother's murderous wishes (both fantasized and real) toward Mei Ling. Guilt over these feelings toward the simultaneously loved and hated object is only beginning to emerge in the treatment.

As she began to settle into her new residence, Mei Ling began to make a host of complaints about various features such as the dry, moldy, smelly air, the noise made by footsteps from the upstairs tenant, the construction going on outside the apartment building, and, most ominously, the putative effects on her health and psychological functioning. These complaints became increasingly pointed and desperate and coincided with incisive self-reproaches for not having taken a condominium she had been interested in the previous year. She had completely repressed that she had uncovered structural problems with the building in which that unit had been housed, which resulted in the withdrawal of her bid. Mei Ling often returned to the mantra that she has purchased "a lemon" and that she knows "nothing about shopping" for herself.

In July 2007, a new employee, Adam, joined the staff at her accounting firm. She described him as young and attractive. At first, she wondered about the appropriateness of dating a coworker. She initially reacted to him by being "rude . . . because I was attracted to him, and I don't want to be that way. It was because I was attracted to him, and I didn't like feeling that and was immediately turned off. Is it okay to be attracted to someone in the work situation?" My reaction to Mei Ling's ambivalence was to take a neutral position and wait for an opportunity to interpret her anxiety regarding intimacy, which she has consistently demonstrated over the duration of the treatment, and to understand its origins and functions for her. Predictably, in the ensuing months, Mei Ling erected other barriers to getting romantically involved with Adam. These barriers included a sizable age difference (he is twenty-three), his presumed interest only in blonde-haired, blue-eyed celebrities (he had made some remarks about the attractiveness of several celebrities), and the differences in their professional goals (he wants to start his own accounting firm someday). In spite of these barriers (or perhaps because of them), Mei Ling's romantic interest in this man continued to develop. Based on her reporting, it seems as though Mei Ling was able to nurture a friendship, perhaps even a mutual romantic interest, with this young man. He gave her a greeting card, instant messaged her throughout the work day from his desk, and shared some of his personal life with Mei Ling.

At the end of the first three months, however, Adam revealed that he had started dating someone. Mei Ling used this information both to erect yet another barrier to developing a mutually satisfying romantic relationship with him and to develop even deeper feelings for him. I began to inquire why it was so difficult for Mei Ling to have a straightforward talk with Adam about her feelings. Mei Ling initially replied that she feared he would reject her—that he perceived her as an "old cougar" trying to catch a young stud. He would ultimately ridicule her for having feelings for someone who was obviously out of her league. Curiously, in spite of Adam's revelation that he was dating someone, his subtle flirtation with Mei Ling continued, much to the bewilderment and pleasure of Mei Ling. She wavered between wanting the flirtatious behavior between them to continue and wanting it to stop altogether. In a recent session, Mei Ling reported that Adam was looking for a gym to join and wanted to explore Mei Ling's gym as a possibility. When asked for her feelings about it, Mei Ling replied that she was going to tell Adam that she did not want him joining her gym. When I pointed out the obvious hostility in this premeditated behavior, Mei Ling replied, "Well, I'm competing with someone and losing." We then explored how she felt that her father had ignored her during childhood and gave all his attention to her mother and sister, with none left over for her. Mei Ling realized that she was recapitulating a painful experience from her childhood.

In a more recent session, Mei Ling's explanation for not expressing her feelings to Adam directly shifted from a fear of rejection to a desire to get Adam to express *his* feelings first so that she can then reject *him*. She stated that she does not imagine settling down with Adam but rather avoiding the embarrassment of the "old cougar" dating a younger man. She lamented that her father was absent from her life as a child and still as an adult—that "he does not have this love for me." My attempt to connect these feelings of absentee or uncaring men with my own recent vacation succeeded in provoking a hostile attack: "I don't even think of you as a man—I neutralize you. . . . I just became self-sufficient. I've survived in New York City because of my self-sufficiency. I think it's really narcissistic of you to say that. You function like a hindrance to me because my mind isn't focused on the real relationships in my life like my father and mother. What you're doing really isn't helping. You always do this and it's really annoying to me." I responded that it sounds as though she has gone back into her protective shell. She replied, "Yeah, well, if I hadn't done that, maybe I would have killed myself. I could have used you on Christmas Eve [her birthday], but you weren't here, so I dealt with it on my own. You want me to admit I missed you. Well, I missed you, okay, but everybody else does things—makes decisions on their own, and they survive. So I just pretended to be fine, and I was." Since the first year of treatment, attention to the transference has seldom aroused this level of rage in Mei Ling. Since moving into her own residence and developing a romantic interest in Adam, however, Mei Ling seems more acutely anxious and perhaps fearful of the delusional contents of her mind (see below). When I am not present as a compensatory structure, Mei Ling becomes fearful of fragmentation and disorganization and blames me for abandoning her in her greatest time of need.

Coinciding with this upheaval in Mei Ling's life, I changed supervisors. The new supervisor underscored the oedipal conflicts Mei Ling is struggling with, while the former supervisor had highlighted Mei Ling's narcissistic vulnerabilities, produced by a symbiotic attachment to her mother and simultaneous cocoon-like protection against her. Indeed, in sessions, Mei Ling provided compelling evidence for a condensation of the preoedipal and oedipal phases of development. She perceived her mother as simultaneously ensnaring her and keeping her from having a "normal" life—with a husband, children, and career. Because she was terrified of her own condominium, Mei Ling began sleeping at her mother's condominium, which sometimes made her feel invigorated and alive. In a different session, however, Mei Ling questioned her decision to sleep at her mother's residence: "She sleep deprives me and manipulates me." Under this supervisory change, I sometimes struggled with choosing the most appropriate interventions to make, given my recent exposure to the perspective that Mei Ling sometimes functions at a higher developmental phase than I had previously given her credit for. In this session in which Mei Ling perceived her mother as a persecutor, I pointed out how

Mei Ling feels like a helpless victim in the face of an all-powerful, torturing mother who prohibits her from having a normal life. Mei Ling sharply disagreed, and said she was tired of hearing "that I can do something about this because it feels that I can't." Had I conceptualized Mei Ling in that moment as a patient struggling to maintain a psychic boundary to ward off a terrifying mother rather than as a patient angry with her mother for spoiling her wishes for a career and family, I would have empathized with Mei Ling's persecutory anxiety and provided a stable good object for her to identify with during these moments of experienced terror. This brief exchange between Mei Ling and me under this supervisory change illustrates one of these empathic breaches based on confusion about the extent of her regression and level of personality organization. Having physically separated from her mother, Mei Ling began to convey a siege mentality in relation to her residence (both a wish for and fear of the mentally ill mother), which coincided with a deterioration in the quality of her thought processes.

Subsequent sessions have demonstrated to both my new supervisor and me that Mei Ling struggles primarily with narcissistic vulnerabilities that under certain conditions produce delusional thinking. Instead of directly challenging this thinking, as I had been doing over the second half of last year under the assumption of a higher level of personality organization, I am now "getting into Mei Ling's bubble with her," experiencing her terror with her and not abruptly introducing reality. This approach seems to be maintaining the connection between us and keeping her from disintegrating altogether. The delusions are somatically based and revolve around her belief that her Staten Island residence was aging her and slowly killing her. The following passage provides a flavor of the content of these delusions: "I just hate my place. I'm slowly aging in there. I wake up with wrinkles on my face. I bought a coffin, and now they're building up around me." I said, "It must be frightening that you feel you've bought a coffin." She replied:

> Yeah, here I am, trying to escape my mother's claws [the prototypical old cougar], and now I'm in a coffin. I'm scared I won't recoup my costs for this apartment, and it sucks to feel this first major decision to do something good for myself has been an unequivocal failure. I've lost time, money, moisture [referring to her face]. . . . I'm almost willing to solve the problem by cutting my losses and save my health. . . . I'm tired of trying to live there because it's just not working. I can't even paint there now because they start construction at 8 a.m. I was [in the neighborhood] when I was harassed by . . . kids. I don't feel safe there. . . . I'm so tired because I never sleep. I feel as though if I go to sleep, I'll die because it's the breath of death [in her apartment]. I feel as though it's hard to go to sleep because I'll die if I do, it's a coffin, there's no air. And I wake up so much older. I gotta get out of there. I have to get out.

In a later session, Mei Ling continued this somatic theme: "I've never felt this unhealthy before. Now, I found something else I'm allergic to [in the apartment]. I have to get out of this apartment. I'm allergic to the detergent." I asked, "What about the detergent?" She replied, "Well, the rusty water interacts with this detergent, and it's destroying my skin. My skin has eczema all over it because it's so dry in there. . . . There's definitely something wrong with the construction of the apartment." My work with Mei Ling consisted of trying to get inside her experience of terror and waiting to see where this experience would lead us next. The lifeline of psychoanalysis eventually stabilized Mei Ling sufficiently so that she could recompensate and continue the painful, frightening individuation process.

Mei Ling eventually moved out of her Staten Island condominium and rented it out. She moved into a luxury apartment in lower Manhattan where she reestablished a psychological equilibrium she had not experienced since living with her mother. Unfortunately, this new apartment also became dangerous to her:

> This new place isn't the comfortable place I thought it would be. It's arguably as uncomfortable as my [Staten Island] apartment. The previous tenant acknowledged he was crazy [for living there] but that he wasn't that bothered by it. . . . I can't find anything good about this apartment. . . . I'm so chilled to the core that I can't even get warm, and I've tried because I'm not sleeping at night. I wake up every two hours. . . . I'm looking at my apartment as a mausoleum—death by pneumonia—and I forget about how beautiful my apartment is. I focus on the dread.

Mei Ling also talked about her perceived lack of appeal to men and attributed it to her lack of warmth—a quality she admires in her older sister. In this same vein, Mei Ling mentioned feeling sick from her cold apartment but not wanting to reach out to her mother for nurturance: "The last person I want to see is my mother because she just sucks the energy right out of you. She feeds you this healthy food while she's feeding on your brain. She sucks you dry mentally. She lived in New Jersey for two years by herself. She just sat in one room with a space heater because she didn't want to spend money heating the house." Mei Ling also criticized the psychoanalytic process as contributing to a sense of "alienation—my feelings are so calculating now. I don't think people feel as comfortable around me. They think maybe I'm above it all. . . . I'm glad I have passion, and I don't want to feel as though I'm a puppet master." I suggested that perhaps she perceives me sometimes as she perceives her mother—sucking the warmth and feeling right out of her, which sometimes makes the psychoanalytic process seem like a dangerous place like her apartment. Mei Ling responded by reciting her personal failures: "What I mean is that I'm just now getting an apartment at age thirty-eight. It's just really late, and I'm making these mistakes that most people make at age twenty-five, and it feels like such a mess, and it's about nothing important." In future work, I will continue gradually to uncover Mei Ling's unconscious identification with her mother and the ways in which this identification keeps Mei Ling tethered to her mother instead of striking out on her own to form a new family, with a new set of interdependent relationships outside the fantasy bubble and outside her mother's orbit.

Chapter Three

The Jellyfish: Processes of Therapeutic Change in an Analysand with Borderline Personality Disorder

CARLY

Chief Complaint at Initial Consultation

"I have problems with intimacy; I've almost always had other partners. . . . I've been depressed all of my adult life."

Brief Personal History

Carly is a forty-nine-year-old co-owner of a restaurant business of Irish American descent who initially presented with symptoms of depression, anhedonia, morbid obesity, excessive alcohol consumption, intense, inappropriate anger and mood lability, unstable interpersonal relationships, and impulsivity. Her chief complaints included dissatisfaction in her current partner relationship of eighteen years and a chronic, low-grade depression that has accompanied her entire adult life. Carly is the second oldest of six children. Her father was a professor at Queens College in accounting, while her mother was mostly a housewife. The family lived in Woodside, New York, in a working-class neighborhood until Carly entered eighth grade, when the family moved to Forest Hills. Around the time of the move to Forest Hills, Carly's paternal grandmother, who had lived just down the street from the family and with whom Carly had a "special relationship," died.

Carly felt extremely isolated in her new school, where she was only "one of two Irish kids among sixty-two Jews and two Hispanics." Carly's grades slipped, and she began to engage in antisocial activities with the few friends she was able to make—shoplifting, destruction of mailboxes, lighting matches and throwing them on piles of leaves, smoking marijuana and ingesting alcohol, and stealing cars for joy rides—from the age of fourteen. Carly did not finish high school, but returned at age nineteen to receive her Graduate Equivalency Diploma. At the encouragement of her father, Carly enrolled at Queens College but dropped out at age twenty-one after her father died suddenly of a massive heart attack at age forty-eight. She never returned to college. After this event, Carly maintained some semblance of stability but felt she could be living a more meaningful life like her professionally and financially successful siblings. She worked as a supervisor at a laundromat for many years, then quit and formed a restaurant business with her lesbian partner for the past thirteen years. In her current relationship, Carly has been monogamous except for one affair three years ago that coincided with the completion of a controversial diet in which she lost 150 pounds. After the affair, Carly regained 70 pounds, and at 5'11" inches tall, weighed 290 pounds at the initial consultation.

As Carly recalls it, her relationship with her mother was marked by profound ambivalence. Carly felt extremely loyal, yet confused and angry, toward her mother. She loved her mother but also felt deeply unloved and neglected by her. In the second year of treatment, Carly began to talk about her feeling unloved and neglected by her mother as a child. Carly's mother contributed to these feelings by frequently hitting Carly or tending to her other five children while neglecting Carly. A dynamic emerged in which Carly would misbehave to ensure some form of attention from her mother—positive or negative. She recalled putting gold stars on her scholastic tests—thus disguising her failures—so that she would gain some recognition from her mother. Similarly, talking back to her mother or shirking her chores also earned her mother's attention—screaming at or hitting Carly. Repeatedly in the treatment, Carly has paraded her misbehavior in front of me—drinking, taking unprescribed pain medication, aggressive driving, smoking marijuana, binge eating—to elicit my concern and, possibly, my active intervention. These provocative behaviors seem designed in part to accomplish a masochistic gratification of what amounts to a beating fantasy. Carly has been successful in her attempts to elicit not only concern but also worry in me, which I have discussed with my supervisor. She has not been successful, however, in eliciting my active intervention to keep her safe, which I believe has been a source of feelings of deprivation, a perceived failure to protect her, a reliving of feelings of neglect, and resulting feelings of anger, which one can hear in the clinical material that follows. Kesha, Carly's lesbian partner of eighteen years, has assumed the role of auxiliary ego for Carly. Kesha functions like the mother of a child, basically running their restaurant business, waking Carly up in the morning for her sessions, taking care of all the finances and household organization, giving her practical advice, and making all the major life decisions. Carly has said that if Kesha died, Carly would drive to their vacation home in Delaware and "crawl into the fetal position."

Carly's perceived relationship with her father has not been a predominant theme of the treatment. She has described him as a tall, large, affectionate, but remote man preoccupied with his academic responsibilities as a professor. Carly explained that her father seldom used physical punishment because "he knew he would kill us if he did." Carly expressed the wish that her father would have intervened more forcefully to stop her mother from beating her. She recalled her father once calling out "Evelyn, Evelyn!" (her mother's name) to stop her mother, which failed. Anger toward her father has not directly emerged. Carly also admired her father for his academic prowess. She decided to enroll at Queens College, where he was a professor, but dropped out soon after he died of a massive heart attack at the school when she was twenty years old. Even before he died, however, Carly often skipped classes to smoke marijuana, perhaps to elicit attention from her preoccupied father.

Carly felt extremely close to her paternal grandmother, who lived just down the street from the family. Carly often ran away from home to her grandmother's house, where her grandmother frequently spoke disapprovingly of Carly's mother. Carly stated that, at times, she felt disloyal to her mother because she was giving her grandmother an audience. What Carly's grandmother gave to Carly that Carly apparently was not receiving at home, however, was her undivided attention, warmth, and availability as a safe haven whenever Carly wanted to flee the chaos of her own home. Unlike her mother, Carly had her grandmother all to herself. This source of security and gratification abruptly ended for Carly at age fourteen, however, when her grandmother died.

Case Formulation

Carly presented with borderline personality organization with identity diffusion, a reliance on primitive defensive processes, and tenuous but generally intact reality testing. Carly's preferred defensive processes included denial, devaluation, and flight into action. At the time of the initial consultation, her tolerance for any unpleasant affect was dangerously low. She warded off even mildly unpleasant affects before she became aware of them. Carly relied on an assortment of external substances and behaviors to assist her in the banishment of these affects from conscious awareness. The substances included food, alcohol, and drugs. The behaviors that accomplished the same purpose included flirting with other women, aggressive driving, and, at times, hypomanic activity related to running her business. These affects were either discharged immediately or numbed with the assistance of these substances and behaviors.

Having grown up in a household of six children in which the child one year younger than she was became an academic and athletic star, Carly lacked the attention she craved. Although Carly has few specific memories of her childhood, she remembers herself always at the center of trouble. Her mother would be tending to household chores or one of the other children while Carly was sitting in the basement alone, eating ice cream and watching television. Her mother did respond to Carly's misbehavior, however, by hitting her in her face and on her body. A mother-daughter dynamic evolved in which (1) Carly felt neglected by her mother and resentful that some of her siblings were receiving more than their fair share of their mother's attention, (2) Carly felt angry toward her mother for this neglect and need to compete with her siblings, and (3) Carly felt guilty about these feelings toward her mother; therefore, she (4) learned to pacify her guilty feelings by punishing herself. The self-punishment both expiated the feelings of guilt and captured the mother's attention, which was the original objective. Carly often got into trouble at school for not completing her homework or for skipping school and shoplifting or going places without permission. Her mother would find out and punish her, which would bring instant relief from guilt as well as the maternal recognition she craved. Carly's overeating, drinking alcohol to excess, ingesting prescription narcotic medication, and smoking marijuana serve to expiate feelings of guilt over her envious, resentful feelings and at the same time elicit caring from others.

From the point of view of separation and individuation, Carly's reliance on external substances and behaviors also creates the illusion that she is symbiotically fused with the archaic mother-breast with infinite supplies who will take care of all her needs and wants. In this state of fusion, Carly can fantasize that she controls the sources of her pleasure and satisfaction without actually having to be aware of her reliance on those around her. Her sense of entitlement to free psychological services and unlimited women for her exclusive sexual pleasure reflects not only compensation for the overwhelming experience of maternal deprivation throughout childhood but also a reinstatement of the omnipotent illusion of infinite maternal supplies—a disavowal of her probable childhood reality of sudden disillusionment and premature individuation in a house of six children, an absentee father, and an overwhelmed, impatient, self-absorbed mother.

Carly only dimly perceives that she sustains this illusion through her dependence on nonhuman or dehumanized external sources of instant gratification. Occasionally, when this perception comes more sharply into focus, Carly characteristically adopts a helpless posture. Like a passive anxious-resistant baby who cries for the mother to return from separation but does not engage in any search behaviors to find her and does not reach for her when she does return (attachment subclassification C2), Carly feels and acts helpless whenever she experiences the unpleasant affects that emerge in the context of bouts of abstinence from these external crutches. She relies on acting helpless as her fallback method of solicitation for help when the illusion of symbiotic fusion fails. The terror Carly experiences when she realizes just how dependent, helpless, and vulnerable she is quite effectively motivates her to avoid dependence on others—or at least the awareness of dependence on others—with the familiar illusion of self-sufficiency and omnipotence.

This illusion, nurtured by her dependence on external sources of gratification, consists of a toy box of "transitional fantasies" (Volkan, 1973, p. 351) employed as "intangible representations of transitional objects" (p. 351). Each one of Carly's addictions—food, alcohol, flirtations—is associated with specific fantasies that combine to provide a powerful alternate attachment relationship for her. This alternate attachment relationship helps her to disavow the profoundly unsatisfying attachment relationship she must have experienced with her mother as a child. When her mother asks Carly for handouts or special treatment, Carly can turn to the alternate attachment relationship for temporary solace and comfort, thus recapitulating the illusory symbiotic fusion with her mother and simultaneously punishing herself for the guilt she unconsciously experiences over the underlying rage and resentment at having been ignored and ultimately overlooked by her mother as the parade of closely spaced babies in the household continued unabated. In this context of emotional deprivation, Carly fended for herself in isolation—eating ice cream in the basement while the rest of the family enjoyed each other's company upstairs—underscoring her separation from a protective, nurturing caregiver and the desperate need to disavow this painful reality.

Carly's illusion of omnipotence and fallback position of helplessness when the illusion falters are encapsulated in two distinctly different self-representations and defensive constellations. On the one hand, Carly portrays herself as an omnipotent, invulnerable force wearing impenetrable armor: the mere thought that her partner has cancer could cause it. Moreover, rather than missing me on vacation, it gave her a chance to sleep in. On the other hand, when this illusion breaks down, Carly portrays herself as a "jellyfish": her partner's death would cause her to drive to their weekend home and "crawl into the fetal position and hope that somebody would take care of me" or simply kill herself. Defensively, the omnipotent self-representation seeks to block objects from making her aware of negative affects, while the jellyfish self-representation invites objects to have mercy on her like a submissive wolf that exposes its throat to a dominant wolf. Intrapsychic boundaries are either rigid and fortified or nebulous and undefined.

The predominant oral metaphor operating at the deepest layers of Carly's personality seems to be "eat or be eaten." Carly can consume her objects and incorporate their nurturance, but in so doing, destroys them as nurturing sources, which elicits an unconscious sense of guilt. Carly can also allow herself to be consumed by her objects, which affords her the potential for fusion but at the cost of her own survival. I believe that in the transference, she wanted simply to consume me rather than internalize my mentalizing function, which simultaneously worried her (see below). She also both wished and feared that I would consume her, which would restore the desired archaic symbiotic relationship but destroy her very self in the process.

Transference-Countertransference Paradigm

The pervasive transference-countertransference paradigm could be summed up by the catchphrase, "Eat or be eaten." The treatment has endured because Carly can simultaneously feel that (1) I am plotting to exploit her by making her dependent on me and enslaving her in psychoanalysis forever and (2) she is exploiting me by receiving virtually free psychoanalysis. The transference often shifts between Carly's perceiving me alternately as the depriving, exploitative mother and the petulant, weak, dependent child whose vulnerability is repulsive. At other times, however, Carly perceives me as the paternal grandmother who gives her undivided attention and love without the mother's emotional limitations. My countertransference reactions have ranged from feeling like a devalued, worthless child to feeling like a depriving, exploitative parent, to feeling like a burdened parent saddled with a special-needs child.

Notably, Carly has succeeded in inducing in me moments of profound helplessness and pessimism, especially when she talks about her latest risk-taking behavior—whether it be smoking marijuana while driving at high speeds without wearing a seat belt, carrying on clandestine cell-phone relationships with females under her partner's searching eye, embezzling thousands of dollars from a former employer, or employing a restaurant staff of undocumented workers and drastically underreporting her income to the Internal Revenue Service. Carly seems to parade these behaviors in front of me to provoke either (1) active intervention—a direct caring response from me that would undermine my mentalizing capacity, (2) criticism, which would align me with her punitive mother, or (3) passive onlooking, which proves that I am uncaring and that she is unworthy of care.

In the first instance, the caring response would be manipulatively extracted rather than freely received, which spoils it. Carly's childhood memory of putting a gold star on failed tests to deceive her mother into giving her praise illustrates this first interaction structure. In the second instance, her mother's criticism would represent a masochistic gratification that assuages Carly's guilt over the rage and resentment she feels toward her mother for the emotional deprivation she experienced. Carly's car thefts in adolescence provoked not only criticism but also violence from her mother. In the third instance, passive onlooking also represents a masochistic gratification that serves to justify her worldview of an uncaring world. Carly's father generally played this role whenever Carly's mother was punishing her. I tended to interpret my role in Carly's mind as a passive onlooker when she reported risk-taking behavior, but this stance usually incurred healthy doses of devaluation. A passive onlooker is too weak, too helpless, and too afraid to assume an active role. At these moments, Carly projected her weak, dependent, jellyfish-like self-representation into me, which she could then attack at a safe distance from her omnipotent fortress of impenetrabilility.

All three of these strategies for provoking helplessness and pessimism in me served to bind us together in a complementary identification (Racker, 1968). In so doing, Carly could avoid the reality of separation, loss, depressive anxiety, and guilt that continually threatened her psychological existence. Carly's desperate need to deny her separation from me provoked underlying wishes to exploit me parasitically, which she then projected onto me and denied. In one session (see below), Carly warned a spider against crawling toward another spider's web on the ceiling. Carly was displaying her fear of getting close to me because she might become too dependent on me and stay forever while I suck her bank account dry.

Predictably, Carly often acknowledged her fear of staying on my couch forever but denied her fear that I might exploit her—even though she often reminded me that she abruptly left her previous therapist when she raised her fee to $80 per session. The therapist's Mercedes Benz became for Carly a symbol of the therapist's exploitation of patients. Carly often asked me what kind of car I drive but always denied the motivation behind her question other than sheer curiosity. In reality, Carly was exploiting me by owning a thriving business, maintaining two homes in exclusive areas, and paying only $15 per session (and getting some of this money back in insurance claims).

I rationalized my feelings of exploitation by reminding myself that I was fulfilling the requirements of my psychoanalytic training and collecting this patient's material for a possible journal article or book chapter. Carly's identification with her exploitative mother, however, remains shrouded behind a defensive fortress that I dare not penetrate on penalty of losing her altogether. As her symptoms continue to improve with additional psychoanalysis, and as she begins to feel gratitude toward me for my tolerance of her sadistic devaluation of me, my patience with her masochistic self-destructive behavior, and my mentalization of her unbearable internal experience, I believe that she will gradually become aware of this identification and risk psychological individuation from her mother.

Description of Psychoanalytic Process

Carly was first seen on July 26, 2004, for an initial consultation. She explained that she had had many psychotherapy experiences since ninth grade, when her school first referred her to Forest Hills Family Services for treatment. Three years ago, she had participated in couples therapy as an outcome of her partner's discovery of the affair. The couples therapy ended, but Carly continued to be treated by the couples therapist in once-weekly individual psychotherapy. Sensing that no meaningful change was taking place, however, Carly began to consider other treatment options. Her first lover and best friend from high school, Nadine, was in psychoanalysis with a member of my psychoanalytic institute. Nadine suggested that Carly try psychoanalysis because Nadine had experienced it as helpful to her. The psychoanalyst had recommended me because Carly had requested someone who could conduct a low-fee psychoanalysis. When asked about these previous psychotherapy experiences, Carly stated that they all seemed to be somewhat helpful, but nevertheless found fault with each therapist. She complained mostly about either boundary maintenance (either my boundaries were too loose or too rigid) or fee increases: "When my last therapist raised my fee, I told her she should have gone into plastic surgery."

Carly came for this initial consultation looking as unremarkable as possible, dressed in blue jeans and a blue flannel shirt with the bottom not tucked in, wearing leather sandals and no make-up. She wore her dark brown hair close-cropped and short. The only remarkable aspect of her appearance was her sheer size: standing at 5'11" and weighing 290 pounds, she evinced a commanding presence. No evidence of femininity was also noted; even her gait appeared to have masculine characteristics. She seemed to exhibit a full range of affect; her mood seemed hypomanic. Carly sat comfortably in her chair. No restlessness or other physical manifestations of anxiety was noted. Rate and volume of speech appeared within normal limits, but she seldom paused to collect her thoughts or give me an opportunity to speak.

Psychoanalysis offered at a frequency of four times per week seemed to be the treatment of choice for Carly because her suffering seemed to be of a longstanding nature, originating in childhood, and because of her motivation and intellectual ability and communication skills. A capacity to reflect on her thoughts and feelings in the context of her life, her personal history, and her current circumstances was not initially evident, but Carly's strengths were sufficiently developed that an attempt at conducting psychoanalysis seemed feasible. Based on her report of symptoms mentioned earlier, particularly the mood instability, pattern of unstable relationships, and impulsivity, I determined that Carly had developed a borderline personality organization and satisfied formal criteria for borderline personality disorder.

Initially, because Carly was new to me, I decided that I would treat her in once-weekly psychotherapy until September 2004, when I would convert the treatment to a four-times-per-week psychoanalysis. This arrangement suited Carly. As the psychotherapy progressed toward psychoanalysis, the treatment quickly took the form of Carly's narrating stories about past lovers and current women in whom she had a romantic/sexual interest. When asked what she liked about having all these relationships, both real and imagined, Carly replied that she enjoyed the conquest. Each relationship would inevitably end, however, when she realized "I didn't want to belong to any club in which I was accepted as a member," which made her lose interest and move on to the next conquest. When she was not regaling me with stories of these conquests, Carly often asked me personal questions such as my birth date, astrological sign, where I was born, hobbies and interests, sexual orientation, and prior clinical experience with treating lesbian patients. While I did answer her question regarding prior clinical experience, I also explained that I would not answer personal questions because this treatment is about Carly, not about my personal life. These questions, however, are meaningful because they reflect an emerging interest in me and what I am like.

By the middle of October 2004, when it became obvious that personal information would not be forthcoming, Carly became passively angry toward me, exhibited in coming late to sessions or being silent. Comments that Carly might be feeling angry toward me because I was not making self-disclosures to her were greeted with denial: "Yes, it's frustrating when you don't answer my questions, but I know that you didn't answer because you don't think it would be helpful. I told you last week, if I were angry, I wouldn't tell you, but I'm really not angry." I replied, "Then how would I know?" Carly stated, "I think I would tell you—you told me, 'Don't censor.'" Gradually, Carly's anger would subside, but denial would often be activated whenever I suggested that she might be feeling angry toward me. Carly experienced no difficulty expressing anger about others, however, whenever she felt slighted or wronged by someone within her inner circle of friends.

I began to feel worried because it seemed as though the framework of psychoanalytic treatment might be too abstinent for Carly's fragile ego to withstand; furthermore, Carly's drinking behavior seemed to be getting worse. She began pouring vodka and orange juice into a thermos to carry around with her during the day as she drove around posting restaurant flyers. I wondered whether it was ethical to treat an alcoholic patient who refused to attend Alcoholics Anonymous (AA) meetings and who was taking a cocktail of psychiatric medications (Lexapro, 20 mg/day for depression; Wellbutrin, 200 mg/day for "sexual dysfunction"; Ritalin, 20 mg/day for distractibility). When confronted about going to AA, Carly replied that her true addiction is food, so Overeaters Anonymous (OA) is where she really belongs. Yet she was not committed to attending these meetings either. Thus, I was worried not only about whether psychoanalysis was the treatment of choice, but also about whether Carly was becoming a chronic danger to herself.

I interpreted these concerns about Carly's self-destructive tendencies in the context of how they might make her loved ones feel. I also interpreted that, in the back of her mind, Carly must believe that her mere attendance at sessions would provide her with a magical solution to her problems; therefore, no emotional work would need to occur outside these sessions. Carly acknowledged the emotional impact that her behavior was having on her partner and on her siblings and friends. Carly thus made a New Year's Day resolution to begin attending OA meetings. Sobriety, however, seemed more difficult for Carly to commit to. After several false starts, Carly took her last drink on March 20, 2005—while I was on a one-week vacation. On March 18, the final session before the vacation, Carly reported that she declined having a drink at a St. Patrick's Day gathering. When asked why she declined, Carly avoided the question and instead stated that she would have taken one if one of her attractive female friends had also attended the gathering. Later in the session, Carly admitted that she had recently thought about buying pot, "but you stopped me." When asked what was going on, Carly replied that she had become tearful in front of a close friend who had asked her how she was doing. She told the friend that "'my therapist tells me I keep distracting myself from my inner pain.' Next week, I'm going to start Weight Watchers." By the seventh month of treatment, it was evident that the internalization of me as a benign superego representation had begun. This benign representation stands in stark contrast to her punitive, sadistic superego that never ceases to punish her for experiencing hostile, violent thoughts directed toward loved ones, including me. In fact, as Carly has moved away from the absolutism of her superego, her affects have become predictably more modulated.

By April 2005, Carly was becoming more directly angry toward me. The numerous complaints seemed to revolve around making sacrifices of food and drink at the altar of therapy, with no obvious payoff; in fact, the abstinence just made her feel angry and depressed. In her words, "Why am I denying myself drinking? I think it would make me feel better." Out of frustration with Carly's seemingly endless litany of complaints and her occasional use of the treatment as a coffee clutch, I once referred to Carly's Harlequin-style romance storytelling as "frivolous": "You use these frivolous stories to avoid your inner pain for forty-five minutes. You can tell me all the he-said/she-said stories, but are they therapeutic? Do they help you confront the feelings you're trying to avoid?" Carly experienced this clumsy comment as a narcissistic injury. She got off the couch and sat in a chair, then left the session four minutes early in spite of my attempt to get her to stay to talk about her feelings.

My attempts in a later session to interpret Carly's anger toward me were greeted with characteristic denials. I stated, "It seemed to me yesterday you started to see me as an enemy." Carly replied, "I don't believe so because if you were an enemy, you'd want to hurt me, and I don't believe you want to hurt me." I continued: "How would you characterize your feelings toward me?" Directly acknowledging her anger toward me for the first time since the beginning of treatment, Carly stated, "I'm pissed off at you, but you're not an enemy." Although directly acknowledging her anger, Carly nevertheless managed to express some of her anger indirectly by telling me that I was wrong about her perceiving me as an enemy. Sensing that Carly was at least partly available for further exploration, I then attempted to help Carly elaborate on her feelings: "Let's talk about your feeling pissed off." Carly risked an elaboration: "That you just said, basically, stop with these 'frivolous stories.' It's like a person drowning and throwing them an anchor and saying, 'How does it feel to go down?'" Wanting to interpret the conflictual elements of this elaboration, I replied, "Earlier, you said you don't see me as an enemy because I'm not trying to hurt you, yet your analogy suggests that I am trying to hurt you—I'm throwing you an anchor while you're drowning." But Carly was not prepared to acknowledge my perceived malice: "You would be wrong. You're taking it too literally. I like to be funny." Carly's capacity for self-reflectiveness was developing at a much slower rate than her symptomatic improvements outside the treatment.

I spent many sessions interpreting the defensive nature of her addictions and the magical solution they seemed to provide for the painful affects concealed beneath the surface. I experienced this work at times as tedious and somewhat circular. To illustrate, in a session at the end of April 2005, Carly stated, "I have tremendous sadness, anger, and confusion." I interpreted these feelings as precisely the ones masked by binge eating and drinking: "Is it possible that these are the very emotions you've been covering up through drinking and overeating?" Evidencing an emerging understanding of this dynamic process, Carly replied, "It's entirely possible. But I'm just getting fatter and more depressed." Her response is not entirely true because she was not gaining weight. Continuing with this theme, I reminded Carly, "So we could expect that if you aren't eating or drinking anymore, that you would start feeling worse sooner or later." Interpreting this comment fatalistically and responding with a feeling of helplessness, Carly asked, "So what am I supposed to do?" I attempted to help Carly elaborate on her feelings: "Well, we can talk about them [your feelings]." Carly accepted this invitation: "Okay, let's talk about them. I'm tired of not feeling good, being angry, battling with myself. I was stupid depressed on Monday; it felt more about anger yesterday." While the increased candor about her "shitty" feelings in the context of abstinence reflects within-session progress, a tone of reproof seemed to permeate her response, as if she were saying, "Okay, I've done my part by giving up booze and food. Why aren't I feeling any better? What are you going to do about it?" Interpreting her self-destructive behavior as punishment over guilt experienced in relation to her anger toward me and other significant people in her life proved difficult because of her frequent denial of feelings of anger directed toward me.

With supervisory assistance, I came to perceive Carly's outright rejections of interpretations as rejections of the nourishment I was providing Carly because accepting this nourishment would make her feel too dependent on me and thus too vulnerable to either attack from me or loss of me. This approach—essentially to interpret the denial of an awareness of a concealed positive transference—was first tested on July 1, 2005. It was a Friday session, and because of the upcoming three-day holiday weekend, I would not see Carly until the following Tuesday. I reminded her of this fact early during the session, and Carly asked me why I was bringing it up. I responded that I knew that she was having a hard time lately. Carly snapped, "Well, it's not that this is helping. You've been saying that I've been devaluing [of you]. Maybe I should watch what I say. Will psychoanalysis help me get out of this place? If I'm steering this ship, I have a lot less confidence that this could help me." I chose to explore Carly's urge to curtail uncensored communication, a threat to the integrity of the treatment: "It's interesting that your response to my pointing out the vacation is that you'll stop talking rather than exploring what you say." Carly characteristically fled into denial: "But I don't feel the way you do about your going away. I don't feel the way you do about my getting angry with you. I've never been angry with you; it's psychoanalysis I've been angry with, not you. What? Do you want me to feel something I don't feel?" I interpreted the denial using the metaphor of rejecting my nourishment: "It seems I give you some food, and you spit it out without even taking it in and seeing whether it's nourishing for you." Carly paused, reflected on what I had said, and replied, "Well, that makes a lot of sense. You have to remind me to do that when you want me to consider a point." Sensing a new openness, I pressed further: "Okay, now, taste this: I think you've grown to depend on me, and it frightens you because it makes you feel so vulnerable, especially when I go away." Carly's response to this interpretation illustrates an emerging capacity for self-reflectiveness and a diminished reliance on denial: "I'm tasting that. I don't think I depend on you, but maybe I do. I'll have to think about that some more." In these sessions, I was feeding Carly through an active interventive stance that will need to be further analyzed when her ego is sufficiently able to tolerate increased levels of frustration.

The twin themes of separation from and closeness to me dominated the therapeutic landscape after this July 1 session. I also weaved these issues into the fabric of her romantic and social lives. Specifically, Carly tries to avoid physical intimacy with her partner, but fantasizes about physical intimacy with some of her female friends. She regulates her feelings of closeness and separateness by wanting to escape her commitment with her partner and flee into fleeting intimacy with these female friends. In doing so, Carly can try to avoid her twin fears of engulfment and abandonment—swallowing up others and thus destroying them, or being swallowed up by others and thus being destroyed herself.

After a series of vacations on both our parts, Carly stated that she wanted to take a break from treatment for the rest of the summer. In early August, I empathized with the anxiety and anger aroused by these disruptions: "You've been uncomfortable here, and I think it started when you came back from Florida. It must be upsetting to have all these disruptions of my going away and your going away." Carly agreed with this assessment: "That's why I wanted a break a couple of months ago—because this is so fractured." Sensing an opportunity, I attempted to help Carly elaborate on the feeling of fracturedness: "I can appreciate how you feel, but perhaps we can explore what makes it upsetting to you." Carly responded by characteristically expressing her anger toward herself rather than me: "Just that it's so fractured. We should have taken a break for the summer, but you said 'no.' I'm angry because I should have listened to myself. I'm angry that I don't have a choice, and it makes me feel that I'll just go until the end of September, and that's it. . . . I don't want to have to deal with all the fracturedness of this treatment." I responded by making her concern directly relevant to the core themes discussed throughout the summer: "I can understand that. But part of this treatment is helping you to deal with separation. My vacation coming up at the end of August won't be my last vacation, and your vacation in Florida won't be your last—unless you end the treatment." Now realizing that something new could be experienced about herself through these separations, Carly replied, "I'm also just angry today. I know you said I tend to make big decisions when I'm angry." In this exchange, it appears that Carly has begun to adopt an analytic attitude toward herself, originating from an internalization of a positive therapist representation. She implicitly understood that her angry mood has resulted in her saying something about termination that she did not really mean. In other words, she has displayed an important component of ego strength—impulse control through an enhanced capacity for self-reflectiveness. It is this capacity that makes this patient analyzable.

By early September, these themes were explored in relation to her partner, whom she periodically expresses a desire to leave for any of a number of sexually attractive female friends. Carly stated, "Isn't my relationship with [name of a female friend] intimate?" I replied, "It really is intimate only in your mind. She's really just a fantasy of yours. Intimacy is waking up to Kesha [Carly's partner] and smelling her breath. That's why closeness with her frightens you so much—you have experienced some feelings of intimacy with her, but they frighten you. . . . Then you turn to these other women to regulate the intimate feelings with Kesha." Perhaps frightened by the accuracy of this interpretation, coming at the end of the session, Carly replied, "I wish we could continue for another forty-five minutes—and remove the Friday session." Seizing the opportunity to bring the material into the transference, I stated, "Perhaps coming here four times per week feels too intimate for you." Carly replied, "It feels we're just getting started today."

This work on intimacy continued. Five days later, Carly spontaneously referred to my comment on intimacy: "I told Kesha what you said about 'intimacy is waking up to somebody and smelling their breath,' and she said, 'He's right.'" She then described the physical sensation of kissing her partner—the discomfort she experiences. Each kiss of her partner feels "obligatory." Carly later characterized her partner as "clingy." I interpreted the defense: "I wonder whether you're using clinginess to mask your own fear of intimacy." The critical moment of this session comes when Carly now brings her own material into the transference even though she suggests that she would be predicting my next move: "And you're going to bring it in here too—you're the clingy one! [laughing]" In the following comment, I interpreted both the projection as well as the underlying wish: "You know on some level I'm not clingy, so we have to wonder why you perceive me that way. I think the reason is that with people you feel intimate with, including me, you are actually *feeling* the intimacy, which frightens you." Feeling overwhelmed and sensing that the session was over, Carly asked, "What time is it?" I replied, "You really want to dismiss what I'm saying, but we really need to consider this issue in earnest in the future." The themes of separation and closeness have continued to emerge and be worked through as the analysis continues to deepen.

In another session, Carly discussed her tender, caring feelings toward an elderly woman whom she regularly visits and her identification between this woman and her beloved paternal grandmother, who died when Carly was age fourteen. She talked about the qualities that made her grandmother so special to her, especially the grandmother's warmth and availability as a safe haven whenever Carly wanted to flee the chaos of her own home. Perhaps this relationship represents an initial effort to excavate the vestiges of a positive grandmother representation now directed toward me—someone Carly can rely on to sustain her attachment to me and to the clinical work. This positive representation could also be used in the service of modulating Carly's punitive, persecutory representation, manifested all too frequently in the first year of psychoanalysis.

In the second year of psychoanalysis, Carly was struggling with her addictions and her depression, which seemed exacerbated by her mother's asking Carly and her siblings to give her a monthly allowance. Carly resented this request because twenty years ago, Carly had given her mother the money to purchase a house in Florida in exchange for her mother's promise to sign over the deed to Carly—which the mother has still not done twenty years later. This resentment presented itself in the treatment as massive deprivation of supplies by Kesha and me, which Carly attempted to mask with unprescribed medication that she was surreptitiously receiving from Kesha's invalid mother, who lives on Staten Island. Kesha's mother colluded with Carly to give her Percocet without Kesha's knowledge, thus confirming the expectation that mothers are corruptible, dangerous, unnurturing, and devoid of genuine emotional supplies. Carly therefore placed me in a no-win situation: if I do not intervene, I too am complicit in Carly's self-harm, but if I intervene, I am overstepping therapeutic boundaries by becoming a "real" person in Carly's life and depriving her of the opportunity to depend on me for self-understanding. Carly often stopped in session and asked me to "steer the ship," meaning that I should say or do something to make her feel better. I would interpret such comments as Carly's needing reassurance from me that I care about her and desire to nurture her with my words.

In one session, this intervention resulted in her devaluing me. Specifically, she accused me of being clingy. I interpreted the projection by telling her that she devalues me "out of fear of closeness." Carly replied, "Look, why would I get invested in you? You might not be here tomorrow." I said, "So you're afraid I'm going to leave you." She replied, "Well, you could raise your fees tomorrow, and that would be a problem for me like it was for Lisa [her previous therapist]." I said, "So I could leave you tomorrow—but it's your difficulty with getting close to me, thinking that I could abandon you, so you protect yourself." Carly replied, "Well, who's going to protect me?" I continued, "I could hurt you." She responded, "Well, sometimes I wonder why you're here. I don't know. I guess you have to help me for your dissertation or whatever—not to negate that you care." She then mentioned the fantasy of bringing me some soup, which I interpreted as her wanting to take care of *me*. Then she mentioned her plan to go away with Kesha for the weekend and wanting to flirt with some of her female friends, which Kesha would disapprove of if she found out. I said, "Let's look at this. You're going to be going away with Kesha for leaf peeping . . . close quarters with her—and that results in your needing to escape the threat of increased intimacy with her by distancing yourself with calls to other women. It's like a law of physics with you, and you're doing the same thing here. You're sitting on the edge of your seat ready to bolt out of here just like you did a few months ago." This intervention resulted in more devaluation of me. In retrospect, I would have introduced the transference element explicitly—that Carly feels that I will exploit her and, ultimately, abandon her, as she fears her mother has exploited and abandoned her. Instead, I focused exclusively on her need to escape the vulnerability implied by the feelings of intimacy experienced in her relationships with her partner and me. In this instance, Carly was unable to do more than mount a devaluing defense against the emerging feelings of vulnerability and her fear of abandonment.

Carly's feelings of helplessness in relation to my separateness, as expressed in the possibility that I could raise my fee over her objection and essentially abandon her, emerged later in the fall of 2005 as she continued to struggle with her mother's financial request. I interpreted, "You're afraid that I'm going to raise my fee and tell you you're out of here." Carly replied, "That's a distinct possibility—that you're done with the school piece. Why are you seeing me at the low fee?" I asked, "Why do you think?" She replied, "I don't know. There are some things I'm a little obtuse. [starts crying]" I said, "Maybe that helps to explain why you don't rely on me so much in here." Carly replied, "That it will end." I said, "Exactly. I also think that you feel guilty over what you pay me even though you feel you can't pay me." Carly responded, "Yeah, just like my mother—I feel guilty not giving her enough, but resentful that I have to give her something." In this passage, Carly spontaneously brings the transferential material into the session, without any prompting from me. She demonstrates an emerging awareness of her need to be taken care of in a symbiotic relationship and a simultaneous emerging awareness that other persons are physically and psychically separate from her and have their own needs.

At other times, in spite of the low fee, Carly perceived me as withholding love and care from her. After talking about her resentment stimulated by the discovery that her partner had started a side project as a professional organizer and had printed business cards without Carly's name on them, Carly asked me what kind of car I drive. I replied, "You set us both up. You know that I don't answer personal questions. Sometimes you put yourself in the deprived child role and me in the role of the depriving, withholding caregiver. I think these are roles you're familiar with." Carly responded, "I hear you, but I think it's just me wanting to be a good guesser. My mom called, and I didn't call her back." I said, "So you reversed roles with her, and you became the depriving one and she became the deprived child for a change." Carly replied, "But I would feel guilty doing that. I just want to give her money and tell her to leave me alone, but it would never be enough." I asked, "Who's that sound like?" She said, "That sounds like me." I responded, "But I think you also see me as depriving. You fear that I might raise my fee and make it impossible for you to continue." Carly replied, laughing, "And you might move to Chicago with your lawyer wife." In this exchange, we see Carly's enhanced capacity for self-reflectiveness after an initial denial ("me wanting to be a good guesser"). She demonstrates an emerging recognition of herself in the sadomasochistic relationship that she has created with her mother, with both of them at different times playing the roles of depriver and deprived.

Leading up to the Christmas/New Year's holiday, Carly focused on her lack of passion for her partner. I commented, "I wonder whether you don't emotionally invest in Kesha or me because we might leave like your grandmother did." Carly responded, "I know—maybe I haven't loved or trusted anyone since her. . . . She used to say bad things about my mother. . . . I think I felt guilty because I was betraying my mother." I said, "I wonder whether you feel that if you expressed hateful feelings about your mother in here, that you might be betraying your mother in here and feel guilty." Carly replied, "I made a negative comment about my mother at OA [Overeaters Anonymous], and I felt bad about it. . . . 'Mothers are the reason we're all in therapy'. . . . What time is it?" I replied, "Why do you want to know?" She replied, "Because I want to know whether to start a new conversation." I said, "Let's stick with this. You feel deprived because you're not trusting Kesha or me, so you turn to Percocet to keep from feeling so deprived—something that's always available 24/7, something you can control." She replied, "Something that will make me feel warm and fuzzy." In this exchange, we observe Carly's punitive superego that does not tolerate any negative feelings toward her abusive mother and the resulting punishment—experienced as guilt—for permitting such feelings to become momentarily conscious. I focused on the Percocet abuse as a substitute for the depriving mother, but I might have also focused on her feeling cut off from my emotional supplies, or the self-punishment implied in this behavior as a strategy for assuaging the guilt over her perceived betrayal of her mother.

On New Year's Eve, Carly had her first alcoholic beverage in nine and a half months. In early 2006, she also began to smoke marijuana on a daily basis. She also stopped the narcotic abuse and refused her mother-in-law's offers. My interpretations focused on her anger toward me for going on vacation during the Christmas/New Year's holiday, her persistent feelings of deprivation and emptiness that need to be filled, and her compulsion to depend on substances (alcohol, marijuana, food) rather than people for support and nurturance because people cannot be controlled and can therefore leave her at any time—like her beloved grandmother. Carly has become increasingly able to tolerate this interpretive work, but her reliance on substances continues. Her alcohol use and diet, however, appear to be less frenetic than when she first entered treatment. She attends occasional Weight Watchers meetings, where she is weighed, and a weekly "chubby girl group"—group therapy for morbidly obese women offered at a local hospital. Carly complained that nothing is helping her, yet continued to attend her analysis four times per week on time as well as these two support groups.

The narcotic abuse stopped after a series of sessions in which we discussed her motives for this behavior. I said, "Maybe your taking drugs at this point is a big fuck-you to me. You're telling me that I don't matter because it would be too scary if I mattered to you." Carly replied, "I just think I need a savior—someone to rescue me. Isn't that one of the criteria for borderline?" I replied, "And in a year and a half, you've figured out that I'm not rescuing you and it's disappointed you." Carly said, "Maybe just a little, but not that much." I continued, "And so taking drugs is a way of saying 'fuck you—you haven't rescued me, so I'm going to show you.'" Carly replied, "I don't think so." Carly is able to acknowledge some negative affect toward me—disappointment—but she is still unable to acknowledge a more intensely hostile affect such as revenge in response to feeling uncared for by me. Less than two weeks later, Carly called to cancel a session and said that I did not have to call her back. In the following session, Carly expressed dismay that I had not called her back but denied feeling any anger toward me. When asked how she interpreted my behavior, Carly responded that "men are obtuse." I interpreted to her that "you end up feeling resentful that your needs aren't being met." Instead of getting defensive as in previous sessions, however, Carly replied, "Yeah, I think it's not wanting to be vulnerable; that's hard for me. By the way, my pills [Percocet] are going to run out soon. I came close to throwing them out." I responded, "You know, it's so tempting to take pills because they can't reject you like people can. You can control them 24/7, and they give you a good feeling when people let you down. They can't make you feel vulnerable; they don't require feeling vulnerable as a condition of love." Carly replied, "I disagree with some of that. I think the pills could control me. I'm a very sensitive person." I said, "And we can be specific and say sensitivity to rejection, which pills can help you avoid." Carly acknowledged, "Yeah, I see that. [Carly's sister] called. I think it's part of growing up in a family of six kids. I don't think my needs could ever be met." Carly began the session feeling angry toward me. In the past, this anger would have interfered with her capacity for self-reflectiveness and would have lasted over several sessions. The process in this session suggests that Carly's recovery time after a moment of affect dysregulation has improved sufficiently within the session itself so that she can reengage in self-reflectiveness and acknowledge her insatiability. I could have added that taking pills is also one of the ways in which she mothers herself.

Helping Carly to tolerate her disappointment and anger toward me for not helping her quickly enough or being there for her all the time has continued to dominate the clinical landscape. Just before my spring vacation, Carly complained of having to spend the Easter holiday with Kesha's family rather than her own and having an urge to obtain narcotics from Kesha's mother. I commented, "Think about this before you respond: I wonder whether you feel angry at me for going away next week and that you want to take drugs to punish me for going away." Carly responded, "The truth is, I felt like canceling our sessions for the rest of the week because I wanted more time off. And the drugs—what about the other 364 days of the year I want to take drugs?" I said, "The drugs are more dependable than your therapist, who takes vacations." Carly replied, "It seems you want me to say I'm going to miss you, I'm going to be so scared, but I don't feel that. If I came every day and I saw this chunk of stone we're chipping away at, and I'm making such progress. . . ." I responded, "Maybe you feel we haven't made progress and so perhaps I don't deserve to go on vacation." Carly replied, "I agree with the first part of that statement. I'm just a weak, stupid, fucked-up, whiny person. They're the only ones in analysis. [crying]" I said, "So then you just beat yourself up about needing help." Carly responded, "But that's the reality." Carly's capacity to reflect on her feelings, wishes, and fears diminishes in the face of overwhelming fear of abandonment such as my impending vacation, and she reverts to hating herself to control her rage and protect me from it. Perhaps I should have interpreted that dynamic here; on the other hand, I sensed that she was no longer available to listen to me reflecting on her motives.

These issues continue to emerge repeatedly. Does her mother really care about her? Do I really care about her? How would she know? Will she be abandoned? After this vacation, Carly wondered whether I am treating her because she poses such a challenge: if I cure her, it would be like hauling in a big fish. Or perhaps she would be hooked on me as her narcotic. I interpreted, "[Earlier] you mentioned that your mother called and complained—again—about having to work and didn't ask how you or Kesha are doing; now, you wonder whether I care about you, whether I'm here for you or for me." Carly responded, "I'm sure on some level you care." I said, "On some level, but you feel something's missing from it." Carly replied, "I just want to hear from you why you're here. . . . What happens when you become a psychoanalyst? Does that mean you raise your fee?" I responded, "I think you have a lot of questions about whether I'm still going to be here for you, but this discussion will have to be continued [end of session]." The concern whether I will always be here at my fee of $15 per session is a constant theme that makes me feel trapped. If I continue to treat her at $15 per session after I graduate from my psychoanalytic training program, I would feel resentful toward her. If I raise my fee, I would feel guilty about betraying her trust, and I sense that she would leave the treatment prematurely. Would I then be considered another caregiver who ultimately abandoned her? I continue to struggle with both my resentment and guilt over the fee. Of course, the situation resembles that between her and her mother: she feels obligated to acquiesce to her mother's demands for financial support but simultaneously feels resentful about it. I had not yet interpreted this parallel process to her, however.

This countertransference reaction sometimes results in my wanting to cure Carly as soon as possible so that I can terminate the treatment with a clear conscience. For example, I have made heavy-handed comments about her self-destructive behavior. Carly mentioned that Kesha complained about Carly's drug use and concluded that her partner "doesn't like it when I'm happy." I said, "So you're assuming she doesn't like you when you're happy, but I wonder whether she gets upset when you try to kill yourself with smoking pot and drinking." Carly responded, "You and Kesha are buzzkills, aren't you?" I said, "You get annoyed when people actually care about your safety. I don't want to go to your funeral next week." Carly replied, "You know, I'm getting a pain right here [she rubs her neck]." I commented, "So I'm a pain in thc neck." She responded, "Well, I'm not going to rub my ass. Don't you know that you can't say that stuff? The gods will hear." I replied, "So then I'll be responsible for your death rather than you if I talk about it." Carly said, "Yeah, you can't talk about that stuff." I responded, "Yeah, we need to keep reality out of this work." Carly replied, "Yeah, you're such a buzzkill. [laughs]" In this sequence, it appears that the heavy-handed approach produced some amusement for Carly rather than self-reflectiveness about her self-destructive behavior. Perhaps I have become the scolding parent showing the concern she craves—a masochistically gratifying experience for Carly. Again, we witness the enactment of the exciting beating fantasy.

In other sessions, I was able to harness my concern. Carly reported a dream in which Carly's mother and partner throw Carly a party in which some men get drunk and become violent. Carly corrals her mother and partner into a separate room and calls security. Carly interpreted that she wants to save her mother and partner from her hurting herself. I pointed out that it is her mother and her partner in danger, not her specifically. When I asked her what she thought I meant, Carly answered, "Well, that they're scared, too; they're in danger." I interpreted, "You left that part out of the dream because you don't want to be aware of the fact that your behavior hurts those you love the most." After Carly asked whether people customarily take their shoes off in analysis, I continued, "It's hard to acknowledge the guilt you feel. In waking life you don't let it affect you." Carly responded, "I do feel bad. . . . I just want to find out who I am."

During the summer months, Carly introduced the theme of "the penis," which she described as "the cause of wars." At certain moments, she would characterize me as a "eunuch," a "girly girl," and "a man with a vagina" to express her unconscious desire to perceive me as a nonthreatening presence. In one session in which she called me a "girly girl," I interpreted, "Women show vulnerability, which is dangerous, so you identify with the masculine role because men don't show vulnerability in your mind." She replied, "I agree with that. . . . But I wonder whether I identify with men because I knew that I would never be the cheerleader. I found it easier to be the athlete. Actually, my mother was the one who was like supermom. I think between my two parents, my mom was stronger. I was twenty when my father died. If I had him around for another twenty years, I would be able to make a more informed decision. He wasn't an athlete; he was an intellect." In a later session, I suggested that Carly might want a penis. She replied, "Men have their pick of the litter. They can pick whoever they want. If you're single when you're thirty, by that time all the guys are taken." For Carly, the penis represents her need for power and control to help her to cope with separateness and vulnerability.

As my vacation approached at the end of August, the theme of my not caring about Carly reemerged. In one session, she complained about a traffic cop not doing his job and not caring that traffic was being backed up: "Nobody cares if people wait in traffic—taking two hours to get over the Triborough [Bridge]. Government not caring, nobody cares." I said, "I think you feel nobody cares about you personally, so you turn to food and alcohol and pot to give you the illusion that you are being cared for." Carly replied, "Yeah, I need to be caring for myself—eating healthy, exercising." I said, "It's hard for you to turn to people to receive care." Carly responded, "Who am I going to turn to? You?" I answered, "Well, yeah, we've talked recently about how it's hard for you to depend on me." Carly said, "Yeah, because I don't know if you're going anywhere. You might leave. [Carly's preadolescent niece] said to me I might be tough on the outside, but I'm really a teddy bear on the inside. I don't have any patience." We continue to work on Carly's anger toward me. In a session following my return from vacation, Carly stated that she thought I would get angry with her for bringing coffee into the session. I stated, "It strikes me that maybe you're feeling angry with me." Carly responded, "Because you haven't fixed me yet." I replied, "Yes." Carly then sat up. I said, "Maybe your sitting up has something to do with my pointing out that you're feeling angry with me." Carly said, "The truth is I'm not angry with you." I responded, "You've made a number of disparaging remarks about the treatment today." Carly said, "Yeah, well, that's how I'm feeling today." She then told the story of a friend's dog, who was being looked after by the friend's brother, and the dog ran into the street and was run over. I said, "Here's a dog that wasn't adequately cared for and got killed." Carly tearfully replied, "I wasn't cared for and so I don't care for myself now, and I'm going to be dead."

Carly continued to work through her fear and rage over her feelings of massive deprivation and potential abandonment by those about whom she cares most deeply. She is becoming more available to using a psychoanalytic process to explore her conflicts and anxieties. The sadomasochistic elements—present since the beginning of treatment—are emerging more clearly now and are therefore more available for us to work on together in the transference. Other issues such as her sexual identity and her rage toward her mother and me are also emerging as central conflicts that Carly is becoming more comfortable talking about. I believe that this increasing psychological availability follows a lessening of superego pressures and represents authentic internal change. We observe a strengthened ego, reflected in greater anxiety tolerance both inside and outside sessions, a strengthened self-structure, reflected in greater feelings of self-worth, and the development of analytic trust with me. Carly no longer collapses when I make interpretations but rather reflects on them and genuinely considers them before responding. Most important, Carly is slowly taking ownership of the analytic process. I anticipate further internal growth as we continue to struggle together with these issues.

During the third year of psychoanalysis, Carly continued to struggle with her pervasive sense of deprivation, the associated feelings of vulnerability, and her pervasive sense of entitlement to special treatment as compensation for this sense of deprivation. Carly has also experienced guilt over her murderous impulses associated with frustration over perceived inadequate emotional compensation. These dynamics manifested themselves in the fertile ground of the analytic relationship, where Carly's maternal transference took center stage in the context of a future fee increase and her mother's current requests for increased financial support from Carly and her other children in spite of clear evidence of her mother's fiscal mismanagement.

Throughout this year, in spite of (or perhaps because of) the intensified transference material emerging in sessions, I have observed Carly's progress measured in fits and starts. Notably, Carly's symptoms have mostly abated. Carly has stopped drinking except on rare celebratory occasions. She has stopped driving recklessly and has started wearing a seat belt. Although Carly has continued to smoke marijuana, her binge eating has diminished considerably and has consequently lost approximately thirty pounds and dipped below the three-hundred-pound mark for the first time in many years. Carly has also recommitted herself to her partner of eighteen years and for the most part has stopped flirting with other women in their circle of friends. The restaurant business owned by her and her partner continues to flourish, and they have purchased a vacation home in Delaware, where they get away on the weekends. In sessions, Carly has demonstrated a greater capacity to listen to my interpretations without responding defensively with devaluation (although defensiveness continues to be an area of occasional difficulty). There is evidence of internalization of me as a new object (see below) that has resulted in increased self-reflection on her impulses to hurt herself and diminished acting on these impulses. Carly continues to experience moments in session where she can consider the integration of split-off self- and object representations even though she cannot yet sustain their integration.

In the beginning months of 2007, Carly began to show signs that she was internalizing me as a new object even though she still felt the need to devalue this achievement when I pointed it out to her. In a session in early February, Carly reported, "I'm wearing my seat belt now, and friends are surprised that I'm doing that. Then I thought that I'm having a birthday at forty-eight, and then I thought of your birthday." I replied, "I think perhaps your associations suggest you feel closer to me—your birthday and my birthday are connected in your mind, and this connection between us is leading you to internalize the caring parts of me for your own use." She responded, "That's stupid." Referring to previous instances when she has devalued me after admitting feelings of closeness, I said, "Whenever I mention closeness to you, you feel vulnerable and criticized, and you jump to criticize me and get me back." Carly modified her original devaluation: "Okay, silly." In this exchange, Carly was reporting to me that she was now wearing her seat belt—an issue we had talked about numerous times the previous year as an illustration of her lack of concern for her safety (along with smoking marijuana behind the wheel). In a sense, she was saying "Look what a good girl I am!" and wanted me to validate her effort. Instead, I pointed out the internalized parts of me and the implication that she was feeling close enough to me to allow me inside her. Conscious awareness of this level of closeness was overwhelming, however, which made her defend against the resultant fear by pushing me out—"that's stupid." Carly has repeatedly shown the ability to continue working in sessions after one of these episodes rather than letting her defensiveness derail the entire session, which had been the case earlier in the treatment. This excerpt is typical of Carly's increasing capacity to modulate her impulses, in this example leavening her anger with a dash of affection, replacing the word "stupid" with "silly."

Another theme that reemerged early in 2007 and coincided with external events involving Carly's mother later in the year was a future fee increase scheduled for sometime in 2008 and her refusal to consider paying a fee higher than her current $15 per session in spite of the financial success that has resulted from her lucrative restaurant business. I should note that Carly had embezzled thousands of dollars from a previous employer, casually acknowledges the inequality in the division of labor in her and her partner's restaurant business, and pays only lip service to the gratitude she feels over paying a low fee to me. In one session, I said, "You feel that two people can't come to some resolution about this through compromise." She replied, "Because I'll feel guilty." I asked, "What's that about?" She said, "That you're charging me $15 a session, and I'm here until you raise it. Then I'm gone." I responded, "It seems there has to be a winner and a loser—you feel guilty for winning—getting treatment for a low fee—or resentful for losing—having to pay a higher fee for treatment." She said, "So I lose either way." I replied, "Exactly, you feel we couldn't compromise on a fee acceptable to both of us." Carly said, "I've had that experience before with Lisa [a previous therapist]." I responded, "And you feel the same thing will happen here." In that previous therapeutic relationship, Lisa raised Carly's fee to $80 per session, which Carly felt was unfair because Lisa owned a Mercedes Benz and therefore could have treated her for less money. We had previously discussed Carly's belief (tenaciously held by Carly until we worked on it together) that therapists should not charge any money for their services because they have taken an oath of poverty like Mother Theresa. We observe here that Carly's sense of entitlement to free care interferes with the reality of psychotherapy—a service rendered for a fee (see Goodman, in press, chapter 3). Carly's fantasy of me as a breast with an infinite supply of milk is directly challenged by the reality of a future fee increase. This conflict between the fantasy of free compensatory care for life and the reality of payment for increased understanding and responsibility for oneself and one's feelings and behaviors continued to surface throughout this third year of treatment.

Because of the exploitative and neglectful manner in which Carly's mother treated her as a child (and continues to treat her), Carly now feels entitled to compensation from caregivers, including me. In the past, she has said that mental health providers, like Mother Theresa, should take a vow of poverty and offer their services free of charge. My projected fee increase contradicts her fantasy of me—and all caregivers—as a breast with infinite supplies, and refutes her expectation that she is entitled to special dispensation from her mental health caregiver. I could have confirmed her expectation and dropped the projected fee increase, but that would not promote any therapeutic change. Proceeding with the fee increase introduced the painful awareness of reality—that I am a separate person with limitations and needs.

In addition to the themes of the internalization of me as a caring object and the resultant fear of fusion and the theme of entitlement to free services and the reality of payment for services rendered, the theme of a lack of sexual excitement in Carly's relationship with Kesha continued to surface. In February, Carly shared that it was the sixteenth anniversary of the day that she had her first orgasm with Kesha. She and Kesha annually celebrate this anniversary together. When Kesha asked Carly whose anniversary is today, Carly first thought of the birthday of an ex-girlfriend, who shares the same date. She lamented that she does not have "toe-curling sex" with her partner and blamed the partner for not being her "sexual soul mate." I said, "Maybe it feels too dangerous to be excited by Kesha." Carly responded, "It's all mechanical, the whole orgasm thing." I said, "I know you know it's psychological—you want to avoid that part of the experience by focusing on the mechanical." Carly continued, "Maybe at the beginning I felt sexual, but I don't know I was ever in love with Kesha." In this session, Carly discussed the lack of sexual excitement with Kesha, but rather than engage in self-examination of her inhibition, she instead attributed the difficulty to some implied characteristic of Kesha. I found it difficult to do much with this material during the few sessions when she discussed her sexual frustration. At times, she resorted to her familiar devaluation of me as a man unable to understand lesbianism. She explained that lesbians are by nature incestuous and therefore assume multiple roles of mother, sister, and lover with multiple partners. I wondered who I was in the transference. Was I the excluded, neglectful father who is supposed to disapprove of or perhaps desire an unbounded mother-daughter relationship, or the naïve, neglectful mother who is supposed to disapprove of or perhaps desire her daughter's lesbian relationship, or someone altogether different? In the intervening months, I attempted various interpretations of this loss of excitement with no change in the actual symptom; however, Carly stopped flirting with other women in her and her partner's circle of friends.

Related to this fear of sexual excitement, Carly exhibited a desperate wish for and fears of fusion with a primitive maternal object. Initially, the vacation home in Delaware represented for Carly the solution to all her problems. She would walk to the beach with the bitter wind blowing in March 2007, find a rock to sit on, put on her headphones, and smoke marijuana. When I asked her what she found enjoyable about that, she said that she wanted to be near the ocean. She recalled memories of her family going to Jones Beach and swimming in the ocean. I pointed out the wish to be close to her mother and the simultaneous fear of it by blocking out the experience of her absence with drugs and music. Carly countered that all she was doing was "enhancing" the experience for herself. She was keeping me out, just as she was keeping the experience of the ocean out. In fact, I often felt as though Carly were faithfully coming to sessions to lie on my couch as though she were lying on the beach, and proceed to erect barriers between us whenever she felt I was getting too close to her. Much of my task as an analyst has been devoted to pointing out to her the moments when she devalues me and exploring the scary feelings that produced these reactions in her. Typically, in these sessions, we concluded that she is feeling too close to me to maintain her comfort zone with me. She therefore abandons me first before I can have an opportunity to abandon her—the inevitable outcome, in her mind, of letting me get too close to her. In our work together, devaluation serves to push me away, but in other areas of her life, Carly has used devaluation as an all-purpose defense against nonspecific unpleasant affects. By the end of the year, Carly was able to devalue me and spontaneously explore the precipitants of the devaluation without any prompting from me. This process demonstrates how Carly has evolved in internalizing my self-reflective function.

The emotional consequences of letting someone get too close were often available for discussion in sessions. Kesha's medical scare, which Carly believed to be terminal cancer but which required only minor surgery, coupled with my vacation, stimulated fantasies of all-or-nothing defensive processes used to protect her from feeling out of control. In a session at the end of February, I made an interpretation: "You have a fear of Kesha abandoning you, dying, but if you were to give that any conscious thought, in the front of your mind, you start to believe it really might happen, so you block out those thoughts with substances—food and drugs—to reassure yourself that you'll be okay. Unlike Kesha and other humans, substances are there for you 24/7, under your complete control." Carly replied, "To a degree, but I wonder what would happen if I consciously thought those things—not good." I responded, "So you sometimes feel very powerful—that your thoughts could actually cause cancer in Kesha." Carly said, "Well, not that I'm powerful, but I do think that sometimes, I don't want to tempt fate. I think Kesha does love me, I think because I'm such a good person." I asked, "Then what makes you afraid she's going to die on you?" Carly replied, "What would I do? What would I do without her? Let's not even talk about the emotional void—I think, I don't even know where all the bills are." I continued, "So you think about the logistics rather than the emotional implications, to protect yourself from the feelings of the emotional loss." Carly responded, "Well, [pause] I'd just crawl into the fetal position and hope that somebody would take care of me.

Maybe I'd kill myself." In this exchange, Carly struggles between a grandiose self that can control life and death and an infantilized self that would become nonfunctional without Kesha.

These two self-representations conjure two distinctly different defensive processes readily observed in the following session in which we discussed my upcoming spring vacation. When I asked her about her feelings about my upcoming vacation, she put on her armor: "I would say I'm just looking forward to sleeping in. But I know if I lose weight, you won't be here to hear about it. I think you want me to miss you, that I'll crash and burn when you're away." I reminded her that she comes here four days a week and shares her deepest thoughts and feelings here, so "it strikes me that you would have no reaction to my departure." Carly replied, "I don't want to be a Nadine [childhood friend in psychotherapy for ten years]—a whiner. I'm never going to get vulnerable because I'm not going to be paying you all this money. I don't want to be in a position of missing you. Whenever we stop, I don't want to be pining after you. I don't want to be a jellyfish." I commented, "So either you are wearing armor in this relationship or becoming a jellyfish and losing yourself. Those are two extremes." Carly replied, "What can I tell you? I'm a person of extremes, but I think I've become better at that. I know I don't have to live in the extremes. . . . Why would I throw caution to the wind and really open up here? If we could be friends afterward, maybe I could be freer here. I want it all, I want everything, but I know that's not possible. But the truth is, I turn to drugs and alcohol because I don't rely on other people in my life anyway." I replied, "I think you've begun to understand these processes at least on an intellectual level, but I don't think you've allowed that understanding to penetrate the deeper emotional layers of your personality." She replied, "I think you're right about that." Here Carly demonstrates two defensive postures—heavily armored, which reflects an aspect of a grandiose self-representation, and jellyfish-like, which reflects an aspect of an infantilized self-representation. The former posture seeks to block objects from influencing her internal and external world, while the latter posture invites objects to have mercy on her like a submissive wolf that exposes its throat to a dominant wolf. In her split-off internal world, Carly's strategy is to stand tall or surrender, conquer or submit, eat or be eaten. When Carly makes contact with the vulnerable aspects of herself, the overwhelming weakness she experiences places her in a situation where she feels that capitulation is the only course of survival. Carly tends to use intellectualization to avoid these helpless feelings. I often use defense interpretations to make Carly aware of this tendency so that she can begin to integrate these split-off self-representations and assume a more modulated posture vis-à-vis separation.

Sometimes Carly uses projection to rid herself of this vulnerable, jellyfish self-representation. In the following session, Carly acknowledged that she would miss me during my vacation. I asked how it felt saying that to me. Carly replied, "Just that I don't want to be a Nadine—that's what comes to mind." I commented, "It seems Nadine represents the unacceptable, vulnerable part of yourself that you put inside her so that you can disown that part." She said, "Nadine sounds so dramatic. . . . She never had parents tell her what to do; her son is going to be as fucked up as she is. I'm helping this elderly person, and Nadine said I'm a really nice person, but helping this person is something Nadine would never think to do." I continued, "I think you put these clingy, needy, dependent, selfish feelings into Nadine so you don't have to experience those feelings, but we see these feelings come out in relation to drugs and food." Carly replied, "I think you're right. Why leave myself to get my teeth kicked in? . . . I do like animals, babies, and old people." I said, "Sure, you give yourself permission to get close to things that can't reject or abandon you." Carly responded, "It's about trying to avoid sadness—that's what the whole smoking/drinking/eating thing is about." For the first time, Carly connected separation and abandonment with feelings of sadness and loss. Our work together continues to focus on the anxiety stimulated by her increasing vulnerability.

This vulnerability blossomed in the summer and fall of 2007 because of two external events: her mother's back surgery and subsequent requests for increased financial support from Carly and my announcement of a future fee increase scheduled for sometime in 2008. Carly wavered between the stance that she is entitled to free or nearly free treatment (grandiose self-representation) and the stance that she is not worthy of this treatment (jellyfish self-representation). Carly responded to this future fee increase by telling me that she would never pay a higher fee and that she was looking forward to sleeping in on weekdays again. In the countertransference, I have shifted back and forth from feeling the pull to become the omnipotent mother who will gratify all Carly's needs to feeling like the neglected, discarded child whose own needs have exceeded the parent's capacity to meet them. I have tried to convey an empathic understanding of Carly's affective displays of resentment and dismissal by tolerating them without reflexively reacting to them—something that the caregivers from childhood were unable or unwilling to do.

In one of these sessions in which we discussed the future fee increase, Carly reminded me that she had abruptly ended her previous treatment after a fee increase. Simultaneously, Carly was struggling with the fact that her mother, who had just had back surgery, was asking her for more money to support a lavish lifestyle. In the process of getting her mother's finances in order, Carly and her siblings learned that their mother had accrued credit card expenses in the neighborhood of $10,000 on nonessential purchases. Carly resented her mother's requests for financial support, not only because the mother did not need it, but also because she unconsciously resented her mother for physically abusing and ignoring her as a child. Because the mother never met Carly's emotional needs, Carly felt that her mother should not now be asking Carly to meet *her* needs. Resenting my projected fee increase next year, Carly has cast me in the role of the old object—her greedy, depriving mother—and herself in the role of the deprived, neglected child.

I needed to use my skill and creativity to show Carly that I understand and empathize with her childhood resentment, its influences on her fantasies of entitlement to omnipotent caregiving, and her painful awareness that I am separate and not omnipotent. At the same time, I needed to show Carly that my understanding of these issues comes out of a position of difference—that I neither share her wish for omnipotent caregiving nor expect myself to be able to fulfill it. In other words, I am tolerating the expression of her wish without actually fulfilling it. In a session shortly after this discussion, Carly requested to move up our Thursday appointment time from 7:15 A.M. to 7:00 A.M. because it would facilitate her work schedule (note that one of her reasons for wanting to end the analysis was to get more sleep). I agreed to the time change. At the end of this session, she asked me to remind her of the Thursday time change in Wednesday morning's session. I reflected back that it was her suggestion to change the time. She responded that she would write down the time change. I could have agreed to remind her, but then I would have been assuming the role of the omnipotent caregiver, and she the role of the perfectly cared-for jellyfish child. I chose instead to invalidate her expectation, which I believe, in this patient with borderline personality disorder, will promote therapeutic growth over time. In previous years, I do not believe that such an intervention would have promoted therapeutic growth because in the early stages of treatment, Carly needed an auxiliary ego just to tolerate being in the room with me. Three years into the treatment, she can now tolerate some separateness without becoming immediately enraged or depressed.

In a later session, Carly was talking about her mother's incessant requests for more financial support. I commented, "We talked about this yesterday: moms should be giving their love unconditionally, and you need to pay for her love. And it comes up here—that you feel you have to pay for my unconditional love and acceptance." She replied, "Well, I don't think my mother would withdraw her love from me if I didn't pay her more money . . . and I do think mental health professionals should charge. It's just that we live in a capitalistic society, and people charge for their services. But I think in an ideal world, the puppies and cats should be fed, there should be free medical and dental care, but we don't live in a socialist society. Everything is relative: if I paid $10 a day for cigarettes, I'd be addicted to nicotine." I replied, "What you seem to be saying is that the therapy relationship we're in is like a harmful addiction that you can't break free of." She said, "You have a point, but I would never want to put myself in that position." I asked, "And if you did?" She replied, "Well, it goes back to the whole pull-yourself-up-by-your-bootstraps thing. I don't want to become so dependent that I become an emotional cripple and I can't leave, like Nadine. I want to hold onto my house in Delaware." I said, "So you can't consider the possibility of some compromise, or explore the emotional reasons for not wanting to consider it?" She replied, "It's not that I wouldn't pay you more than $15, but I wouldn't pay *that* much more." I commented, "So there's a contradiction here: on the one hand, you've said in previous sessions that there's nothing more valuable to you than your mental health. It's so valuable to you, in fact, that you feel everyone should have it. Yet at the same time, you're unwilling to pay much more than $15 a session for it. How do you reconcile this tension?" Carly identified with the jellyfish/capitulated self-representation: "I don't—my brain doesn't work right. You know that—that's why I come here." Carly's perceived entitlement to emotional supplies is coupled here with the expectation that she must extract these supplies by herself and for herself. She does not deserve to have them for herself. On the other hand, her dependence on these supplies would devolve into a parasitic relationship in which she would be drained of all her own resources. In the countertransference, I have shifted back and forth from feeling like the exploitative mother making unreasonable demands on my child to feeling like the unappreciated child whose generosity goes largely unnoticed. Later in the year, Carly also mentioned experiencing dormant feelings of guilt over having paid so little for this treatment over the years. Yet these feelings of guilt have not changed her mind about the fee structure.

In another session, Carly mentioned that Nadine was paying for her son's expensive private education: "It's nice to pull $80,000 out to do this for your kid. . . . It's only available to people who can afford it. . . . It's like you're canceling me—getting nervous about cancellation." I asked her if I could give her my thoughts about this story. She replied, "You're going to say it has to do with the money issues between us, but I don't want to waste the time over the next year talking about this. Am I right?" I said, "Close—I think it means you feel that the treatment is only for the wealthy, and you're feeling nervous and angry that I might cancel you." Carly replied, "I think there's a bit of truth in that. I don't know what else to say about it. You said compromise, but sometimes that means nobody wins. It's not important who wins and loses. Part of me feels when money comes into play, I lose sight of everything else. It means money becomes the whole thing. I was thinking this morning—I had said mental health should be free. I know that's not the real world." I asked, "How do you see a compromise as unfolding between us?" Carly said, "I would feel cheap. You're worth $150 [a session], but I'd never pay that. Then it becomes a personal thing. . . . I might pay $75 [a session], but I would pay that for only one session. I would come once a week, or whatever, but I wouldn't get involved in paying a lot of money. . . . There's the part of me that says mental health professionals shouldn't get paid, and little animals shouldn't get tortured—utopia. This is a professional relationship." I asked, "Meaning?" She replied, "Antiseptic—it's strange to say I can't really count on you because you're not forever, and it keeps me from being fully involved and trusting here." I commented, "On the one hand, you say you have achieved peace of mind through this process, yet you aren't willing to pay for it." She said, "Well, I don't want to be here forever. I could sell my house and pay you for ten years, like Nadine, and stay the same." I replied, "So it's the black and white thinking. Either you pay $15 a session, or you'll be selling your house and staying here for ten years. There's no middle ground. . . . On the one hand, I'm a kindly, caring, compassionate therapist who has helped you. On the other hand, I'm an exploitative therapist who will be soaking you for all your money. You've said that perhaps therapists get their patients to pay them lots of money like Nadine's therapist." She countered, "Yeah, but not all therapists are altruistic like you, charging $15 a session. A lot of therapists do that to get more money." I responded, "You've said there's a part of you that thinks I have ulterior motives for treating you, and you bring up Nadine's therapist as an illustration of what you're afraid of. So you are struggling between an image of me as good, compassionate, and caring and another image of me as exploitative, money-grubbing, and incompetent because I have not cured you after three years." Carly replied, "No, I think you're a decent person. I don't think you're exploitative." With more time in the session, I could have explored the nature of her resistance at that moment to seeing me as exploitative—the need to preserve her idealistic image of me as the altruistic, infinitely giving breast and perhaps the need to preserve my self-esteem.

In the following session, Carly expressed some guilt because she feared that her refusal to agree to a reasonable fee increase would hurt my feelings: "You're worth everything you would charge." I focused on her need to take care of me, which reflects her own wish for me to take care of her. Carly then spoke of her fear of hurting her mother's feelings by refusing her requests for a higher monthly allowance. She continued, "I think this has been a problem with my mother ever since I started making money. I don't have the balls to confront my mother. If I want to give you a Mother's Day present, you have to put a dollar sign on it." I said, "You see me asking you for more money and your mother asking you for more money, and you feel we're both exploitative." She said, "Well, there are a lot of therapists who do exploit and keep their patients forever. . . . I would like to come in every now and then and just having you fix me." I commented, "Like a big breast where you can feed whenever you want and not have to pay." She acknowledged, "I know that could never happen, so it's not even worth talking about. We can just move on because I know that you deserve to be paid." I said, "I think it's important to acknowledge the fantasies here. The disappointment that these fantasies can't be fulfilled is too painful to bear sometimes, so you avoid them with food and drugs." Carly replied, "I wish I had a zillion dollars too, but I know that's never going to happen, so why dwell on it? I guess your point is that I avoid the disappointment of it with these other things. I can understand that." I ended the session by pointing out that "this is very hard work—it's hard to acknowledge and feel disappointment and loss." In this session, I felt it was important for me to uncover the underlying wish for unlimited, symbiotic caregiving and her efforts to avoid the painful awareness of this wish by turning to nonhuman substitutes that give the sensation of fusion.

The overwhelming sense that Carly's powerful dependency needs make her exquisitely vulnerable to financial exploitation and emotional captivity continued to manifest itself later in the year. Following a discussion of the nature of our relationship, Carly exclaimed, "Oh, look! That spider is on the ceiling. Don't go near that web, spider—that's not yours!" I responded, "And you don't want to go near this web—me—because you feel you'll get caught like Nadine in a never-ending analysis." Carly replied, "Yeah, I don't want this to go on forever. Can we talk about me coming twice a week?" I responded, "Once you admit it's a real relationship we have, you get terrified, and you immediately have to think about moves to limit our contact with each other." Carly stated, "This relationship isn't going to last forever; I've had to struggle with that." Carly is struggling with an unconscious fantasy of an omnipotent, malevolent caregiver who emotionally enslaves the weak and dependent for their own purposes. As we explore this fantasy together, Carly will begin to examine her own parasitic tendencies. Her attitude toward her sense of entitlement to compensate for her perceived victimization has become more modulated over the past year. Carly's identification with her exploitative mother, however, remains embedded in the deepest layers of Carly's personality and will likely become a more prominent focus of the treatment in the months ahead.

Carly continued to press the issue of coming only once a week. In one of these sessions, I told her, "I wouldn't be able to see you at $80 a session for once-a-week therapy because you are successful in your career and can realistically afford to pay more. I would certainly charge you less per session if you were to continue in four-times-per-week psychoanalysis, but I could not see you for $80 once a week. I think you must feel disappointed in me for not continuing as we are at the same fee." Carly replied, "I think you deserve that, but I shouldn't have brought up the money thing." I interjected, "You've been thinking about it." She responded, "I've been thinking about not coming four times a week for a long, long time—check your notes. I want to come three times, then two, then one, then none." I asked, "How do you understand this weaning process you're describing?" She replied, "I don't want to jump off the cliff. How do people go from four times a week to none? . . . It's like a mommy bird and a baby bird, and I had a dream the baby birds were being fed by the mommy bird, and a baby bird falls, and I try to catch it." I said, "So I'm going to kick you out of the nest." She replied, "Well, that's self-evident, but I'm just not going to pay that." I commented, "I think your fear is I'm going to drain you of all your financial resources, and you'll have nothing. It's like your mother sticking her hand out and demanding to be taken care of, and you resent it. It's devour or be devoured." Carly replied, "I understand that you might be taking this personally; you're not an IBM machine." I said, "You'd prefer to make this into my issue, but there's a gap in your thinking here. These three statements don't go together: (1) 'I think you're worth every penny,' (2) 'my peace of mind is worth more to me than anything else,' and (3) 'I'm not going to pay more than half your regular fee for one session a week.'" Carly replied, "What don't you understand?" I continued, "I can appreciate that you don't think I understand, but one of those statements doesn't belong with the others, and I think you don't want to pay a higher fee because you have a fear that I'll be draining you of all your financial resources, and you'll have nothing left." Carly replied, "I just don't want to pay $150 every week or even *close* to that—that's $6,000 a year!" The fear that I will be exploiting her, and the wish to continue to exploit me, continue to constitute a prominent theme in this treatment.

Six days later, Carly tearfully admitted that she wants to begin reducing the frequency of treatment because "you have really helped me, and . . . I don't want to jerk you around until next year and then leave." I said, "So you feel guilty." She replied, "Yes, I feel guilty about it." I commented, "This was an issue with your previous therapist. You left over a fee increase, so this is an opportunity to work through these issues." Carly responded, "Well, if the goal would be to get me to pay you more money, I don't want to go there. When I was with Hanna [a previous therapist], I kept thinking I was paying $2 a minute. . . . I have all this shit coming up with work, and I don't want to be dependent on these workers [her restaurant staff]." I replied, "And you don't want to be dependent on me." Carly said, "Well, if I'm not going to see you in a few months." I asked, "A few months?" She replied, "Part of me says I can't wait until next year; part of me says I should have more backbone and stand up for myself and not come on Wednesdays [i.e., reducing to three times a week]." I could have added to this formulation that Carly uses the fear of exploitation to ward off the fear of the sudden loss of me as a good, reliable object. By wanting to wean herself off me through a gradual reduction in session frequency, she is trying to protect herself from having to experience my loss and all the longing and depressive anxiety that normally accompany a termination.

Carly experienced a change of heart about weaning off treatment in the fall after having spoken to her high school gym teacher, who had been in therapy for eighteen years. The gym teacher had advised her to leave when she is ready to leave and not focus on the money. In this same session, Carly also described an argument with her older sister in which Carly felt like calling her back to make up: "I really wanted to tell you about it yesterday. . . . I thought you would say, 'Why would you want to call her back?'" I responded, "It seems you've internalized me, which is a goal of our work together." Carly replied, "That's exactly right—I *have* internalized you. . . . Kesha said you're doing good work with me, and it's true—it's all coming together now."

Carly's sense of gratitude to me for the improvements I have helped her to make in her life has begun to emerge in the context of rage against me for the inevitable loss of me as an external object in her life, who attends to her and her emotional needs. On the eve of my winter vacation, she was describing the death of her older sister's mother-in-law. I pointed out that she had slipped and said "mother" rather than "mother-in-law" and asked her for her thoughts about it. Carly vehemently denied that she had slipped and accused me of mishearing her and stubbornly refusing to believe her. She then began to devalue me with a vengeance I had not observed in years. I tried to connect the devaluation with her need to protect herself from the pain of my going away on vacation and abandoning her. Unfortunately, Carly was unavailable for exploration for the remainder of the session. As Carly continues to struggle with her feelings of murderous rage toward her mother and me for perceived exploitation and abandonment, both now and in the future, I hope that she will be able to integrate this image with the other powerful image of an idealized breast filled with infinite emotional supplies so that she can ultimately identify with the essential goodness of her caregivers while simultaneously recognizing their obvious limitations. Carly still needs to realize that her needs for dependency and for autonomy can exist in harmony with each other rather than in mortal conflict. At the time of this writing, Carly has begun to demonstrate an emerging capacity to mourn the loss of me and my caregiving function and to tolerate a more integrated view of me and of our relationship.

SUMMARY

Mei Ling (see chapter 2) and Carly were able to benefit from intensive, exploratory clinical work that included aspects of mindfulness, psychological mindedness, and mentalization in the context of a containing attachment relationship to me. I believe that both patients will sustain the gains they have made over the past three and a half years because they have made these changes at the structural level of the personality. I am continuing to work with both Mei Ling and Carly in helping them to consolidate these gains, separate from their mothers, and develop secure relationships with others based on interdependence instead of fusion masquerading as self-sufficiency. With continued treatment, both patients will gradually move from alternating preoccupied and dismissing modes of relating to a secure mode of relating. The protective bubble will not burst but rather gradually evaporate in the sustained light of understanding.

Chapter Four

"I Feel Stupid and Contagious": Two-Person Clinical Supervision of Fledgling Therapists Treating Patients Who Have Negative Therapeutic Reactions

Patients who are prone to having negative therapeutic reactions seem to be increasingly common in clinical practice. These patients pose special problems for graduate students, psychoanalytic candidates, and other therapists who are struggling with anxiety regarding their new role and feelings of incompetence and helplessness associated with the belief that their therapeutic efforts will result in treatment failure.

The fledgling therapist thus provides fertile ground for this kind of patient to project her or his concerned, depressed, guilty self-representation into the therapist. The fledgling therapist, owing to an incomplete integration in her or his own internal world of insecure attachment relationships, is also capable of projecting dead or damaged and dying object representations into this kind of patient, who sometimes responds by withdrawing from the attachment relationship to the therapist or severing this attachment relationship by leaving treatment altogether. I will argue that although we must acknowledge the limitations of our therapeutic technique with this kind of patient, identification and interpretation of projective identification are essential to increase the likelihood of therapeutic success. Finally, I recommend rigorous education in severe psychopathology, exploration of one's intrapsychic conflicts, and participation in individual or peer clinical supervision, as well as an interpretative emphasis on both the deeply buried love for the internal world of insecure attachment relationships as well as its destruction.

As a clinical supervisor over the past nine years, I have watched clinical psychology graduate students become demoralized when patients get worse and drop out of treatment. Graduate students experience guilt and disillusionment, wondering whether clinical psychology was indeed their calling after all. Teaching, nursing, and computer science all begin to look more appealing after that first patient suddenly leaves treatment, either having not improved or actually becoming worse after the students worked so hard to keep the patient engaged in treatment. As a child psychoanalytic candidate treating my first control case, I also fell victim to a disturbing sense of inadequacy when my patient failed to show signs of improvement. I want to propose that a certain kind of patient is prone to making fledgling therapists feel demoralized. Graduate students, psychoanalytic candidates, and other inexperienced therapists need to become aware of the existence of this kind of patient so that when they begin to feel depressed, hopeless, and unsure of their skills, they might use these signs as diagnostic indicators and apply therapeutic techniques that could keep this kind of patient engaged in treatment. I am referring to patients who flee treatment, not because the therapist has aroused their intolerable feelings of envy (a worthy subject in its own right), but because these patients in treatment experience intense unconscious guilt over both their aggression toward their loved internal objects, to whom they are insecurely attached, and their failed attempts at reparation of these insecure attachment relationships.

In 1936, the Kleinian psychoanalyst Joan Rivieré wrote a groundbreaking paper, "A Contribution to the Analysis of the Negative Therapeutic Reaction." Extending Freud's 1923 observations on patients "who get worse during the treatment instead of getting better" and set themselves "against their recovery" (p. 49), Rivieré further explored the meaning of the "negative therapeutic reaction" and the patients who experience it. Anyone wondering whether the passage of seventy-two years has eliminated these kinds of patients from our clinical purview or from society altogether need look no further than the song lyrics of some of today's most popular songwriters. In 1991, Kurt Cobain, considered by many to be the voice of his generation, and his band Nirvana released an album appropriately titled *Nevermind.* In "Smells like Teen Spirit," the song that singularly defined the *Zeitgeist* of that decade, Cobain's voice crescendos to the chorus, where he spews his despair and vulnerability: "I feel stupid and contagious." And in "Lithium," Cobain further expresses his feelings of alienation, self-loathing, and cynicism: "I'm so happy 'cause today I've found my friends—they're in my head—I'm so ugly, but that's okay 'cause so are you." The multi-platinum album touched a raw nerve and proved to be the rallying cry for Generation X and beyond. Cobain poignantly summed up this self-doubting, detached, hopeless philosophy of the 1990s and beyond: "Oh well, whatever, never mind."

Whatever the sociocultural reasons behind the massive popularity of this philosophy, greater numbers of disaffected youth seem to be showing up at our offices, clinics, and hospital doorsteps. These patients (typically diagnosed with narcissistic, borderline, or antisocial personality disorders) pose special problems for fledgling therapists, who, because of their clinical inexperience, might be unable to see the contributions that these patients make to their own doubting perceptions of self-as-therapist and feelings of failure generated by these patients when they leave treatment.

Briefly, Rivieré's (1936) thesis is that many of these patients use primitive defense mechanisms—omnipotent denial, mania, projection, and splitting—to protect themselves from awareness of massive guilt and depression. These patients are unconsciously terrified of losing control, because losing control signifies for them the emergence of the guilt and depressive anxiety they are struggling to defend against. Therapeutic change, therefore, becomes a danger, because it means relinquishing the status quo, of losing control of what unstable psychic equilibrium they have left. The patient prone to having a negative therapeutic reaction guards herself or himself against the dangers of the depressive position because, through the treatment, those dangers "may prove to be a reality, that that psychical reality in his mind may become real to him through the analysis" (p. 312).

Every treatment requires the uncovering of depressive anxiety. Rivieré asked why this uncovering often results in a negative therapeutic reaction and the breaking off of treatment in these particular patients. She contended that these patients live with the conviction that they have already destroyed all their internal objects. The treatment would reveal this truth to them, and it would mean psychic death. It would also spell the end of any shred of hope they have that the treatment could actually resuscitate their intrapsychic object world. The patient thus "clings to analysis, as a forlorn hope, in which at the same time he really has no faith" (p. 315). Finally, the patient fears that she or he will destroy the therapist just as she or he has destroyed all the internal objects. The patient will "add [the analyst] to the list of those [the patient] has despoiled and ruined. One of [the patient's] greatest unconscious anxieties is that the analyst will be deceived on this very point and will allow himself to be so misused. [The patient] warns us in a disguised way continually of his own dangerousness" (p. 317). In the mind of the patient, then, treatment becomes a danger to the therapist, who must be saved from the patient's aggression by the patient's withdrawal from the therapeutic relationship or even by leaving treatment.

Rivieré informed us that this kind of patient also often feels unworthy of treatment. "Why should I allow the therapist to cure me, when my attachment relationships to all my internal objects—objects *I* am responsible for damaging—remain damaged and in need of reparation?" The patient often feels indebted to cure the objects in the internal world, who are all so much more deserving of cure than she or he is. Trying to convince the patient that she or he cannot repair these internal objects until she or he is first repaired ultimately fails because the patient treats this idea as an invitation to betray and abandon these internal objects, leaving them dead or damaged and dying. The manic omnipotent defensive structure convinces this kind of patient that she or he has the self-sufficient capacity to repair the internal object world without outside assistance (see chapters 2 and 3). The solution to this predicament suggested by Rivieré is to uncover the love and unconscious guilt associated with the imagined destruction and, ultimately, to integrate the love for these internal objects with the destructive, murderous hatred directed toward these same objects.

In the final two sentences of this paper, Rivieré alluded to the countertransference reaction stimulated by this kind of patient: "[The transference] tends to rouse strong depressive anxieties in ourselves. So the patient's falseness often enough meets with denial by us and remains unseen and unanalyzed by us too" (p. 320). As we therapists become tuned into the underlying depression and guilt disguised by these patients, we begin to act like our patients and protect ourselves from experiencing these same emotions—until they leave treatment, when the emotions often hit us full force. Those of us prone to using a deactivating attachment strategy are particularly at risk of protecting ourselves from experiencing these emotions (see Goodman, in press, chapter 6).

It is the identification with these depressive anxieties—and the resulting unconscious denial of them through the use of a deactivating attachment strategy—that graduate students, psychoanalytic candidates, and other fledgling therapists are especially prone to experiencing when treating these patients. One might observe that the contemporary songwriters of this generation are more capable of using their intuitive artistic talents to empathize with the self-debasement, guilt, and depression unconsciously experienced by Generation X and their younger siblings.

In retrospect, it is important to speculate why Rivieré stopped short of discussing the countertransference. In the first place, it would be another ten years before Melanie Klein (1946) would formulate the concept of projective identification in perhaps her most important paper, "Notes on Some Schizoid Mechanisms," which would later allow for a more penetrating understanding of countertransference by her students (e.g., Bion, 1959; Heimann, 1950; Rosenfeld, 1952; Winnicott, 1950). This kind of patient is prone to engaging in projective identification with the therapist, making her or him feel inadequate, disillusioned, and hopeless. From an attachment perspective, one could view projective identification as one manifestation of an attachment relationship.

In the second place, Rivieré was probably writing about her own experience as a patient in psychoanalysis with Freud (First, 1999). During his analysis of Rivieré, Freud used her as a translator, ostensibly to assist with her reparative processes. But as Rivieré (1936) pointed out in her paper,

"Recognition and encouragement by the analyst of the patient's attempts at reparation (in real life) allay them merely by the omnipotent method of glossing over and denying the internal depressive reality—his feeling of failure" (p. 320). First (1999) suggested that Rivieré must have conducted a self-analysis to arrive at the insights formulated in her paper. Because Rivieré was probably writing about herself as a patient, it would have been difficult for her to conjecture what Freud might have been feeling toward her during the analysis. How terrifying it would be to speculate about the contents of the mind of your analyst—or your mother or father—that perhaps she or he might be feeling depressed, hopeless, or even despairing because of what you might be projecting into them! Mentalizing these contents on behalf of the patient, and returning them to the patient in metabolized form, allow the patient to tolerate their guilt, depression, and hopelessness (see volume I, chapter 6). Perhaps for both theoretical and personal reasons, Rivieré stopped short of exploring the countertransference reactions stimulated by the kind of patient who is prone to having a negative therapeutic reaction.

If we apply Klein's (1946) concept of projective identification to Rivieré's (1936) insights regarding the patient who is prone to having a negative therapeutic reaction, the results are particularly relevant to inexperienced therapists already uncertain of their therapeutic talents and the value of the treatment they have to offer. Because of the debilitating psychic pain stimulated by the depressive anxieties associated with the belief that the attachment relationships in the internal object world are dead or damaged and dying, this kind of patient often projects into the therapist the concerned, depressed, guilty part of herself or himself for safekeeping, as it were. Otto Kernberg (1984) masterfully described this process:

> Because the analyst stands for the patient's weak, frail, submerged [I would add here concerned, depressed, and guilty] self, the patient may project his good or idealized self representations onto the analyst, almost "for safekeeping," and yet need to attack them under the effects of aggression and envy, originally self-directed. Racker (1968) has stressed the high risk, in such circumstances, that the patient will successfully reinforce whatever masochistic traits the analyst may still retain. (p. 269)

Kernberg explained that the therapist is able to identify not only with the patient's projected object representations, but also with her or his own self-representations projected onto the patient, activated in the transference. With intrapsychic representations being projected both ways in the course of a treatment or even a session, it becomes exceedingly difficult to know which representations belong to whom. Betty Joseph (1987), a contemporary Kleinian, has further developed these ideas by characterizing projective identifications in these kinds of patients as primitive forms of communication and a potential mechanism of psychic development. I would add that projective identifications are the mental tentacles that attach the patient to the therapist, just as neurotransmitters bind to synaptic receptors. One could thus view projective identifications as one manifestation of an attachment relationship.

The task of working with such patients is especially difficult for fledgling therapists, who are often identified with preexisting self-representations of incompetence, guilty over anticipated sins to be committed as a result of their incompetence, and depression over their inability to help the projected object in front of them. Graduate students, psychoanalytic candidates, and other inexperienced therapists provide fertile ground for a projective identification from a patient who wants to expel her or his concern for her or himself and her or his damaged objects and the subsequent depression and guilt that accompany this concern. Fledgling therapists can easily identify on an unconscious level with this projected self-representation coming from the patient.

One common response I have noticed in clinical supervision is the therapist's construction of omnipotent denial—a deactivating attachment strategy—to defend against these projected feelings: "The treatment is going fine. The patient is expressing anger toward me, so she must be connected to me and to the treatment. I feel great that she is able to do that." Or worse, the supervisee reports that the patient is cooperative with her or him in sessions, but is destroying relationships outside the treatment. In both cases, the therapist could be defending against depressive anxieties stimulated by a projective identification on the part of the patient and identified with by the therapist. This omnipotent denial often takes the form of reassurance offered during sessions. Feldman (1997) observed that "patients often recognize such actions, that we all engage in, as expressions of the analyst's own anxieties and wishes, and they similarly increase the patient's uneasiness about the analyst's strength and capacity to contain his projections" (p. 337)—which could convince them to leave treatment.

Inexperienced therapists with damaged internal objects are also at risk for projecting any of these self- or object representations into the patient. These therapists therefore need to cure the patient as an external representative of an internalized object in the therapist's intrapsychic world. This phenomenon therefore clashes with the patient's need not to be cured first. The patient interprets the fledgling therapist's attempts to cure her or him as a betrayal of all those internalized objects who so desperately need help before her or him. The need to flee treatment intensifies. In both situations—the therapist's unconscious acceptance of, and manic defense against, the patient's projective identification into the therapist, and the therapist's projective identification into the patient—the treatment is at risk of becoming imperiled.

Kernberg (1984) argued that clinical inexperience cannot be classified under the rubric of countertransference reactions, and dismissed its psychodynamic importance: "Errors owing to lack of experience or knowledge are just that, not countertransference" (p. 268). Although I agree with Kernberg that lack of experience is not synonymous with countertransference, I have argued, and will attempt to demonstrate, that lack of experience nonetheless makes a therapist vulnerable to accepting projective identifications that resonate with a currently active self-representation as incompetent, helpless, and guilty. Similarly, such a therapist is also vulnerable to projecting damaged self or object representations into the patient, whom the therapist will then try to repair. Both situations can cause a reaction in the patient to sever the attachment relationship and leave the treatment prematurely. Thus, fledgling therapists who are treating patients prone to having a negative therapeutic reaction are more likely to experience treatment failure than more experienced therapists. The reason is that fledgling therapists are more likely to be identified with an incompetent, helpless, guilty self-representation that proves to be fertile ground for the projective identification favored by this kind of patient. Kernberg (1987) described this phenomenon as resembling "a compromise formation that includes elements both from the patient and from one's own self" (p. 81).

Fledgling therapists are also less aware of their own projective identifications of damaged internalized objects into their patients, who might experience the vigorous attempts at curing these objects as a betrayal of their own damaged objects and leave the treatment. Lack of experience can thus act as a catalyst for a negative therapeutic reaction to occur—even, as we shall see, in the work of a psychoanalytic candidate with considerable experience as a psychotherapist. Awareness of these mutually reinforcing processes on the part of both fledgling therapists and clinical supervisors can serve to prevent some of these treatments from derailing. We must keep in mind, however, that the effectiveness of our therapeutic techniques in working with such patients is modest at best. We must neither omnipotently declare the unlimited potential of our craft (deactivating attachment strategy) nor cynically join our patients in bemoaning the helplessness of their situation—or ours (hyperactivating attachment strategy).

EXAMPLE 1

I would like to illustrate these phenomena with three examples taken from the clinical experiences of three therapists—the first two conducting psychoanalytic psychotherapy and the third conducting his first control analysis.

Although the first two examples underscore the feelings of incompetence of two therapists early in their professional careers, the proneness to experiencing such feelings would equally apply to more experienced therapists just beginning treatment of their first control case in psychoanalytic training, as illustrated by the third example. The first therapist was a thirty-two-year-old clinical psychologist. After his one-year psychology internship, he had taken off two years from clinical work to complete a research fellowship and had just begun a two-year clinical fellowship on an inpatient psychiatric unit specializing in the treatment of severe personality disorders. Dismissing the analogy that learning how to conduct psychotherapy is like learning how to ride a bicycle, he was feeling incompetent and concerned about whether he could benefit the seriously emotionally disturbed patients he would be treating. Three months after beginning the fellowship, he was assigned a twenty-one-year-old woman (L) with a history of ten previous psychiatric hospitalizations as well as a history of self-destructive behavior that extended back to early adolescence. The treatment regimen included three-times-per-week individual psychoanalytic psychotherapy conducted by the therapist, an intensive milieu program that included frequent psychotherapy groups, and a highly structured schedule of daily therapeutic activities. L's chief complaint stated the obvious: "I have a history of self-abusive and suicidal behavior. I have a borderline personality disorder, and I thought with the right information and willpower I could get better." These two sentences seem to reveal three things about L: (1) she had assimilated the psychotherapeutic jargon used by her previous treatment providers with no obvious benefit; (2) she was denigrating her previous treatment providers by implying that they had not provided her with the "right information"; and (3) she was still invested in an omnipotent manic effort to save her dead or damaged and dying internal world with "willpower."

L estimated that during the previous three years, she had cut herself over thirty times on the arms and legs, and preferred to use sharp objects to make deep cuts often requiring stitches. L also admitted that she had lied to previous treatment providers about her perceived level of safety. In the initial sessions, L reported that her parents tended to minimize or deny her feelings, but, in spite of this acknowledgment, denied having any angry feelings toward them. The therapist constructed a psychodynamic formulation in which L mutilated herself as a form of self-punishment for the unacceptable aggressive impulses she doubtless experienced unconsciously toward her parents, while simultaneously gratifying aggressive wishes toward the parents. L herself confirmed the idea of self-mutilation as both self-punishment and gratification of aggressive wishes toward the parents when she related that the sight of blood from her arm or leg meant that she had sufficiently punished herself for her sins. She also reported a dream in which her father took a hunting knife and cut himself on the chest.

The therapist, not wanting to take a passive, indecisive stance with this patient that would resonate with his own fears of incompetence and mounting helplessness, immediately began to interpret the obvious aggressive aspects of the previous behavior, which had hurt her, upset her parents, and sabotaged the attempts of previous treatment providers to help her. L responded to this group of interpretations by denying any hostile feelings directed toward her parents or previous therapists. In subsequent sessions, she became more withdrawn and combative as the therapist vainly attempted to interpret her resistance. The treatment seemed to come to a standstill.

L then began to allude to a secret that she was keeping from the therapist. The therapeutic alliance seemed to be rupturing. Interpretations that L seemed to enjoy dangling a morsel of knowledge—the secret—in front of the therapist only intensified L's sarcasm directed toward the therapist. The aggression had infiltrated the transference, but the therapist was experiencing difficulty knowing what to do with it. The nursing staff finally discovered that L had scratched herself with a staple and a piece of her watch on her lower right leg, left ankle, and lower back. In subsequent sessions, the therapist confronted L on her dishonesty toward him, the nursing staff, and peers. The therapist also interpreted to L that perhaps his previous interpretations regarding aggression directed toward her parents had made her feel guilty, which resulted in the self-punishing behavior. L acknowledged that, indeed, the previous interpretations had made her feel guilty, but refused to rule out future cutting incidents.

At this point, our fledgling therapist, now clearly worried about L's safety, his capacity to help her, and his own reputation, observed that L had become fixated on a female member of the nursing staff. L now reported sadomasochistic fantasies in which this nurse would strip off L's clothes, pull her legs apart, and "repeatedly jam [a] metal tube up inside me, laughing evilly all the while." In other sessions, L simply nodded off to sleep. How could a patient, obsessed with sadomasochistic fantasies and posing a chronic danger to her own safety, simply fall asleep in a psychotherapy session where she was supposed to be getting help? L had successfully projected into the therapist her concerned, caring, guilty self-representation. What was left was her sadomasochistic, denying, indifferent self-representation. It is critical to point out that a therapist more experienced with this kind of patient might have become aware of the attempted projective identification, and interpreted L's need to rid herself of concern and love for her internal objects to avoid feeling guilty. Instead, this inexperienced therapist, concerned about his lack of clinical skills, defended against the awareness of this lack through overactive interpretation of aggression, neglecting the deeply buried love and concern L also must have felt for her internal objects. Why punish herself if she were not so concerned about the effects that her aggression had produced on her internal world of attachment relationships to her loved objects? L therefore found fertile ground in this therapist for this projective identification.

The results of this approach were devastating. Early one morning, the therapist was walking down the long hallway of the unit. Patients were sitting around, drinking their coffee as usual, but something was different. All eyes were focused on the therapist as he made his way into the nurses' station. A nurse quickly informed him that the night before, immediately after fifteen-minute checks had been completed, L had unscrewed a light bulb from a lamp in the hallway, crawled into her wardrobe closet, broke the light bulb, and slit her throat from one end to the other. Fifteen minutes later, she was found scrunched up in the closet, profusely bleeding, with a glib smile on her face. L was rushed to a medical hospital, where she received thirty-two stitches. Within twenty-four hours, L returned to the unit, and subsequently lobbied for a transfer to a state hospital, which was granted to her.

One could argue that no fledgling therapist would have stood a chance of helping L integrate her murderous and loving impulses, repair the massive damage caused to her internal world of attachment relationships, and diminish the overwhelming guilt feelings that drove her to self-mutilation. In the face of such intense self-destructive impulses, we must acknowledge the limitations of our clinical skills and our therapeutic technique. Yet an awareness of the projective identification—and the therapist's corresponding self-representation as incompetent, helpless, and intensely concerned, which was already primed for activation in the transference—might have allowed the therapist to take more time to let the treatment unfold, interpret aggression in the context of the deeply buried love and concern for the internal world of attachment relationships, and metabolize the guilt feelings the patient was so motivated to ward off through her self-mutilation. This example illustrates how the confluence of inexperience and projective identification can derail a treatment, leading to an abrupt termination, or in this case a serious suicide attempt.

EXAMPLE 2

The second therapist was a twenty-four-year-old second-year graduate student in clinical psychology treating her first case. She too was feeling incompetent and concerned about whether she could benefit her first patient. In addition, she had an emotionally disturbed brother five years younger on whom she had expended an enormous amount of emotional energy trying to help, and who figured prominently in her choice of career. The patient was a seventeen-year-old boy who had lived in a therapeutic group home for four years. Sometime before his fourteenth birthday, X was testing the limits of his alcoholic mother, staying out long past curfew, getting into arguments, and engaging in other behaviors that X refused to discuss. His mother had convinced the legal authorities to file a PINS (person in need of supervision) petition for him. When this move did not have the intended effect, his mother placed him in a diagnostic treatment center for one month. The day he returned from the diagnostic treatment center, X once again stayed out past curfew. The next day, his mother was hospitalized and died of cirrhosis of the liver, precipitated by many years of drinking. In the absence of any relatives who wanted to take responsibility for him, X was placed in a residential treatment center for a year and a half, then a group home. During his approximately two years in this group home, X had received once-weekly individual psychotherapy from three previous graduate students. The therapist was X's fourth graduate student treating him. The treatment regimen consisted of once-weekly individual psychoanalytic psychotherapy, which X knew would end after one year, when he would be transferred to another graduate student.

X appeared withdrawn and closed off about the circumstances surrounding his admission to the group home. He provided only cursory details about his mother, her alcoholism, his conflicts with her, and his father's multiple prison terms for drug dealing. Instead, X focused on his relationships at the group home and his interest in becoming an emergency medical technician (EMT). After the first couple of months of treatment, X withdrew from the therapist, who had made several interpretations regarding his pushing away the staff and his peers at the group home. The therapist had good reason to make these interpretations—one evening past bedtime, X was blasting his stereo in his room. His peers complained to the staff, who confronted him in his room. X told them, "Whatever you do, you'd better not touch my stereo!" The staff explained to him that he could turn down the stereo without their needing to touch it. He refused. Staff therefore turned down the stereo, and as a result, X needed to be restrained. X constantly complained about the staff and his desire to be on his own.

As we observed from the previous clinical example, however, the therapist omitted X's feelings of dependence on the staff, and the consequent feelings of vulnerability and concern, from her interpretations of aggression. These other feelings were evident, however, in a later incident in which X suffered a serious asthma attack (an attachment-activating situation; see Bowlby, 1973) while staying with a relative for the weekend. The relative called the group home staff to alert them, and then took him to a hospital emergency room. After receiving treatment and being released, X became enraged that the group home staff never showed up—even though the relative appropriately took care of him without staff intervention. The rage reflected X's underlying love for his attachment figures, who bitterly disappointed him with their absence.

Through intensive work in clinical supervision, the therapist stopped making the interpretations of aggression and worked harder on establishing a therapeutic alliance. X began to bring into the treatment music he liked to listen to or poems he had written. One of these poems considered the death of his mother. Written from the perspective of someone in the intensive care unit, the author described the heart monitor flatlining and the medical personnel coming into the room, trying to resuscitate her, and ultimately covering her face with a sheet. X became tearful in session for the first time after reading this poem. He could not—or would not—comment on what he had just read, or confirm whether he really witnessed or only imagined these events.

In subsequent sessions, X began to complain about the treatment's interfering with his other activities. For example, he wanted to take an EMT course that conflicted with his scheduled sessions. At the same time, he expressed a wish to drop out of the final semester of his senior year of high school. The therapist became worried that she was losing the patient, and berated herself for saying and doing the wrong things. In particular, she worried that she had said or done something during that pivotal session in which X had shared the poem about the death of his mother. The therapist tried to explore with X the meaning of that session. He refused. In one session, he even called therapy "a waste of my life." Here again, we observe the therapist's becoming overly concerned and even worried about the fate of the treatment, while the patient is calmly talking about not caring about anything. In this example, however, it is possible that the therapist projected her own object representation into the patient at a moment when the patient provided fertile ground for it and was able to identify with it.

This possibility was discussed in supervision, and the therapist was able to acknowledge that X reminded her of her own brother, whom she had been engaged in trying to save from childhood onward. The brother and X were both roughly the same age, the same height (very short), and of stocky build. Both boys experienced depression and defiant behavior. In addition, both boys aroused in the therapist concern, worry, guilt, and a strong need to repair. The therapist became aware that X had finally made himself vulnerable, sharing his experiences regarding his dying mother and feeling the obvious guilt he must have unconsciously been defending against because of his repeated disobedience, which in his mind eventuated in her ultimate death. Through the transference, X had activated an internal object relationship in the therapist, who must have responded with increased worry, concern, and activity. These internal experiences took the shape of her brother, whose representation she then projected into X. X, however, unwilling to wear this mantle of dependence and concern because of his supreme unworthiness of the therapist's love and concern, responded with omnipotent denial and narcissistic withdrawal (a deactivating attachment strategy), and threatened to sever the attachment relationship and leave the treatment. How could he possibly be worthy of saving, when, through his own aggressive wishes, he murdered his own mother? He would rather forsake his own reparation, and instead go about the impossible task of resuscitating his mother on his own—perhaps through becoming an EMT and saving the lives of others.

EXAMPLE 3

I was the third therapist, a forty-two-year-old candidate in a child psychoanalytic training program treating my first control case. In spite of having practiced child psychotherapy as a licensed clinical psychologist for eleven years, I was feeling ambivalent about beginning my first control case. It felt like starting something I knew so little about, even though I had read extensively about child psychoanalysis and had been practicing psychoanalytically oriented child psychotherapy since my days as a graduate student. Psychoanalytic candidates seldom treat patients who have the potential to develop negative therapeutic reactions; they are often excluded from the control-case pool because they often pose the very challenges this article addresses, and often raise questions of analyzability. Because of the widespread paucity of child training cases and because of changes in psychoanalytic training curricula that now include courses that focus on severe psychopathology and its treatment, however, these exclusion criteria are often relaxed, and almost any child whose parent is willing to transport her or him to sessions four times per week now qualifies as a control case. Thus, I was able to begin psychoanalysis with a child whose mother would develop what I am calling a "vicarious negative therapeutic reaction."

The patient, M, was a six-year-old boy who was experiencing toilet-training difficulties. He had bowel movements during the day and night and urinated at night in his underwear. These accidents occurred at school, on the school bus to and from school, and at home. M could sit in his own products for hours and not seem uncomfortable. When a classmate asked him what that smell was, M told him, "Just ignore it." He also experienced interpersonal difficulties. M needed to control all his interactions with his peers as well as with adults. Other children did not want to socialize with M because the play had to take place on his terms, with his choice of activity and his rules. The parents and teacher reported that M often refused to follow directions, particularly when he was asked to transition from one activity to another (e.g., watching television to going to bed, eating breakfast to leaving for school, playing with peers to sitting at circle time).

Most disturbing to his parents was M's aggression directed toward his brother, who is two and a half years younger. When his brother wanted to inspect one of M's toys, M would hit him hard enough to make him cry. When M's mother changed his brother's diaper, M would sometimes hit his mother. M's use of aggression was not limited to his brother or mother; he also sometimes hit his school peers when they refused to play his games by his rules.

This aggression was not always reactive. In school, M once threw a live rabbit against a wall for no apparent reason. When I asked about the incident in the following session, M expressed anger that the teacher later refused to allow him to hold a baby chick. M then demonstrated this sadistic impulse *in vivo* by gleefully knocking a Russian matryoshka of cats onto the floor, which he referred to as a mommy cat with her baby cats. He then took an action figure and got down on the floor to play with the cats. M then narrated a fantasy story in which the baby cats got inside the mommy for protection from "the bad guy" action figure. The bad guy then overpowered the mommy, and the baby cats fell out and died. They returned to life, however, and battled against the bad guy, who then died. Then other bad guys came and "touched the insides" of the cats, who were filled with "boiling hot liquid soap." Each bad guy was scalded and died. Then the baby cats got inside the mommy again for protection as before against the original bad guy, who had returned to life. The bad guy then savagely attacked the mommy, who died along with her babies, who had fallen out. At the end of the session, M instructed me to clean up all the toys because "I like to order you around."

During other sessions, M demonstrated other aspects of himself. While playing Uno or board games, M. would often upset the game board and fling all the pieces and the board itself all over the office without warning. He called this event "Hurricane Floyd." I later learned from the parents that, at age two and a half, M and his parents had fled their home during Hurricane Floyd, which terrified him. When asked about this incident, M reported that he remembered Hurricane Floyd and how loud the thunder and wind were. He also remembered his parents' looking "scared." He concluded with a statement that he immediately retracted: "God was trying to get me and my mommy." M's baby brother was born only four months earlier. Another intriguing aspect of M's personality centered on his making homemade greeting cards for his teacher and school peers. Some of them read, "I'll never hurt you again. Be my friend again." He also gave them stones he believed represented some value to them. I considered these behaviors to represent unsuccessful attempts at undoing, reflective of a sense of guilt over his mistreatment of them and his need to reestablish some sense of closeness to them.

In my early work with M, I tried to contain his chaotic, hurricane-like feelings of anxiety and rage by empathizing with him. I made nonthreatening interventions such as "Gee, that hurricane must have been really scary—you weren't feeling protected." M responded to this containment by becoming more organized in his play; the hurricanes eventually disappeared. M's accidents, however, continued unabated. Both parents expressed impatience and frustration with the lack of immediate results; they needed the accidents to stop as soon as possible. During a collateral session, M's mother clearly articulated the emotional impact of this symptom on her: "I want to kill him!" Simultaneously with my treatment, M's mother decided to take M to a series of experts: an "encopresis specialist," a gastrointestinal specialist, a neurologist for an EEG (which was negative) and psychostimulant medication (which was prescribed), a neuropsychologist, a school psychologist, a urologist, and a nutritionist. M's mother also mentioned that the neurologist had suggested that M has Asperger's disorder and therefore needed a different kind of treatment. She had conducted some Internet research and had drawn the same conclusions. In the session that followed, M was preoccupied with saying "bye-bye" over and over again. I told her that although I am not a neurologist, I did not believe that the psychostimulant medication would be helpful. She snapped back, "Well, nothing else seems to be helping!" I tried to empathize with her frustration and impatience—how humiliating and frustrating it must be to be changing M's underwear at age six. I calmly explained that M does not have Asperger's disorder, and sat down alongside her as I reviewed the diagnostic criteria in the *DSM-IV* (American Psychiatric Association [APA], 1994) and discussed them with her one by one. By the end of the collateral session, she agreed that M. did not have Asperger's disorder. In this example, we observe what might be labeled a "vicarious negative therapeutic reaction." M is demonstrating some improvement in psychic organization during sessions, but the primary symptom remains unaffected. M's mother is responding to the lack of improvement in the symptom for which she sought treatment for her son by parading in front of me the symbols of her lack of confidence in me and the therapy—a cadre of other professionals who she expects will provide the "magic bullet" that will immediately cure M of his accidents. The negative therapeutic reaction is going on inside the mind of the mother—and I was acutely feeling its effects. Was I failing in the treatment of my first control case of a highly intelligent boy from a middle-income, intact family? Should I be making more confrontational interpretations of M's sadism and his need to get rid of his brother and punish his mother for betraying his love for her by having a second baby? Should I be telling him that he was also punishing himself for these aggressive impulses by sitting in his own cold, wet, smelly products for hours? This is exactly what I did. And the result was dramatic: M began to withdraw in sessions, playing with Legos by himself or working on construction-paper projects without my help. Self-sufficiency—a deactivating attachment strategy—replaced a secure attachment relationship to me.

I was feeling intense pressure from this exasperated mother to solve the problem of the accidents quickly; otherwise, she would surely end the treatment, as M suspected ("bye-bye"). I responded by stepping up my interpretation of the aggression I felt certain was unconsciously responsible for this boy's refusal to be toilet-trained. Simultaneously, I moved away from the relationship-building work that proved so effective earlier in the treatment. M responded by withdrawing from me—a kind of iatrogenic negative therapeutic reaction. I fell victim to the mother's projective identification of her own feelings of incompetence, inadequacy, and disillusionment partly because I was experiencing those very feelings as a fledgling analyst prior to the beginning of the analysis. My vulnerability was exploited by the mother's projection into me of unwanted aspects of her own parental representation.

Through my own training analysis, I gained insight into these dynamics. I was also two and a half years old when my sister was born, and, according to my parents, my adjustment to her existence was difficult. My family often told me the story that soon after she was born, I bit her toe because she was "making too much noise." My father sent me to my room with no dinner—only one example of his inability to tolerate angry feelings, much less understand them, in me. M's mother exerted pressure on me to identify with those aspects of my representation of my father and project my own self-representation of the resentful, spiteful brother onto M. The unconscious purpose of the confrontational interpretations was to coerce M to start behaving properly rather than to help him to mentalize his affects. M's mother and I were sending him to his room with no dinner. Fortunately, M's desire to come to sessions never wavered; instead, he protected himself during sessions through withdrawal.

My clinical supervisor was also helpful to me. He noticed the frequent interpretations of aggression and the corresponding shift in M's behavior during sessions. He suggested that I focus on M's need for a secure attachment relationship, his desire to feel close to me, his enthusiasm for coming to the sessions. My supervisor observed that neither M's mother nor I was noticing M's desire for love. From this point of view, M's accidents were also unsuccessful attempts to regain his mother's love and reestablish a secure attachment relationship, now perceived as lost to his brother. If he could just act like his brother, his mother would lovingly clean up his accidents too. Empathizing with his mother's frustration, impatience, and devaluation of the treatment and me, without acting on the pressure she was exerting on me to change my method of working with M, became my primary challenge. M has since begun to interact with me once again and reveal his internal world to me, and his mother seems to be experiencing less frustration and impatience. This example illustrates how the feelings of incompetence and inadequacy engendered by the circumstances of beginning one's first control case can interact with other psychodynamic factors such as the psychoanalytic candidate's personal childhood experiences and the parent's vicarious negative therapeutic reaction to create a stagnating treatment in which the patient withdraws in the interest of self-protection, thus producing an iatrogenic negative therapeutic reaction.

Commentary

Patients who are prone to having negative therapeutic reactions seem to be increasingly common in clinical practice. These patients pose special problems for fledgling therapists in two ways. First, projective identifications from the patient are more likely to find fertile ground in the psyche of these therapists, already primed to doubt themselves, their skills, and their capacity to help their patients. Lack of awareness of this defensive process can result in premature termination of the treatment. Second, fledgling therapists, themselves less likely to be aware of their own intrapsychic conflicts, are prone to use projective identification in their clinical work. Lack of awareness of one's own conflicts, and their influence on the patient, can also result in premature termination. Finally, I have argued that these phenomena are most likely to become activated in work with this kind of patient in treatment with an inexperienced therapist.

What can a fledging therapist do to help protect the treatment of these patients? First, she or he can acquire an education about severely disturbed patients—specifically, a theoretical understanding of these patients' personality organization and cognitive, affective, and behavioral dysregulation—as well as techniques of structural assessment and diagnosis and clinical treatment. Over the past twenty years, psychoanalytic training programs have expanded their curricula to include courses that focus on severe psychopathology and its treatment. Second, she or he can enter—or reenter—analysis to uncover blind spots—the fertile ground for patients' projective identifications. Inadequate or malignant self-representations can be uncovered, and the circumstances under which they could be activated in one's psychoanalysis of this kind of patient could be identified and understood.

Third, she or he can find a clinical supervisor familiar with the processes of projective identification who can aid in their identification and interpretation. Kernberg (2003) suggested that excellent clinical supervision is the single most important aspect of psychoanalytic training. Clinical supervision can be helpful as a secure base, not just for inexperienced therapists but also for therapists who work with these patients at all levels of training—from graduate students and psychoanalytic candidates to senior training analysts. I am proposing that in a two-person supervision, the clinical supervisor can serve the function of an attachment figure, who can contain the projective identifications (misinterpreted as feelings of incompetence), sort them out, and metabolize them for the supervisee on behalf of the patient, who in turn can receive these communications back from the therapist in a tolerable form.

The Kleinian psychoanalyst Ronald Baker (1989) recommends peer supervision with such cases:

> The analyst who has the opportunity to share such material with his colleagues has, in my view, a distinct advantage over those who work more or less in isolation with these difficult patients. In the private sector there is some evidence that analysts who work under such duress for one or another reason lose or drop patients when the countertransference becomes unmanageable. The presence of a support group potentially militates against countertransference identifications, normal and pathological, with analyst and patient, which fluctuate quite remarkably at different times. (p. 39)

In these settings, the patient's projective identification, through the person of the therapist, has the opportunity of acting on the group members (serving in a supervisory role), who are then able to share their vicarious experiences of the patient with each other and the therapist. In so doing, the therapist gradually becomes aware of the psychic impact and meaning of the patient's primitive communications.

I must note that the outcome of the patient in example 3 was more positive than the other two outcomes, perhaps because psychoanalytic candidates, unlike most graduate students and postdoctoral fellows, have all three of these resources—a rigorous education in severe psychopathology, a personal psychoanalytic experience, and an intensive, self-reflective supervision—automatically at their clinical disposal, along with greater clinical experience to rely on as a holding environment of sorts whenever countertransference dilemmas arise. In addition to obtaining the assistance of these three resources for the purpose of becoming aware of and interpreting the experience of projective identification and its effects on both therapist and patient, what else can fledgling therapists do to retain this kind of patient in treatment? In all three clinical examples reported, the therapist attempted to interpret the aggression toward the object world without simultaneously emphasizing the deeply buried concern and love, depression, guilt, and attempts at reparation that coexisted in exquisite tension with the aggression. Interpretations of aggression were not incorrect, but simply incomplete.

Albert Mason (Grotstein and Mason, 1995), a Kleinian psychoanalyst who worked with Melanie Klein and was analyzed by Wilfred Bion, remarked, "If the patient threw shit in [Klein's] face, she would first compliment [the patient] on his aim." Aggression never exists in a vacuum; it is an ingredient of every attachment relationship (Goodman, 2002). We ignore this great psychological truth at our peril when we treat the patient who suffers from the conviction that she or he has destroyed the entirety of the internal world of attachment relationships to the loved ones whom she or he is killing herself or himself desperately trying to save. We must offer the hope of integration of bad and good objects, murderous and loving impulses, and reparation of insecure attachment relationships if we are to bring relief to the patient who is prone to having a negative therapeutic reaction. We must recognize in this kind of patient the wish to love and to be loved, as well as the wish to destroy and be destroyed, as Karen Finley (1990) poignantly reminds us in her poem, "The Black Sheep": "Sometimes Black Sheep are chosen to be sick / so families can finally come together and say / I love you. Sometimes some Black Sheep are chosen to die / so loved ones and families can finally say—Your life was worth living / Your life meant something to me!" (p. 143).

Chapter Five

Quantitatively Based Methods of Assessing Competence in Clinical Supervision and the Clinical Curriculum

Clinical supervision can harness the power of quantitatively based methods to assess the competence of supervisees. These methods could provide an objective assessment of: (1) the extent of the supervisee's knowledge base of technique; (2) the appropriateness of the supervisee's typical interventions given the patient's presentation; and (3) the supervisee's improvements over time—regarding growth of knowledge as well as increased specificity of interventions in response to the patient's verbal and nonverbal behaviors. The Psychotherapy Process Q-Set (PQS; Jones, 2000) and Child Psychotherapy Process Q-Set (CPQ; Schneider, 2004; Schneider and Jones, 2004; Schneider et al., in press) are two powerful and easy-to-use instruments that help therapists and researchers quantify auditory or auditory/visual observations of the psychotherapy process. The PQS and CPQ items were carefully constructed to capture descriptively three elements of psychotherapy process: (1) the patient's attitude and behavior or experience; (2) the therapist's actions and attitudes; and (3) the therapist-patient interaction, or the climate or atmosphere of the encounter. The resulting PQS and CPQ profiles of adult and child psychotherapy sessions can uncover previously hidden aspects of the psychotherapy process and make them available for discussion.

I used these instruments in two ways. First, I applied the PQS and CPQ to psychodynamic clinical supervision with four clinical psychology doctoral students. All four students attested to these instruments' value not only for improving their knowledge of psychodynamic technique but also their observations of their patients' verbal and nonverbal behaviors, their interaction patterns with their patients, and their own interventions. Specific transference-countertransference paradigms were identified by examining the Q-sort profiles of the students' sessions. Awareness of these paradigms produced positive changes in students' interventions, and, in turn, increased awareness in the patient (see also Goodman, 2007b). Second, I applied the PQS and CPQ to the work of third-year doctoral students enrolled in a course designed to help them prepare a psychotherapy case for presentation to a review panel. These students use the PQS and CPQ not only to test their knowledge of their preferred theoretical orientation but also to assess their adherence to this theoretical orientation in a sample psychotherapy session. In summary, the PQS and CPQ are versatile, quantitatively based methods that can be used to assess students' knowledge base and the conduct of their clinical interventions and their mutual impact on patient change.

My twenty-four-year-old second-year clinical psychology doctoral student looked worried. She was treating her first case, a seventeen-year-old boy who had been living in a therapeutic group home for four years. Her patient called therapy "a waste of my life." She wanted to reach her patient, to help him talk about his disappointment in her, his caregivers, and himself, but she felt incompetent in her efforts to help him to recognize the value of what she was offering him. Together, we eventually figured out that this patient was making the doctoral student identify with a hopeless, dying part of himself that had discouraged previous therapists and caregivers from caring about him. In effect, this patient was getting my doctoral student to feel what a part of him insidiously experienced all the time: "I feel stupid and contagious."

This pattern of interaction took time to unfold in the therapy and to identify in clinical supervision. We needed to rely on my doctoral student's description of her countertransference feelings with this patient in our clinical supervision to uncover what was going on in the therapy and formulate a strategy of intervention. This student was involved in her own therapy and, fortunately, had access to these feelings of incompetence and hopelessness. Over time, she developed a barely perceptible understanding that perhaps the patient was inducing these feelings in her, and that, because of her own fledgling status as a therapist, she was providing fertile ground for this induction process known to psychodynamic therapists as "projective identification" (Goodman, 2005b). But what would have happened with a less articulate doctoral student whose unconscious anxieties, resentments, guilt, and conflicts were less accessible to her? What would have happened had she not been in her own therapy, like so many doctoral students? What would have happened had she not had a secure, trusting attachment to me and consequently withheld her feelings from me?

Clinical supervision can harness the power of quantitatively based methods to assess the competence of supervisees. Transference and countertransference phenomena can be enormously helpful tools in empathizing with our patients and providing them with transforming insight (Tansey and Burke, 1989), but when these phenomena remain undetected and elusive, they become instruments of enactment and, ultimately, futility. Quantitatively based methods can be used to identify transference-countertransference paradigms in supervisees' psychotherapy sessions that could limit the effectiveness of their clinical work. Identifying these paradigms in clinical supervision can especially help fledgling therapists find intervention strategies that facilitate rather than hinder psychotherapy progress.

Different models of clinical supervision exist in the literature. How would quantitatively based methods of assessing supervisee competence in clinical supervision fit into this existing literature? One model (Gonsalvez, Oades, and Freestone, 2002) suggests that supervisors and supervisees together select appropriate objectives for both the clinical supervision and therapy, appropriate assessment of supervisee competence, and appropriate evaluation of supervision efficacy. Because supervisors and supervisees can have different objectives, a discussion between both parties needs to occur to arrive at a concordance. Quantitatively based methods of assessing competence in clinical supervision could facilitate the application of this so-called objectives approach to clinical supervision. These methods could provide an objective assessment of: (1) the extent of the supervisee's knowledge base of psychodynamic technique; (2) the appropriateness of the supervisee's typical interventions given the patient's presentation; and (3) the supervisee's improvements over time—regarding growth of knowledge as well as increased specificity of interventions in response to the patient's verbal and nonverbal behaviors. As the American Psychological Association (APA, 2002a, 2002b) increasingly advocates that clinical psychology doctoral programs systematically assess students' competencies across a variety of domains, there will be an increased demand for quantitatively based methods of assessment.

A second model of clinical supervision (Milne, 2006) suggests a systematic analogy between psychotherapy and supervision such that the therapeutic relationship could be used as a template for supervision. The common thread is an emphasis on problem solving within the context of a working alliance. A supervision experience during my postdoctoral fellowship illustrates a limitation of this model. My psychodynamically trained supervisor spoke only in reference to my process notes and freely interpreted my unconscious dynamics. At times, I felt the supervision would be better conducted on the couch. I did not find that experience helpful, either professionally or personally. This personal example underscores how a model of clinical supervision based on a model of psychotherapy can be taken to an extreme. Quantitatively based methods of assessing supervisee competence can be used in such situations by identifying specific interaction patterns between the supervisee and the patient that might also be going on in the relationship between the supervisor and supervisee, commonly known as "parallel process." Using quantitatively based methods to identify this process objectively could help diminish the potential for defensiveness of both supervisee and supervisor because they would be completing an instrument used to characterize these interaction patterns (see below). In my personal example, using such an instrument might have identified an interaction pattern between my patient and me simultaneously operating in the supervision.

Several literature reviews on supervision have been conducted (Ellis, Ladany, Krengel, and Schult, 1996; Ladany and Muse-Burke, 2001; Russell, Crimmings, and Lent, 1984; Tsui, 1997; Watkins, 1997). These reviews underscore the serious methodological weaknesses that characterize these studies as well as the paucity of knowledge gained from them. These weaknesses are particularly concerning as the emergence of empirically supported treatments (ESTs) elevates the importance of clinical supervision in establishing therapist competence and adherence to specific treatment manuals. A major aim of randomized controlled trials (RCTs) is to establish an empirical basis for treatment efficacy. Clinical supervision is critically important to RCTs because it is one of the main mechanisms used to ascertain that all patients enrolled in these treatment studies are receiving exactly the same intervention as prescribed in the treatment manual. While the generalizability of such studies has been sharply questioned (Westen et al., 2004; see also volume I, chapter 2), RCTs continue to be the mainstay of psychotherapy research. The validity of RCTs largely depends on the quality control of therapist interventions, which in turn largely depends on the quality of clinical supervision administered to the therapist-participants. One of the numerous flaws embedded within the medical RCT model is the inadequate supervision provided for its therapist-participants. Of course, in chapters 2 and 3 of volume I, I argue that naturalistic studies of rank-and-file therapists not in supervision can yield more valuable information than information gathered from RCTs because naturalistic studies can inform us about "conditions on the ground," while RCTs inform us only about conditions in the lab. The systematic study of clinical supervision, however, can assist us with training imperatives in graduate programs where future therapists are being trained.

Clear guidelines that articulate the particulars of the clinical supervision conducted with RCT therapist-participants would be critical because the hallmark of rigorous research is replicability. To my knowledge, only one study in the literature (Fehrenbach and Coffman, 2001) has discussed issues related to the clinical supervision of RCT therapist-participants. Therapists in this study participated in two National Institute of Mental Health–funded clinical trials of couples therapy and depression. No researcher who has conducted an RCT has yet developed a manual that systematizes the delivery of clinical supervision to therapists who participate in RCTs, or even an instrument to assess the competence of the supervision. Contrary to the spirit of manualized treatment packages, RCT therapist-participants have been shown to deliver more eclectic amalgams of theoretical orientations than the manuals stipulate (Ablon and Jones, 1998). Quantitatively based methods of assessing competence in clinical supervision could rectify this methodological weakness by offering systematic feedback to therapist-participants seeking to follow a particular theoretical orientation in their treatment delivery.

FOUR AREAS OF SUPERVISEE COMPETENCE IN CLINICAL SUPERVISION

I would like to propose four areas of supervisee competence that quantitatively based methods could be used to address in clinical supervision. First, clinical supervisors could use a gold standard of therapist technique (as agreed upon by a group of experts) to assess the supervisee's knowledge of the preferred theoretical orientation (i.e., therapist competence). This method would allow clinical supervisors to determine whether the supervisee is able to execute this technique during treatment delivery with high fidelity to the overarching principles of their preferred theoretical orientation without alloying techniques foreign to the orientation (i.e., therapist adherence). Thus, for example, fidelity to the overarching principles of psychodynamic technique *without alloying nondynamic techniques* would be the hallmark of therapist adherence in a psychodynamic treatment.

Second, clinical supervision should attend to the therapist's specific interventions—whether they indirectly or directly serve the therapeutic goals agreed on by the therapist and patient (McWilliams, 1999). Do the therapist's interventions flow out of the patient's clinical material, serve the therapeutic goals, and reflect psychodynamic technique?

Third, clinical supervision should include concordant observations between supervisor and supervisee about the patient's verbal and nonverbal behavior. A wide discrepancy between the clinical supervisor's and the supervisee's perceptions of the same clinical material indicates a possible countertransference reaction that would need to be identified and, ultimately, used in the service of the therapeutic goals.

Fourth, clinical supervision should attend to the interactional matrix co-constructed by both therapist and patient to determine which transference-countertransference paradigms might be operating in the treatment. Jones (2000) referred to these paradigms as "interaction structures," a construct that conceptually overlaps with Luborsky's (Luborsky and Crits-Christoph, 1998) "core conflictual relationship theme." The term "interaction structures" implies that the therapist's countertransference reactions also significantly contribute to the dyad's pattern of engagement. Josephs and his colleagues (Josephs, Anderson, Bernard, Fatzer, and Streich, 2004; Josephs and Fatzer, 2006) have used longitudinal research to demonstrate some ways in which therapist interventions influence these patterns. Ideally, clinical supervision would focus on all four of these areas of supervisee competence. Quantitatively based methods provide the means with which to assess these four areas of supervisee competence, identify specific needs for improvement, and, ultimately, improve the quality of the therapist's interventions and, in turn, the patient's outcomes.

THE PSYCHOTHERAPY PROCESS Q-SET (PQS) AND CHILD PSYCHOTHERAPY PROCESS Q-SET (CPQ)

The PQS (Jones, 2000) and CPQ (Schneider, 2004; Schneider and Jones, 2004; Schneider et al., in press) are two powerful and easy-to-use instruments that help therapists and researchers quantify auditory or auditory/visual observations of the psychodynamic psychotherapy process. Supervisors, therapists, and researchers can begin to use these instruments to assess processes of therapeutic change in adult and child psychotherapy. The PQS and CPQ each consist of one hundred items and use an entire audiotaped or videotaped forty-five-minute psychotherapy session as their unit of analysis.

Q-sort methodology has existed since the 1930s as an alternative to Likert-type scales. In Likert-type scales, items are assigned a score along a continuum (e.g., 1–5). The score assigned to each item is independent of the scores assigned to all the other items. For example, if item 1 is assigned a score of 3, item 2 could also be assigned a score of 3. Q-sort methodology, however, requires the rater to assign a specified number of items a particular score (Block, 1978). All items are therefore ranked in comparison with each other rather than rated independently of each other, as is the case with Likert-type scaling (see Block, 1978, for additional information regarding Q-sort methodology and procedures). Raters of the PQS and CPQ assign scores of 1–9 to all one hundred items. A score of 1 indicates that the item is most uncharacteristic of the session being rated. A score of 9 indicates that the item is most characteristic of the session being rated. A score of 5 indicates that the item is neither characteristic nor uncharacteristic of the session. A specified number of items is assigned to each score. All one hundred Q-sort items are sorted into nine piles ranging from most uncharacteristic to most characteristic of the psychotherapy session being rated. This forced-choice (ipsative) distribution is illustrated below (table 5.1). A Q-sort takes about forty-five

Table 5.1. Forced-Choice (Ipsative) Distribution of Q-Scores

Item Scores:	1	2	3	4	5	6	7	8	9
		Most Uncharacteristic		←		→	Most Characteristic		
# of Items:	5	8	12	16	18	16	12	8	5

minutes to complete. The prearranged number of items assigned to each score forms a normal distribution that facilitates statistical analysis.

The PQS (Jones, 2000) and CPQ (Schneider, 2004; Schneider and Jones, 2004; Schneider et al., in press) Q-sort items were carefully constructed to capture descriptively three elements of psychotherapy process: (1) the patient's attitude and behavior or experience; (2) the therapist's actions and attitudes; and (3) the therapist-patient interaction, or the climate or atmosphere of the encounter (Jones, 2000; Schneider and Jones, 2004). Approximately one-third of the items for both instruments were designed to assess each of these three elements. For example, item 64 of the CPQ assesses the child's behavior: "Child draws therapist into play." If this item is highly characteristic of the psychotherapy session being rated, *relative to the other ninety-nine Q-sort items*, it would be placed in one of the highest piles (8 or 9). Item 100 of the PQS assesses the therapist's interventions: "Therapist draws connections between the therapeutic relationship and other relationships." If this item is highly uncharacteristic of the psychotherapy session being rated, *relative to the other ninety-nine Q-sort items*, it would be placed in one of the lowest piles (1 or 2). Item 11 of the PQS assesses the therapist-patient interaction: "Sexual feelings and experiences are discussed." Again, this item is placed along the continuum from 1 to 9, *relative to the other ninety-nine Q-sort items* (for a complete list of the PQS and CPQ Q-sort items, see Jones, 2000, and Schneider and Jones, 2004).

The resulting PQS and CPQ distributions of adult and child psychotherapy sessions have a variety of uses. A factor analysis of the one hundred Q-sort items can be conducted with a minimum of fifty sessions (Jones, 2000, p. 266). The resulting factors depict psychodynamic psychotherapy process related to a particular patient or group of patients with a particular psychiatric diagnosis (Jones and Pulos, 1993; Josephs and Fatzer, 2006). These process factors can then be used to predict both symptom outcome measures such as the Symptom Checklist-90-Revised (SCL-90-R; Derogatis, 1983) and structural outcome measures such as the Social Cognition and Object Relations Scale (SCORS; Westen, 1993). With the PQS and CPQ, the empirical question of most interest shifts from "which psychotherapy works?" to "how does it work?"

The PQS has also been used to construct ideal prototypes of adult psychotherapy sessions from several theoretical orientations. In constructing the

PQS prototypes, two groups of experts widely recognized for their expertise in psychodynamic psychotherapy ($N = 11$) and cognitive-behavioral therapy ($N = 10$) were asked to rate the PQS Q-sort items according to the process that occurs within a prototypical psychotherapy session conducted from their theoretical orientation (Ablon and Jones, 1998). These Q-sort distributions were then composited within each theoretical orientation to form two prototypical Q-sort distributions that reflect the ideal psychotherapy process from a psychodynamic orientation and a cognitive-behavioral orientation. Correlations between the Q-sort distribution of each psychotherapy session and the prototypical Q-sort distribution comprised of the experts reflect the extent to which a particular session adheres to the ideal principles of a particular theoretical orientation. These adherence correlations can then be treated as scores used to predict outcome measures. A similar process was followed for constructing the CPQ prototypes.

ASSESSING THE FOUR AREAS OF SUPERVISEE COMPETENCE IN CLINICAL SUPERVISION USING THE PQS AND CPQ

I would like to demonstrate how clinical supervisors can use quantitatively based methods—namely, the PQS and CPQ—to assess the four areas of supervisee competence in clinical supervision described earlier. Over the past two years, I have used the PQS and CPQ in my own psychodynamic clinical supervision with four clinical psychology doctoral students. All four students have attested to these instruments' value not only for learning psychodynamic technique but also for improving their observations of their patients' verbal and nonverbal behaviors, their interaction patterns with their patients, and their own interventions. My supervisees and I have been able to identify specific transference-countertransference paradigms by examining the Q-sort profiles of their sessions. Awareness of these paradigms produced positive changes in supervisees' interventions, and, in turn, increased awareness in the patient.

At the beginning of the first year, I was assigned three second-year doctoral students from our clinical psychology doctoral program for one-hour-per-week psychodynamically oriented supervision. These supervisees were treating individual outpatient psychotherapy cases in their first externship. None of these students had ever conducted individual psychotherapy. One student (Student A) was assigned a sixteen-year-old adolescent girl, another (Student B) a seven-year-old girl. The third student (Student C) was not assigned a patient because our program's clinic did not have enough patients to assign to all students. I asked Student A to sort the PQS, which is used for adults and late adolescents, and Student B to sort the CPQ, which is used for children and early adolescents. I also asked Student C to sort the CPQ. First, I gave each student instructions on Q-sorting; then I told each one to sort the items according to the process occurring within a prototypical psychotherapy session conducted from a psychodynamic orientation, *as they currently understood this orientation.* I also sorted both the PQS and CPQ. After collecting the students' Q-sort distributions, I correlated their prototypical Q-sorts with both my own as well as the composite prototypical Q-sort comprised of the psychodynamic expert raters (obtained from Stuart Ablon).

My own PQS and CPQ ratings were highly correlated with the psychodynamic prototypes ($r = .80$ for both) and uncorrelated with the cognitive-behavioral prototypes ($r = -.01$ and $r = -.10$, respectively). The correlations between the three students' prototypical Q-sorts and my own varied widely. While the correlations between Student A and Student C and me were similar ($r = .50$ and $r = .49$, respectively), the correlation between Student B and me was much higher ($r = .73$). Student B's exceptional standing as a student, as well as her strong interest in psychodynamic theory, could account for her high correlation with me. In supervision with each student, I reviewed all the Q-sort items in which the student and I experienced discrepancies greater than 3. For example, Student A placed PQS item 45 ("Therapist adopts supportive stance") in pile 8, while the psychodynamic experts and I placed this item in pile 2 (a discrepancy of $8 - 2 = 6$). Student A had assumed that psychodynamic therapy was characterized by a high degree of therapist supportiveness (approval and encouragement). We discussed the theoretical reasons for this discrepancy, including the idea that a patient could interpret the therapist's supportiveness as a subtle form of evaluation that could stifle disclosure of negative material. I used this review process to teach each student the essential elements of psychodynamic psychotherapy process and to help them to consider how they might further the goals of psychodynamic treatment.

In January (the midpoint of the academic year) and again in July (the endpoint of the academic year), I asked all three students to complete prototypical Q-sorts. I used these Q-sorts to determine whether their basic understanding of psychodynamic psychotherapy process improved. Student C, who was not supervised, served as a control. As expected, Student A's and Student B's correlations with the psychodynamic prototype improved, while Student C's correlation with the psychodynamic prototype remained essentially unchanged. I attribute the learning curve of Student A and Student B to psychodynamically oriented supervision and the use of the PQS and CPQ. This example, drawn from my own supervision experiences, underscores one

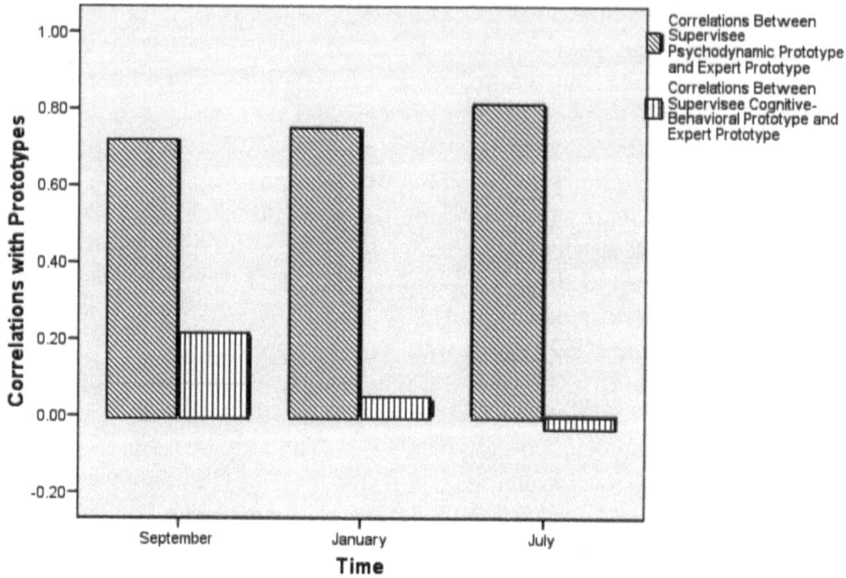

Figure 5.1. Mean Knowledge of Two Prototypes across the Academic Year

way that clinical supervisors can assess the degree of a supervisee's competence in their knowledge about therapist technique from their own preferred theoretical orientation using the PQS and CPQ.

I decided the following academic year to repeat this supervision method with two additional supervisees from my program. The prototype data of the four supervisees (Students A and B and the two new students) are represented in figure 5.1. Although the mean differences across the three time points are not statistically significant, the reader will notice that the supervisees' knowledge of psychodynamic process improved across the academic year, while their confusion of psychodynamic process with cognitive-behavioral process diminished, as illustrated by the decreasing bars indicating the supervisees' diminishing correlations with the cognitive-behavioral prototype across the academic year. The mean difference between the psychodynamic process and the cognitive-behavioral process was, of course, statistically significant, paired samples $t(11) = 8.97$, $p < .001$. I attribute these trends across the academic year to weekly exposure to psychodynamically oriented supervision and the use of the PQS and CPQ.

I also required all four supervisees to Q-sort their own weekly psychotherapy sessions. I have also been using the PQS and CPQ in weekly psychodynamically oriented supervision with these four supervisees. Each supervisee completes a Q-sort immediately following his or her session

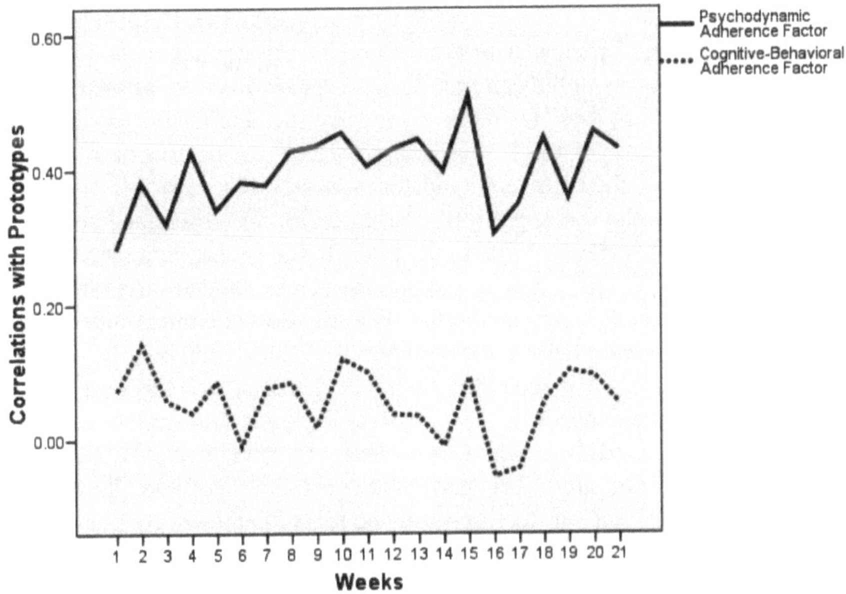

Figure 5.2. Plot of Mean Adherence Factors by Weeks of Treatment

based from memory or from viewing their own video recording and then e-mails me the Q-sort distribution prior to our supervision appointment. Figure 5.2 illustrates these supervisees' adherence to psychodynamic process and cognitive-behavioral process across twenty-one sessions of treatment. The reader will notice that their mean adherence to the psychodynamic prototype in the conduct of these twenty-one sessions is significantly higher than their mean adherence to the cognitive-behavioral prototype, paired samples $t(20) = 23.83$, $p < .001$. The correlation between the number of sessions and the supervisees' weekly adherence with the psychodynamic prototype approached significance, $r = .38$, $p = .09$, while the correlation with the cognitive-behavioral prototype was not significant, $r = -.22$, *ns*. Collectively, these findings suggest (1) that the supervisees adhered to psychodynamic process more closely than to cognitive-behavioral process in their actual clinical work, and (2) that their adherence to psychodynamic process increased over time, while their essential nonadherence to cognitive-behavioral process remained essentially unchanged. Again, I attribute the improved adherence to psychodynamic process to weekly exposure to psychodynamically oriented supervision and the use of the PQS and CPQ.

Clinical supervisors could also ask the supervisee to provide them with an audio or video recording of each session, which the supervisor could then Q-sort. Then the supervisor could correlate the supervisee's Q-sort with his or her own and review item discrepancies within supervision. Because of time constraints, I simply review with the supervisee during supervision the ten items he or she places in the extreme piles—1 and 9. Because of their placement at the extremes, these ten items essentially characterize the psychotherapy process of a session. Because it is impossible for a supervisor to review with the supervisee the entire audiotape or videotape of a session, I often ask the supervisee to play back portions of the session of particular interest or difficulty. Later, I review with them the ten extreme Q-sort item placements, which give me an overall sense of the process across the entire session.

Using quantitatively based methods in this way during clinical supervision has proved enormously helpful to the supervisee and, I imagine, the patient. For example, Student A placed PQS item 3 ("Therapist's remarks are aimed at facilitating patient speech") in pile 9, item 7 ("Patient is anxious or tense [vs. calm and relaxed]") in pile 1, and item 15 ("Patient does not initiate topics; is passive") in pile 1. This particular constellation of item placements told me that the patient was feeling calm and relaxed and was spontaneously pursuing topics; however, the therapist was feeling compelled to encourage the patient with responses such as "mm-hmm," "sure," and "right." In our discussion of these items, Student A confided that these encouraging responses helped her allay her fear that the patient would stop talking and fall silent. Of course, one would hope that an attentive supervisor would catch these issues when listening to or watching a session, but the PQS and CPQ use the therapist's own observations to identify the salient characteristics and alert the supervisor to technical errors, transference-countertransference paradigms, and the like. These instruments could also harness audiotaped and videotaped observations to disconfirm the student's item placements, which might reflect a countertransference that could be distorting the student's perceptual capacity. Objective measures of psychotherapy process such as the PQS and CPQ can be used to test the subjective impressions offered by the student.

In another example, Student A played an audiotape in which the patient was discussing fears of elevators, flying, heights, needles, and roller coasters. Student A placed item 7 ("Patient is anxious or tense [vs. calm and relaxed]") in pile 1. I pointed out to Student A that the session's content—a litany of situationally based anxieties—stood in stark contrast to the patient's presentation in session as markedly calm and relaxed. Student A was then able to discuss this discrepancy with the patient—to facilitate the patient's ability to reflect on these seemingly compartmentalized mental states. In this way, the PQS and CPQ can also be used to lay the groundwork for enhancing the patient's (and therapist's) mentalization processes (Fonagy et al., 2002; see also volume I, chapter 6).

ASSESSING STUDENT COMPETENCE AND ADHERENCE TO THEORETICAL ORIENTATION IN THE CLINICAL CURRICULUM USING THE PQS AND CPQ

I coteach a required doctoral-level course that assists our third-year clinical psychology students in their preparation to present a psychotherapy case from their externship training to a review panel. Over the past two years, all students enrolled in this course have completed prototypical Q-sorts from their preferred theoretical orientation (i.e., psychodynamic or cognitive-behavioral). These students have discovered how much they actually know about the psychotherapy process of their preferred theoretical orientation. Figure 5.3 indicates their mean knowledge levels of the two prototypes as a function of their preferred theoretical orientation. The psychodynamically oriented students (*n* = 16; left half of figure 5.3) have a strong knowledge of psychodynamic process, as indicated by the far left bar. The short third bar from the left indicates that these students' confusion of psychodynamic process with cognitive-behavioral process is trivial. Similarly, the cognitive-behaviorally oriented students (*n* = 10; right half of figure 5.3) have a strong knowledge of cognitive-behavioral process, as indicated by the second bar from the right. The nonexistent fourth bar from the right indicates that these

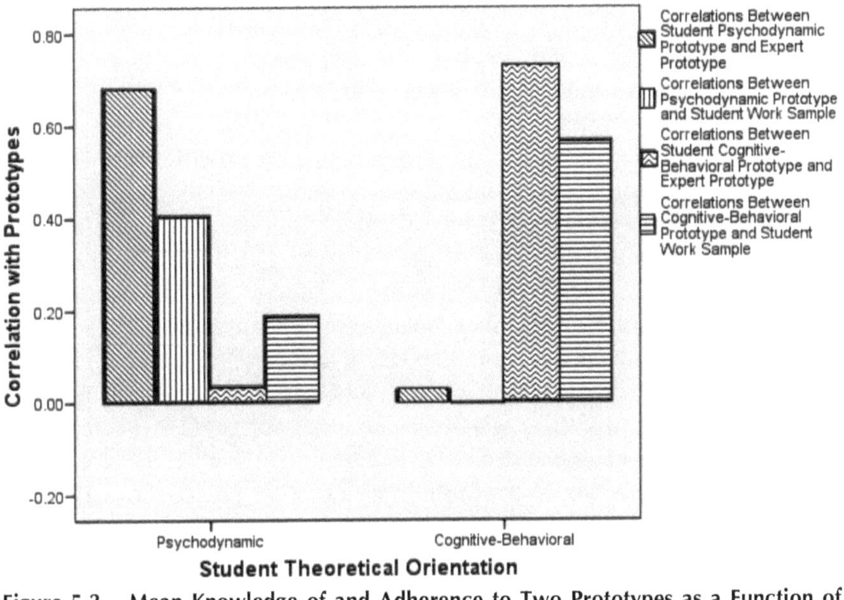

Figure 5.3. Mean Knowledge of and Adherence to Two Prototypes as a Function of Preferred Theoretical Orientation

students' confusion of cognitive-behavioral process with psychodynamic process is similarly trivial. Collectively, these data suggest that both groups of students indeed have a strong knowledge of their preferred theoretical orientation and are not confusing them with the nonpreferred theoretical orientation.

These students also must Q-sort an actual session from the psychotherapy case they will be presenting to determine how closely they adhered to their preferred prototype during that session. As illustrated by figure 5.3, the psychodynamically oriented students are only moderately adherent to the psychodynamic prototype (second bar from the left), while the cognitive-behaviorally oriented students are closely adherent to the cognitive-behavioral prototype (far right bar). The difference between the psychodynamically oriented students' knowledge of the psychotherapy process of their preferred theoretical orientation and the conduct of this process in an actual session was statistically significant, paired samples $t(25) = 4.00$, $p < .001$, while the difference between the cognitive-behaviorally oriented students' knowledge of the psychotherapy process of their preferred theoretical orientation and the conduct of this process in an actual session was not statistically significant. Collectively, these findings suggest that psychodynamically oriented students are less adherent to the psychotherapy process of their preferred theoretical orientation than cognitive-behaviorally oriented students are. Correlations between students' knowledge of psychotherapy process and their conduct of this process were high for both the psychodynamic prototype, $r = .76, p < .001$, and the cognitive-behavioral prototype, $r = .76, p < .001$. Taken together, these findings suggest that students' adherence to the psychotherapy process of their preferred theoretical orientation varies according to their knowledge of it. In all likelihood, students' knowledge of psychotherapy process improves their chances of practicing it in their sessions.

I will present two interpretations of these findings. First, the fact that in spite of a strong knowledge of their preferred theoretical orientation, psychodynamically oriented students do not adhere as closely to psychodynamic process as their cognitive-behaviorally oriented counterparts suggests that these students are more responsive to their patients' needs and are therefore more likely to combine cognitive-behavioral process when necessary (fourth bar from left). Cognitive-behaviorally oriented students, on the other hand, are typically chained down to a treatment manual that prescribes specific techniques—not much latitude to try other approaches (third bar from right). The flexibility among the psychodynamically oriented students and treatment-manual-bound rigidity of the cognitive-behaviorally oriented students could account for the significant difference in adherence between these two groups of students. One recommendation derived from this interpretation is to train students of both theoretical stripes to adjust their techniques to "conditions on the ground" rather than to adhere rigidly to a treatment manual.

Second, it is important to keep in mind that these students are novices. When in doubt, they readily turn to a cookbook or some other authoritative source that tells them what to do to allay their anxiety. Cognitive-behaviorally oriented students have a cookbook to turn to, while psychodynamically oriented students have no such cookbook. The differences in adherence between these two groups of students could simply mean that the psychodynamically oriented students are more likely to flounder in their application of theoretical orientation than their cognitive-behaviorally oriented counterparts. One recommendation derived from this interpretation is to provide more support for students receiving psychodynamic supervision by making existing treatment manuals for psychodynamic approaches available to them (e.g., Bateman and Fonagy, 2004; Clarkin et al., 2006). Anecdotally, students in clinical supervision with me often say they feel frustrated because they do not grasp what it is I want them to be doing in sessions. That could be because I am a poor clinical supervisor. More likely, however, it could be because the therapeutic encounter is inherently unpredictable and therefore does not lend itself readily to prescriptions. I tell these students that tolerance for ambiguity is a necessary attitude for the psychodynamically oriented therapist to have. Some students accept this state of affairs and continue along this path, while others later declare their allegiance to the cognitive-behavioral orientation. Using the PQS and CPQ in my course helps students of both theoretical orientations sort out what their strengths and weaknesses are and whether they should present their Q-sorted session as evidence of their exemplary clinical work for their case presentation.

Low correlations have shocked some students into selecting a different session or even a different case altogether to present because low correlations suggest unacceptably low adherence to their preferred theoretical orientation. Of course, students can use case material to argue why they strayed from the psychotherapy process most characteristic of their preferred theoretical orientation. We instructors should value flexibility of approach if a student can provide a rationale for implementing techniques foreign to the theoretical orientation he or she is using. This quantitative approach to learning psychotherapy process has been helpful to our students and welcomed by the American Psychological Association reaccreditation site visitors as they evaluate our program on our methods for assessing clinical competence among our students.

DIRECTIONS FOR FUTURE RESEARCH

For her dissertation, one of my students will be using her CPQ psychotherapy session Q-sorts to examine the effects of countertransference on psychodynamic child psychotherapy process. She will be completing the Countertransference Questionnaire (CTQ; Betan, Heim, Conklin, and Westen, 2005), while two independent raters will be Q-sorting her videotaped psychotherapy sessions. We are hypothesizing that the discrepancies between her Q-sort distributions of her sessions and those of the independent raters will be positively correlated with her countertransference reactions as measured by the CTQ after each session. These discrepancies will also be used to predict changes in the patient's symptom levels throughout the entire year of treatment. In summary, the PQS and CPQ are versatile, quantitatively based methods that can be used to assess supervisees' psychodynamic knowledge base and clinical interventions and their mutual impact on patient change. I hope that someone will construct a clinical supervision process Q-set (CSPQ) in which supervisor-supervisee interactions can be systematically observed, assessed, and used to predict changes in psychotherapy process and treatment outcome. The effectiveness of clinical supervision on students' psychodynamic interventions and on their patients' improvements is an area of research in need of attention. Using the methods proposed here, doctoral students (and their clinical supervisors) could begin to feel a little less stupid and contagious and a little more competent and hopeful about the impact of their interventions on therapeutic change.

Chapter Six

Processes of Therapeutic Change in a Spirituality Group for Inpatients with Borderline Personality Disorder

Nine psychiatric inpatients diagnosed with borderline personality disorder participated in a psychodynamically oriented, exploratory spirituality group. Through drawings and group process, the patients uncovered and elaborated on their representations of God. Two patterns of representations were identified: (1) representations of a punitive, judgmental, rigid God that seemed to reflect directly and correspond with parental representations, and (2) representations of a depersonified, inanimate, abstract God entailing aspects of idealization that seemed to compensate for parental representations. Interestingly, the second pattern was associated with comorbid narcissistic features in the patients. Those patients who presented punitive God representations were able to begin the process of re-creating these representations toward more benign or benevolent images in the context of this group, while those participants who presented depersonified God representations seemed unable to do so. I suggest that a spirituality group can facilitate the re-creation of representations of both God and self among spiritually curious borderline patients.

In the early years of life, the child develops a range of self- and object representations that soothe the child when alone, aid in the delay of instinctual gratification, and warn of potential danger situations in external reality. One of these early object representations is the representation of God. Winnicott (1971, pp. 1–25) traced the origins of the God representation to the young child's world of transitional objects created in the intermediate area of experience (potential space), where illusion and reality simultaneously dwell. This intermediate area of experience, "unchallenged in respect of its belonging to inner or external (shared) reality, constitutes the greater part of the infant's experience, and throughout life is retained in the intense experiencing that belongs to the arts and to religion" (p. 14).

The psychoanalyst Rizzuto (1979) conducted a meticulous study of object representations and God representations among four psychiatric inpatients, hypothesizing that such an investigation might "provide an unsuspected projective test of childhood object relations which the patient has unknowingly transformed into his God image" (p. 8). Based on her findings, Rizzuto posited that the representation of God is constructed out of a range of representational materials: "Like the transitional object, God is heavily loaded with parental traits (those objects the child finds). But as a creation of the child he has other traits that suit the child's needs in relating to his parents and maintaining his sense of worth and safety" (pp. 208, 209). By comparing responses to two separate questionnaires regarding one's parents and God, Rizzuto was able to identify patients' specific parental representational materials that corresponded with their representation of God.

While her case studies were able to demonstrate a correspondence between the structure and content of parental and self-representations and those of the God representation, Rizzuto (1979) did not address whether a therapeutic exploration of the person's representation of God could provide insight into or integration of one's unmodulated parental or self-representations and lead to greater self-understanding and self-acceptance. Kirkpatrick (1999), however, does raise this possibility: "In cases [of] religious change . . . does one's orientation toward interpersonal attachments then change concomitantly? If so, this knowledge might provide a useful basis for the development of therapeutic strategies for dealing with relationship-based difficulties, particularly in religious populations" (p. 819). Could an exploration of one's representation of God produce global therapeutic benefits in some clinical populations?

Kirkpatrick (1999) further suggested that representations of God might not always correspond with the parental representations established in early childhood, at least in a direct way. In addition to the "correspondence" hypothesis, God representations might be formed to compensate for insecure or otherwise deficient parental representations—the "compensation" hypothesis. Thus, under certain unspecified circumstances, the quality of God representations "might be expected to correlate inversely with contemporaneous outcome measures" (p. 818) as well as the quality of parental representations. Consistent with this idea, having an avoidant internal working model of attachment to the mother was significantly associated with the experiencing of a sudden positive religious conversion during adolescence and adulthood (Kirkpatrick and Shaver, 1990). Kirkpatrick (1999) concluded: "For people who seek and value close relationships, but who have difficulty developing and maintaining them due to fears of being unloved and/or abandoned [and thus avoidant of attachment], it is easy to see how God's unconditional (or easily earned) love may be perceived as immensely attractive, and how the experience of finding such a relationship may be emotionally powerful and deeply rewarding" (p. 816). Kirkpatrick seems to be suggesting that the formation of the God representation could be modified beyond the preschool years and used to defend against perceived disappointments inherent in the parental representations established during early childhood.

This line of research has recently been elaborated by others (Beck and McDonald, 2004; McDonald, Beck, Allison and Norsworthy, 2005) who have suggested that persons insecurely attached to parents are more likely to cultivate a relationship with God than are those who are securely attached to parents as a form of compensation. These researchers found, however, that the insecure attachments to parents eventually negatively influence the nature of the relationship to God, following the correspondence hypothesis. Specifically, they found that lower levels of family spirituality (r = -.34), of family intimacy (a dimension of parental attachment; r = -.28),and of family support for autonomy (a second dimension of parental attachment; r = -.21) were associated with a dismissive stance toward the importance of attachment to God. The authors concluded, "Comparisons between parental variables and attachment to God appear to support a correspondence between working models of parents and God" (McDonald et al., 2005, p.26).

Clearly, more work is needed to sort out what may be complicated relationships between parental and God representations and to identify under what conditions the compensation versus correspondence processes operate. In the context of a process-oriented spirituality group, I clinically pursued these ideas by soliciting the representations of God held by borderline inpatients and assessing their relationships to patients' parental representations. I was also interested in exploring whether changes could occur in these representations in the context of the potentially safe space of the group. I present the organization of the psychodynamically oriented, exploratory spirituality group and a sampling of the drawings of the God representation made by the participants. I also describe a portion of the group process reflecting the openness to change in these representations, at least by some participants during the course of the group.

THE SPIRITUALITY GROUP

The fourteen-session spirituality group (loosely based on a model presented in Gallagher, Manierre, and Castelli [1994]; see also Goodman and Manierre, 2008), was co-led by a male clinical psychologist and a female hospital chaplain in a long-term, psychodynamically oriented psychiatric unit dedicated to the treatment of inpatients diagnosed with borderline personality disorder.

These inpatients were admitted to this unit because they satisfied diagnostic criteria (APA, 1994) and because they posed a danger either to themselves or others. The group was advertised in the unit as an opportunity to talk about participants' images of God, what God means to each participant, and how these images influence their lives. Nine out of twenty-five female inpatients agreed to participate in weekly forty-five-minute sessions. Because group participants were inpatients and thus a "captive audience," all of them regularly attended sessions. Only one participant dropped out prior to the completion of the fourteen sessions.

Participants were informed that the group's purposes were threefold: (1) to increase awareness of spirituality—particularly conscious and unconscious images of God—held by each participant; (2) to place these images and associated feelings and beliefs in the context of their current and past life situations and psychiatric symptoms; and (3) to provide an opportunity for participants to explore and discuss each other's image or images of God, thus potentially facilitating a re-creation and modification to a more integrated and benevolent image. I had hoped that the participants would also begin to develop attachment relationships with my coleader and me that would provide them with a secure base (Bowlby, 1982) from which to explore these images of God (see Goodman, in press, chapter 3). The resulting sense of safety would permit them to confront unintegrated, frightening images of God that would otherwise produce a sense of discomfort and avoidance in other contexts.

In the initial session, participants were requested to take ten minutes to make a drawing depicting their image of God as they believe God to be. Each participant then elaborated on her drawing in the group, an exercise designed to stimulate group discussion. I was struck by the observation that the drawings seemed to fall into two broad categories: (1) a punitive, judgmental, rigid God who shows love only to those who follow his rules and refuse to question his authority; and (2) an abstract and nebulous, impersonal, or depersonified life force that serves as a positive energy source in the universe. Five participants drew pictures depicting a punitive God, while the other four drew pictures depicting a depersonified, formless God. These two categories were unrelated to participants' specific religious backgrounds; all nine participants came from traditional Judeo-Christian religious backgrounds.

To illustrate these two categories of depiction, the drawing made by Jasmine (all names used are pseudonyms) depicts yellow rays of sunlight emanating from a pleasant-looking blue cloud at the top. Orange and yellow pointy flames of fire rage at the bottom. Black stairs descend from the blue cloud in the upper left corner to the top of the flames in the lower right corner. On the bottom stair, just above the flames, is a stick figure lying down. Separating the stick figure from the heavenly blue cloud and rays of sunlight

Figure 6.1. Jasmine's Drawing

above is a sheet of black (see figure 6.1). When asked by the group to elaborate on her drawing, Jasmine stated that she is lying on a trap door to hell and that a black cloud separates her from God. She added that her priest told her that people are guilty because Adam and Eve ate the apple. She explained that one has to be deserving to have a relationship with God. One participant suggested that the black cloud represents the church's rules or teachings.

By contrast, the drawing made by Hudson depicts a long, flowing, winding, and curving path constructed out of tiny words written as a stream-of-consciousness poem: "Maybe this is moving falling flows breaking flows still and in the wide wash the ever into is were am feeling in an ever in a moving winter spring blue woven fabric space the longing filling longing breathing ever and am able when I breathe the mist the evening layers over when a color fuses into trees the leaving water falling hands and hair out flying swinging center and a whisper and a child every smile open eyes and dark and whispers to the edge and black and falling into nothing into water into flowing" (see figure 6.2). When asked to elaborate on her drawing, Hudson stated that God is flowing in and out, rhythmic, moving, not good or bad, not pleasurable or unpleasurable. God encompasses everything, but not nothing, and definitely does not include judgment.

Figure 6.2. Hudson's Drawing

Over the first three sessions, Jasmine explained that she would like to stop believing in the Catholic religion but would first need permission from her priest. She then launched into a massive attack on priests and their "silly" beliefs about God, such as the burning bush, the distinction between venial and mortal sins, and the categorization of cursing as a sin. One of the group leaders suggested that Jasmine was placing the priest in a double bind: if the priest were to refuse her permission, then she would perceive him as rigid and authoritarian; if he were to grant her permission, then she would perceive him as collusive. One of the other participants added that Jasmine might also be placing God in a double bind. Jasmine listened thoughtfully without responding.

Associating to this material, one of the group leaders asked to what extent participants felt as though their illness was a form of punishment or a hell that God has assigned them to for not following the teachings. Both Jasmine and Jessica strongly endorsed this view. Jasmine added that she felt as though she had no choice about what to believe. One of the group leaders drew the analogy of Jasmine as a prisoner, with God as the jailor holding the key. Jasmine replied that perhaps the Catholic Church is the jailor, not God. It was pointed out that, earlier in the session, she said it was God who would be sending her to hell. Jasmine laughed nervously and said she was not sure. One of the group leaders mentioned that although four of the nine participants were raised as Catholics, all four had vastly different feelings toward church and God. One of the participants suggested that these different feelings might originate in cultural and family differences.

In another session, Jasmine read a passage about a boy whose first teacher taught him the "right" way to draw a flower but whose second teacher allowed him to draw his own flower. Jasmine explained that she identified with the boy because her parents and the Catholic Church told her how to think, act, and feel, and what she should believe about God. She thought she would be going to hell for all the mortal sins she had committed. One of the group leaders asked Jasmine whether God could be forgiving. Jasmine replied that the priests had also said this, but she questioned that view. What kind of God would have all these rules and regulations? She said that she had done wrong in her life and deserved hell. She explained that she had never experienced forgiveness before. The group leader asked whether she could accept God's or anyone's forgiveness, or forgive herself. She was not sure. She had done horrible things to people. Why would God like her or want to forgive her?

Another group participant suggested that Jasmine was too concerned about other people's approval. One of the group leaders asked whether Jasmine had created God in her parents' image. She answered that maybe she had because it was hard to trust God and others when all the people in her life had been untrustworthy. Jasmine asked how she could begin to trust again—she wanted answers. One of the group leaders suggested that Jasmine wanted him to draw the flower for her. She and the other participants laughed. This group leader then asked Jasmine what her ideal image of God would be like. She responded that he would be like the second teacher—letting the child draw the flower as he sees it. It would be hard to imagine such a God, however, because she had the feeling that God was going to judge her someday. The group leader responded that it would be hard to imagine that God could be any more judgmental of her than she was of herself. She thought for a moment, understanding that her image of God was similar to her experience of her parents.

Reacting to this material, Hudson offered that she liked her own image of God as water because water is pliable, not rigid like dogma. Water always flows to the lowest point; it is balanced. Her image of God is neither masculine nor feminine, a life force, "being"—a verb rather than a noun. Meagan read a passage that attributed such qualities as kindness, generosity, compassion, and love to God. Samantha, who had drawn God as formless watercolors, responded that she had tried to live a perfect life but developed obsessional eating habits that led to her hospitalization. Hudson agreed with this characterization, adding that she wanted to see these attributes in herself as well but could never achieve them. She said she was dying for forgiveness and no longer wanted to strive for perfection. Later in the group, she read a passage by a Buddhist monk depicting the life force as a river, with each individual as a whirlpool or identity in the river. Hudson explained that each person could flow within and without the river; individuals can be either in resonance or out of resonance with the life force. Another patient commented that the passage sounded beautiful but lonely. In that world, she would need to take a detour-return to her old (and self-destructive) behaviors for excitement. One of the group leaders asked whether cutting oneself (a preadmission symptom experienced by many group participants, including Hudson) was living in or out of resonance with the life force. Hudson responded that it was being "out of synch" because it was a destructive act, not a creative act. The leader posed the question "How does one shift from being in synch to being out of synch and vice versa?" Hudson replied that she made choices. She emphasized that cutting was not necessarily wrong. This choice was conditioned by the judgments and criticisms of others. Raising her voice, she declared that her image of God had nothing to do with judgment or evil. One of the group leaders later read a passage about the loss of a loved one that questioned God's presence. One of the other patients said it was cruel to read something so sad. Hudson, on the other hand, stated that there was beauty in loss—that somehow the longing and pain associated with the loss make the loss more poignant.

Some Thoughts about the Group Process

Drawings from five of the patients depicted a punitive, judgmental, and demanding God who shows love only to those who follow his rules and refuse to question his authority. These patients struggled with parental representations that sounded strikingly similar to their descriptions of their images of God. For example, Jessica reported that she struggled with a schizophrenic mother who kicked her out of the house at age fourteen and strictly prohibited anger from being expressed in the household. A similar object relationship was repeated with her abusive husband. On several occasions, she declared that God does not tolerate anger. In another example, Jasmine reported that her mother and father had been physically abusive toward her, and her two brothers had sexually abused her while God idly stood by or perhaps even directed this activity. Perhaps in the interest of preserving some morsel of goodness in her parental representations, Jasmine began to perceive herself as inherently flawed, unworthy of her parents' love and deserving of her abuse. She could rail against the God/parents who threatened her existence through abuse and neglect, yet later in the course of the group, she disclosed underlying feelings of inherent badness by quietly admitting that she really did deserve hell.

The drawings of the other four patients depicted an abstract, formless life force that serves as a positive energy source in the universe. These God representations seemed to serve primarily defensive functions, reflecting a disavowal of characteristics signifying personhood. For example, Samantha struggled with anorexia and the sense that her mother failed her, yet she drew God as formless watercolors and characterized God as a mystical power that will fulfill all her needs once she gives in to it. It is easy to imagine that her image of God signified a massive idealization of a perfectionistic, demanding mother representation who finds Samantha lacking.

Struggling with feelings of longing, Hudson mentioned the death of her father and wondered whether he was still present in some way, just as she wondered whether her dear friend who had committed suicide was still present in some way. Without prompting, she denied that she was feeling any anger toward this friend. Continuing this theme of denial, Hudson engaged in a massive reaction formation that moved her to declare that there was beauty in loss and that her image of God had nothing to do with judgment or evil. During another session, however, she revealed that she was dying for forgiveness for her lack of perfection and wanted to see perfection in God, as if God were actually a person. Yet later during this same session, she drew the analogy of God to water—not dogmatic, but pliable and balanced. Hudson's struggle as manifested in the group centered on her need to idealize God to compensate for overwhelming sadness and loss.

In essence, then, for five participants, their drawings of God corresponded rather directly to their views of their parents as harsh, angry, and abusive. For the other four patients, their drawings of God seemed to reflect defensive denial and idealization as well as a distancing by depersonifying. I discovered that all four participants who presented a depersonified representation of God were diagnosed with comorbid narcissistic features in addition to their primary Axis II diagnosis of borderline personality disorder. None of the other five participants had such a diagnosis. This observation between the quality of God representation and the absence or presence of narcissistic psychopathology seems consistent with Kernberg's (1986b) concepts of pathological narcissism, the pathological grandiose self, and associated defensive processes of idealization and devaluation. This pathological organization, observed in narcissistic personalities with underlying borderline personality organization, robs the superego of good, modulating elements, and permits some ego integration at the cost of a deterioration of object relationships. Unacceptable self-representations are split off in combination with "widespread, devastating devaluation of external objects and their representations" (Kernberg, 1986b, p. 262). Based on this theory, I speculate that the depersonified, inanimate, nebulous representations of God offered by those borderline inpatients with pathological narcissistic features suggest a distancing from the unconscious God representations formed during early childhood—consistent with a dismissing internal working model. Via idealization and denial, a punitive, demanding God can be transformed into something harmless, bland, or even mystical, as in Hudson's image of flowing water. A mystical power can never find fault; on the contrary, one's needs will be magically gratified without having to acknowledge another person's existence. In a related fashion, the four borderline inpatients with comorbid narcissistic features offered less information regarding their parental representations than the others, perhaps reflecting a denial of their influence or very existence. Thus, I am suggesting that narcissistic psychopathology is associated with the formation of defensive, "compensatory" God representations. Of course, the God representations of the other group also contain defensive aspects, but the "correspondence" of these representations to the parental representations quickly became obvious, often to the participants themselves.

In addition to these clinical observations from the group, I wondered whether the group could begin a process of transforming representations of God into more benevolent and personified forms. For example, in the beginning, Jasmine could not conceptualize God as anything more than the sum total of all the rules, regulations, and punishments imposed on her by her parents and priests. Jasmine was not permitted to question God, just as she was never permitted to question her parents. God does not accept skeptics, and mothers do not accept children who question their authority. By the end of the group, however, Jasmine risked articulating her ideal image of God—someone who would benevolently allow her to define her own identity. She was helped to this point in her exploration by the group leaders' and other participants' suggestions that her parents helped to create her God image for her and that she herself had created God in her parents' image. In the Winnicottian spirit of the transitional object, we observed the paradox that Jasmine was re-creating an image of God who could give her permission to re-create both her images of God and herself.

I also observed that a group therapy setting seemed to facilitate this transforming work because the exposure to different religious experiences shared by the participants enabled them to question their own religious assumptions and adopt a sometimes playful approach to their exploration and critical examination of their God representations. Without this group exposure, the openness to question the historical and emotional basis of these representations might not have developed so readily. That the two group leaders represented two different disciplines also permitted participants to observe the group leaders' openness to their own different spiritual experiences, which validated the participants' own spiritual exploration.

Finally, the group's observations of the sometimes striking similarities between a participant's God representation and her parental and self-representations increased participants' awareness that the God representation could both differ from and even transcend parental and self-representations. Interestingly, however, this awareness did not seem to help participants to modify their parental representations. Perhaps parental representations seemed too real and therefore more resistant to modification, while the obviously projective nature of the God representation (and perhaps also the self-representation) was openly acknowledged and accepted.

We believe, however, that the group leaders' willingness to discuss openly the relations between representations of God and personal experiences profoundly influenced participants' motivation to examine their understanding of all their mental representations—including but not limited to God, parents, and self. That changes in parental representations were not observed in the group process does not necessarily mean that the group process did not produce changes in these representations, or at least in reflective functioning pertaining to these representations (Fonagy et al., 2002; see also volume I, chapter 6). I believe that the secure base that my coleader and I provided for the participants also facilitated the openness to the group experience observed in the patients without narcissistic features (see Goodman, in press, chapter 3).

Remarkably, we did not observe any openness to re-creation of the representations of God or parents among the four participants who presented depersonified representations of God. In fact, their mental representations did not appear open to change at all during the course of the group. Kernberg (1980, pp. 135–53) suggested that the pathological grandiose self, observed in narcissistic personalities with underlying borderline personality organization, does not permit the intrapsychic vulnerability necessary to benefit from psychotherapy. Only in middle age, when their youth and beauty begin to fade and the narcissistic supplies begin to dwindle through the loss of their associates, do narcissistic persons seek out and benefit from psychotherapy. Perhaps these borderline inpatients were unable to make themselves sufficiently vulnerable or decrease interpersonal distancing and devaluing to benefit from the group process, at least in this time-limited context.

I want to note that the validity of the conclusions drawn from this study are limited by: (1) the small group of participants (n = 9), and (2) the lack of an empirical method used for studying these representational phenomena. A larger number of borderline patients could be assessed for their levels of narcissism and placed into narcissistic and nonnarcissistic categories. Their drawings of the representation of God, along with their descriptions of them, could be blindly assigned by raters to the punitive and depersonified categories suggested here. A statistical association could thus be calculated. The assessment of change in one's representation of God resulting from participation in a spirituality group would require a systematic method for measuring the quality and complexity of this representation (e.g., see Blatt, Chevron, Quinlan, Schaffer, and Wein, 1992).

In spite of these limitations, we believe that these clinical impressions can serve as preliminary evidence in support of the idea that a psychodynamically oriented, exploratory spirituality group can help patients identify and potentially reconstruct images of God, which, in turn, can facilitate change in other mental representations. While this clinical work did not appear to re-create parental representations, or to re-create any mental representations of borderline inpatients with comorbid narcissistic features, some participants were able to embark on a process of re-creating their representations of God and of themselves. These persons were able to encounter a God whom they could re-create, and, in doing so, a self whom they could re-create, in the potential space provided by a spirituality group.

Chapter Seven

Attachment-Based Processes of Therapeutic Change with Prepubertal Children: The Impact of Parent, Child, and Therapist Mental Representations on Intervention Points of Entry

Attachment theory has significantly influenced psychoanalytic developmental theory, from infancy to adulthood, yet, until recently, little has been written about clinical intervention using attachment theory. Some authors (Mayseless, 2005; Waters and Cummings, 2000) have suggested that this paucity of literature reflects the relative lack of theoretical attention John Bowlby, attachment theory's founding father, paid to any developmental period beyond the preschool years. Although attachment-based interventions with mothers and infants are beginning to flourish, guidelines for developing attachment-based intervention with prepubertal children are lacking. This chapter remedies this lack by discussing two areas: (1) potential intervention points of entry with prepubertal children based on attachment theory, and (2) the impact of parent, child, and therapist characteristics—notably mental representations (also known as internal working models)—on the potential intervention points of entry being targeted. In contrast to attachment-based early intervention, in which parental characteristics are targeted, attachment-based intervention with prepubertal children must include the child as well as the parents. Therapists attempting an attachment-based intervention with prepubertal children must take into account the quality of the child's mental representation as well as their own quality of mental representation to provide an effective clinical experience (Goodman, 2007a).

Prepubertal children (defined here as children ages five to twelve) are often referred by parents, school officials, and pediatricians for intervention services. The symptoms that these referred children experience are often of sufficient frequency, intensity, and duration to meet formal criteria for one or multiple childhood diagnoses contained in the *Diagnostic and Statistical Manual of Mental Disorders* (*DSM-IV*; APA, 2000). Perhaps the most troubling symptoms a prepubertal child can experience are aggression and depression.

Familial, interpersonal, and individual risk factors have been identified to account for childhood aggression (Katsurada and Sugawara, 2000; Warrick-Swansen, 1999) and depression (Gazelle and Ladd, 2003; National Institute of Mental Health, 2000; Williams and Harper, 1979). Although parental hostility and depression are known risk factors for childhood aggression and depression (Brent et al., 2002; Katsurada and Sugawara, 2000; Lyons-Ruth, Easterbrooks, and Cibelli, 1997; Pfeffer, Conte, Plutchik, and Jerrett, 1979; Warrick-Swansen, 1999), the literature is indecisive about which variables might mediate their influence, and which interventions might work with which parents and children. In this chapter, I will discuss the design and implementation of attachment-based intervention with prepubertal children predisposed to significant psychiatric dysfunction such as aggression and depression because of an underlying attachment disorganization.

Attachment theory has evolved from a theory of infant socioemotional development first proposed by Bowlby (1958, 1982) into a grand blueprint for early clinical intervention in the mother-infant relationship (Bakermans-Kranenburg, van IJzendoorn, and Juffer, 2003; Berlin, Ziv, Amaya-Jackson, and Greenberg, 2005; Bowlby, 1988, 1989; Egeland, Weinfield, Bosquet, and Cheng, 2000; Lieberman and Zeanah, 1999; Stern, 1995; Stern-Bruschweiler and Stern, 1989; van IJzendoorn, Juffer, and Duyvesteyn, 1995). Attachment theory has even been used to understand the intricacies of clinical intervention with adults (Bosquet and Egeland, 2001; Diamond et al., 1999; Dozier, 1990, 2003; Dozier, Cue, and Barnett, 1994; Dozier and Sepulveda, 2004; Dozier, Stevenson, Lee, and Velligan, 1991; Fonagy et al., 1996; Horowitz, Rosenberg, and Bartholomew, 1996; Korfmacher, Adam, Ogawa, and Egeland, 1997; Slade, 1999; Tyrrell, Dozier, Teague, and Fallot, 1999). Unfortunately, in spite of these impressive efforts, virtually nothing has been written about clinical intervention with prepubertal children from an attachment theory perspective. Greenberg (1999) attributed the lack of research in this period of development to a "measurement roadblock" (p. 486); that is to say, assessments of attachment are only beginning to be validated for this age range (see also Solomon and George, 1999b).

In a recently published volume (Kerns and Richardson, 2005) that seeks to rectify this omission in the attachment literature by focusing exclusively on prepubertal childhood, Mayseless (2005) follows Waters and Cummings (2000) in suggesting that this paucity of literature reflects the relative lack of theoretical attention Bowlby (1977, 1988) paid to any developmental period beyond the preschool years. While such a volume is desperately needed for attachment theory to close what I would call the "prepubertal childhood gap," none of its twelve chapters addresses clinical intervention for children from this developmental period. Thus, attachment-based intervention with prepubertal children needs to be designed and implemented to reduce their increasing levels of aggression and depression and other forms of psychopathology.

POTENTIAL INTERVENTION POINTS OF ENTRY BASED ON ATTACHMENT THEORY

Perhaps the central question asked by attachment researchers who have both studied and designed attachment-based early intervention programs for mothers and infants is "Where should one intervene to improve the infant's attachment security?" Regardless of the researcher, two answers always seem to be offered: either (1) at the level of maternal mental representation, or (2) at the level of maternal behavior. For example, both van IJzendoorn et al. (1995, p. 227) and Berlin (2005, p. 4) present almost identical models of attachment transmission that predict that maternal mental representation of her attachment relationship to her parents influences maternal behavior, especially sensitivity and contingent responsiveness, which in turn influences the infant's attachment security. This developmental pathway simultaneously privileges the quality of the mother-infant relationship as the foundation of infant attachment security and later socioemotional adaptation (Weinfield, Sroufe, Egeland, and Carlson, 1999) and illustrates the means by which the quality of attachment is believed to be transmitted intergenerationally.

All attachment-based early intervention programs seem to focus exclusively on the maternal mental representations or behavior as the agents of change. One group of researchers explained that "as an adult, the caregiver has more degrees of freedom in changing patterns of attachment-caregiving interactions than does the child" (Cooper, Hoffman, Powell, and Marvin, 2005, p. 141). This top-down approach to understanding the origins of infant attachment security has become a core tenet of attachment theory (Sroufe, 1985). The mother is believed to be providing emotional "training" to the infant "through her behavioral and emotional reactions to her baby [which] is thought to build the child's working model of attachment, and thus lays the foundation for the expectations the child has concerning his or her relationship with the mother" (Cassidy et al., 2005, p. 38).

Conceptualizing maternal sensitivity as the mediator between the maternal mental representation of her own childhood attachment experiences and the infant's attachment security has been questioned, however (De Wolff and van IJzendoorn, 1997). This transmission gap (van IJzendoorn, 1995) has been explained in several ways: inadequate assessment of maternal sensitivity, need for greater focus on constructs related to but not identical with sensitivity (e.g., reflective functioning, secure-base provision), inadequate theory, and infant temperament (Berlin, 2005; Cassidy et al., 2005; Goodman, 2002; Slade, Grienenberger, Bernbach, Levy, and Locker, 2005). As the child becomes older, his or her mental representations of the parental relationships become increasingly resistant to change as past interactional experiences become habitual, expected, and reliable forecasters of future caregiver behavior (Bowlby, 1980; Bretherton, 1985; Main et al., 1985). Thus, when considering attachment-based intervention for children beyond preschool, do the assumptions of caregiver-focused interventions still apply?

An attachment-based model for understanding potential intervention points of entry for prepubertal children is presented in figure 7.1. This model includes the two traditional intervention points of entry (A and D) as well as five other points of entry either recently targeted (B and C) or not targeted at all (E, F, and G) in current attachment-based early intervention programs. Each of these points of entry will be discussed.

Intervention Point of Entry A

Intervention point of entry A—the parents' mental representations (also known as internal working models) of their attachment relationships with their own parents—has been traditionally targeted by attachment-based early intervention programs (e.g., Benoit, Madigan, Lecce, Shea, and Goldberg, 2001; Carter, Osofsky, and Hann, 1991; Cicchetti, Toth, and Rogosch, 1999; Cohen et al., 1999; Cramer et al., 1990; Egeland and Erickson, 1993; Erickson, Korfmacher, and Egeland, 1992; Heinicke et al., 1999; Heinicke et al., 2000; Heinicke, Fineman, Ponce, and Guthrie, 2001; Lieberman, Weston, and Pawl, 1991). Most proponents of this intervention point of entry cite Fraiberg and her colleagues (Fraiberg, Adelson, and Shapiro, 1975) as the inspiration behind the modification of parents' mental representations. The theory behind this approach is that parents' mental representations are haunted by the ghosts of the past—unintegrated memories of painful interactions with their own parents during early childhood that never got resolved. These unintegrated memories often have an unintentional impact on the parents' own parenting behavior, often in the context of those same kinds of interactions that first produced the unintegrated memories.

Let us take, for example, a mother who as a toddler was scolded and spanked by her own mother whenever she urinated in a new diaper. Now the mother scolds and spanks her own daughter whenever she urinates in a new diaper. The mother has no idea why she behaves in this manner toward

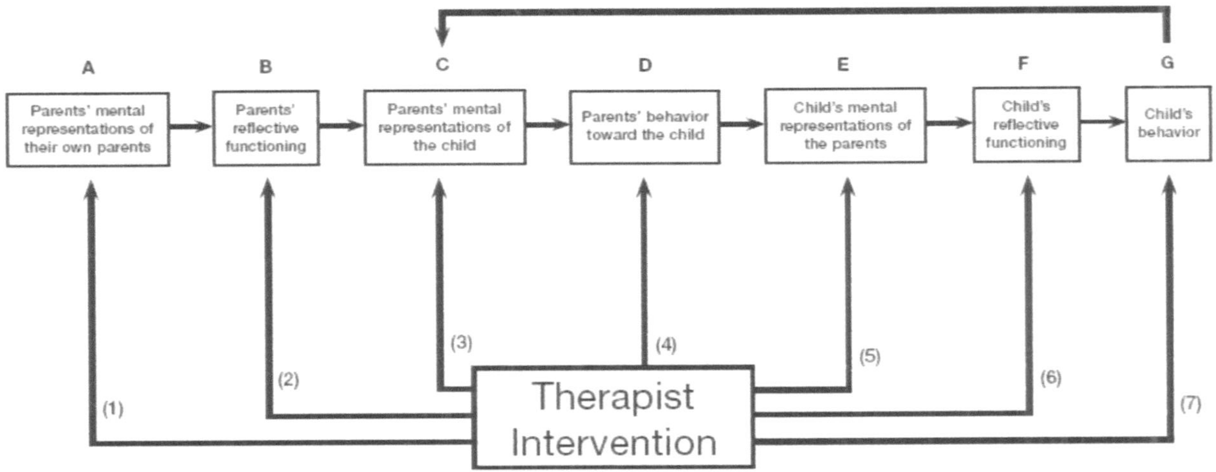

Figure 7.1. Potential Intervention Points of Entry Based on Attachment Theory

her daughter in this context. This behavior, however, is interfering with the daughter's sense of security in her mother's protectiveness and comfort. The daughter now becomes frightened whenever the mother approaches to change her diaper. Or perhaps the daughter attempts to retain her urine or feces because she has associated her mother's anger with her own urination and defecation. The daughter thus develops a symptom. These unintegrated memories of the mother's painful interactions with her own mother are the ghosts that need to be exorcised, or at least confronted and metabolized, by working with the mother on her mental representation of her relationship with her own parents.

According to the theory, if the mother can remember and work through (Freud, 1914) these memories rather than repeat them in her own caregiving, then she will become a more sensitive caregiver, even in those contexts in which she had provided insensitive caregiving. This enhanced sensitivity will result in the child's development of a more secure mental representation of his or her relationship with the parents, which has been previously associated with a wide range of desirable socioemotional outcomes (Weinfield et al., 1999).

In considering the socioemotional needs of prepubertal children, however, it is an empirical question whether this approach alone can modify the developmental trajectory already set in motion by countless previous interactions with the parents. If through intervention a parent can resolve ancient conflicts from childhood relationships with his or her own parents, would the resulting changes in caregiving behavior have the same impact on the prepubertal child's mental representation that it might have had on this structure at an earlier developmental period? As mentioned earlier, Bowlby (1980) suggested that mental representations become increasingly resistant to change. Expectations of specific parental responses to the child's behavior—particularly during moments of distress when the child's attachment system is activated (separation, injury, illness, fear, or punishment)—gradually move from the realm of episodic memory into the realm of semantic or procedural memory (Main and Goldwyn, 1994). Stern (1985) referred to this process as "representations of interactions that have become generalized" (RIGs). This process continues throughout childhood, like slow-drying cement, into adulthood, when personality organization is considered stable and classifiable (Kernberg, 1986a, 1996). Perhaps beyond the preschool years the child's attachment security cannot be changed solely through the intervention point of entry of the parents' mental representations of the relationships with their own parents. Other points of entry—including the child as the subject of intervention—need to be considered.

Intervention Point of Entry D

Intervention point of entry D—the parents' behavior toward the child—has also been traditionally targeted by attachment-based early intervention programs (e.g., Anisfeld, Casper, Nozyce, and Cunningham, 1990; Barnett, Blignault, Holmes, Payne, and Parker, 1987; Dozier, Dozier, and Manni, 2002; Dozier, Lindhiem, and Ackerman, 2005; Lyons-Ruth, Connell, Grunebaum, and Botein, 1990; Spieker, Nelson, DeKlyen, and Staerkel, 2005; van den Boom, 1994, 1995). The theory behind this approach is that mothers can become more sensitive and contingently responsive to the infant's attachment-relevant cues and thus enhance the infant's attachment security—without having to bother with modifying the parents' mental representations of the relationships with their own parents. In other words, intervention at this point of entry "will be successful in promoting secure attachments . . . *without the need to alter the caregiver state of mind* [mental representation]" (Dozier et al., 2005, p. 189). The general method used to circumvent the parents' mental representations is "to help caregivers override what may be their own natural response to turn away from a distressed infant" (Dozier et al., 2005, p. 179). Another technique used is to train the parent to "become more focused in the interaction with the child by monitoring the child's behavior (as was practiced in the intervention), and thereby diminish . . . dissociative processes in the presence of the child" (van IJzendoorn, Bakermans-Kranenburg, and Juffer, 2005, p. 304).

Let us take again our example of the toddler who is retaining her urine out of fear of her mother's reaction. Helping the mother to focus on her insensitive behavior during diaper-changing episodes can provide her with the opportunity of "overriding" her impulse to scold and spank her daughter as she was scolded and spanked as a child during those same situations. In considering again the socioemotional needs of prepubertal children, however, it is an empirical question whether sensitivity training alone can modify the developmental trajectory already set in motion by countless previous interactions with the parents. Assuming that the mother can indeed modify her behavior in the context of diaper-changing through this behavioral approach, would these modifications have the same impact on the prepubertal child's mental representation that they might have had at an earlier developmental period?

A mother severely restricts her nine-year-old son's mobility in their quiet neighborhood. In response, he defies her restriction and fails to return after fifteen minutes. As the mother becomes increasingly punitive toward her son, in defiance he extends the time spent in the neighborhood to dangerously long intervals, and now ventures outside the neighborhood. A sensitivity intervention targeting the mother by the time the child reaches his eleventh birthday might work for her, but it might not do anything to modify his defiant behavior. Sensitivity training could improve the mother's sensitivity in one developmental period, but might not generalize to later developmental periods (van IJzendoorn et al., 2005). As mentioned earlier, other points of entry—including the child as the subject of intervention—need to be considered.

Intervention Points of Entry B and C

Intervention points of entry B and C will be considered together. These approaches have only recently been targeted by attachment-based early intervention programs (e.g., Cooper et al., 2005; Cooper and Murray, 1997; Grienenberger, Kelly, and Slade, 2005; Heinicke et al., 1999; Heinecke et al., 2000; Slade, Sadler, and Mayes, 2005). The theory behind these approaches is that mothers can become more sensitive and contingently responsive to the infant's attachment-relevant cues and thus enhance the infant's attachment security through modifying their mental representations of the relationships with their infants and increasing their reflective functioning related to their caregiving behavior.

After the publication of Main et al.'s (1985) landmark article that introduced an innovative approach to the assessment of mental representation of attachment, attachment researchers began to identify other representational structures that could be measured. One of these representational structures was the parent's mental representation of the relationship with the infant. Four groups of researchers have developed instruments that assess this construct (for a review, see Goodman, 2002; see also Goodman, 2005a). Attachment researchers have begun to recognize the importance of these more proximal mental representations to the parents' behavior as opposed to the more distal mental representations of the parents' childhood attachment relationships. To the extent that the therapist can help the parent modify his or her mental representation of the relationship with the infant, then the consequent caregiving behavior can be similarly modified.

Related to the parents' mental representations of the relationship with the infant is the process of reflective functioning, first identified by Fonagy and his colleagues (Fonagy, Steele, Steele, Moran, and Higgitt, 1991) and subsequently discussed as a potential intervention point of entry by others (Cooper et al., 2005; Heinicke et al., 1999; Heinicke et al., 2000; Slade, Sadler, and Mayes, 2005; Truman, Levy, and Mayes, in press). The origins of this concept can be traced back to cognitive theory's metacognitive knowledge (Flavell, Green, and Flavell, 1986) and psychoanalytic theory's observing ego (Freud, 1933). Fonagy et al. (1996) defined reflective functioning as the person's "capacity to understand mental states [of self and other] and their readiness to contemplate these in a coherent manner" (p. 24). Their rating scale based on this concept "assesses the clarity of an individual's representation of the mental states of others as well as of their own mental states" (p. 24).

Elsewhere, Fonagy and Target (2000) described reflective functioning as "*the capacity to make use of an awareness of their own and other people's thoughts and feelings*" (p. 72). Reflective functioning has been shown to be negatively associated with parental psychopathology (eating disorders and borderline personality disorder) and mediates the influence of parental mental representations on their children's attachment security (Cooper et al., 2005; Fonagy et al., 2002; Fonagy et al., 1996; Grienenberger et al., 2005; Slade, Grienenberger, et al., 2005). Thus, helping the parent to develop this reflective functioning could in turn modify his or her behavior toward the child and thereby change the child's expectations of comfort and protection from the parent.

These two intervention points of entry (B and C) pose certain advantages over the traditional points of entry (A and D). The therapist can focus on increasing the parents' awareness of and making meaning out of the infant's internal states and intentions—in other words, to speak for the baby (Carter et al., 1991; Fraiberg et al., 1975). For example, the therapist says to the mother, "Look how he turns and reaches up to you when he sees me. I bet he's telling you that he wants to feel safe when an unfamiliar person is around and that you're just the person who can pick him up and make him feel safe!" The other aspect of this work is to increase the awareness of the parent's own internal states and intentions in response to the infant's internal states and intentions. A mother's discomfort with her son's bids for contact, and the message that her discomfort might convey to him, would be explored.

This work directly influences the parents' mental representations of the relationship with the child, without necessarily activating the anxiety and resistance commonly associated with conjuring the ghosts of the childhood caregivers. In other words, intervening at points of entry B and C obviates the necessity of modifying the parents' mental representations of the relationships with their own parents (point of entry A). At the same time, modifying the parents' mental representations of their relationship with the child stands a better chance of generalizing the parents' sensitivity and contingent responsiveness to a variety of developmental periods than sensitivity training alone, conducted during a single developmental period (point of entry D).

At later periods of development such as prepubescence, however, the child's mental representation of the relationship with the parents has already been formed. The child is now behaving in accordance with this complex mental organization that includes historically derived expectations of parental behavior in attachment-relevant situations as well as defensive processes that serve to ward off discomfort when attachment security is not forthcoming (Goodman, 2002). As mentioned earlier, intervening at any of the four parental intervention points of entry (A–D) might modify parental sensitivity but not necessarily the prepubertal child's mental representation or behavior.

Intervention Points of Entry E and F

Intervention points of entry E and F will be considered together. Notably, these approaches have not been targeted by attachment-based early intervention programs, probably because these programs have been traditionally focused on mother-infant and mother-toddler dyads (see Bakermans-Kranenburg et al., 2003; Berlin et al., 2005; Egeland et al., 2000; Lieberman and Zeanah, 1999; van IJzendoorn et al., 1995). Working directly with an infant or toddler on modifying his or her mental representation of the relationship with the parents would be at best a dubious endeavor. Bowlby (1988), Silverman (2001), and Slade (1999) have written with clarity and insight about how to apply attachment theory to clinical work with adults, but little systematic work has been published regarding clinical work specifically with prepubertal children from an attachment theory perspective (but see Goodman, 2002).

In spite of the paucity of clinical application to children from this developmental period, the basic concepts identified by Slade (1999) as central to attachment-based clinical work with adults—transference, countertransference, defensive processes, and affect regulation—closely resemble the clinical concepts used in clinical work with prepubertal children carried out by therapists who espouse more traditional clinical perspectives (e.g., Altman, Briggs, Frankel, Gensler, and Pantone, 2002; Lanyado and Horne, 1999; Pine, 1985; Spiegel, 1989). The clinical distinctiveness of attachment theory underscored by Bowlby (1988) and Slade (1999) lay in the recognition that the therapist represents an attachment figure—a secure base from which a person can explore the depths of his or her wishes and disappointments and to which the person can return for safety and solace when this exploration becomes overwhelming. The pattern of attachment that the person might form with the therapist might resemble the pattern of attachment that the person formed with the first attachment figures: the parents. The theory behind this approach is that modifying the mental representation of the relationship with the parents will directly modify the person's behaviors and improve a wide range of socioemotional outcomes.

The prepubertal child might defend against wishes for closeness and emotional intimacy by minimizing the importance of the therapist and the therapeutic relationship out of fear of rejection or unavailability, just when the child might need the therapist most, such as moments of distress or emotional vulnerability. The child might be demonstrating to the therapist in the transference just how he or she defended against expectations of rejection in the parental relationships. The therapist's countertransference reaction might consist of feeling rejected or unacknowledged by the child and a resultant urge to disregard the child without recognizing the underlying need for connection.

A different prepubertal child might also express neediness directly to the therapist by clinging at the end of sessions, refusing to leave the therapist's office, calling or e-mailing the therapist between sessions, or, more seriously, threatening to hurt himself or herself when the therapist announces an upcoming vacation. The child might be demonstrating to the therapist in the transference expectations of feeling overwhelmed and confused in response to the unpredictability in the parental relationships. The therapist's countertransference reaction might consist of feeling overwhelmed and confused by the child's emotional dysregulation and a resultant urge to abandon the child and take more vacations without recognizing the underlying need for containment.

A third prepubertal child might also express bitter disappointment or even terror at never having experienced his or her attachment needs gratified by trashing the therapist's office, making threats of harm against the therapist or self, or actually assaulting the therapist or self during sessions. The child might actually enjoy the experience of inflicting pain, which simultaneously disguises deeply buried, split-off needs for personal safety and emotional wholeness. The therapist's countertransference reaction might consist of wanting to beat the child to a pulp, or of wanting to banish the child to a disliked colleague without recognizing the underlying needs for connection as well as containment.

Related to the child's mental representation of the relationship with the parents (point of entry E) is the process of the child's reflective functioning (point of entry F). Fonagy and Target (1997, 2000) have offered some ideas about how to modify reflective functioning in the prepubertal child. First, the child needs to learn how to observe his or her own emotional states, which takes place by helping him or her to label specific emotions, identify conscious and unconscious links between these emotional states and their behaviors, and notice moment-to-moment changes in the child's internal states within the therapy sessions.

Second, pretend play between the therapist and child allows for the sharing of internal states between both parties and a shared understanding of a world that is considered neither real nor fantasy—a potential space (Winnicott, 1971) both discovered and created by the child. This potential space is populated by a common set of objects symbolically held in the minds of both parties. The varieties of play and the challenges of playfulness facilitate the development of reflective functioning in the prepubertal child. In older children, this playfulness can take place in the potential space of discourse.

Third, paying close attention to the transferential relationship offers what Fonagy and Target consider "the most effective route towards acquiring mentalizing [reflective] capacity" (Fonagy and Target, 2000, p. 87). The authors point out, however, that the nonreflective child transfers repudiated self-representations, not parental mental representations. The therapist works in the here and now, using interpretations to place emotions in a context of sequential mental experiences. In so doing, the child begins to "find himself [or herself] in the mind of the therapist as a thinking and feeling being" (p. 88). This process is believed to enhance the child's emotional regulation and impulse control, which in turn is believed to modify behavior.

Intervention Point of Entry G

Attachment-based early intervention programs, again because of the limited age range of the child participants, have not targeted intervention point of entry G—the child's behavior. We know that infants' and toddlers' behavior cannot be directly modified to improve socioemotional functioning. Behavioral and cognitive-behavioral therapists, however, tend to work directly with the prepubertal child on behavior modification, which usually also includes work with the parents and family (e.g., Graham, 1998; Greene, 1998; Reid, Patterson, and Snyder, 2002; Watson and Gresham, 1998). Although working directly with the prepubertal child to modify behavior has its advocates, all psychoanalytic theories, including attachment theory, presuppose a mind that mediates behavior and its functions. A child's behavior can be directly modified; however, without uncovering the meanings of this behavior and the purposes it serves in the child's mental organization, the likelihood that the behavior modification will generalize across socioemotional contexts and developmental periods is reduced. Moreover, attachment theory is fundamentally a theory about the formation of relationships and their role in affect regulation. It would make sense to use a form of therapy that focuses on the relationship between therapist and child as the curative agent in affect regulation rather than behavior modification.

The child's behavior also reciprocally influences the parents' mental representations of the child, which in turn influences the parents' behavior toward the child in a feedback loop (see figure 7.1). Therapists who intervene at point of entry G need to understand and anticipate the impact of the child's behavioral changes on the parents' mental representations and on their own behavior. One would expect that changes in the parents' mental representations would lag behind the child's behavioral changes because the parental expectations that comprise these mental representations have developed over time and become resistant to change. Moreover, other factors such as birth order, physical appearance, physical health, gender, and personality and intellectual attributes unrelated to the child's behavior influence these parental expectations. For all these reasons, parental changes made at the representational level—without direct intervention at point of entry C—will naturally take time to observe.

Generally, relationship-focused therapies (e.g., McWilliams, 1999) hold promise for restructuring the representational landscape that influences the child's thoughts and feelings about the self and others as well as the child's behaviors. Attachment-based intervention that focuses on these relationships—either with the parents in reality or with the therapist as a symbolic representative of the parents or the child himself or herself—can work toward resolving the underlying affect dysregulation and conflict related to attachment insecurity, fear of emotional closeness, and mistrust. This intensive and challenging work needs to occur to establish a sense of internal and external security. A therapist treating a prepubertal child from an attachment theory perspective would therefore more likely consider intervention points of entry E and F for conducting an attachment-based intervention, or consider combining all three child intervention points of entry (E–G) in a multipronged approach that might also include the parental intervention points of entry (A–D). The most effective attachment-based intervention with prepubertal children would ideally consider addressing all intervention points of entry (A–G).

THE IMPACT OF PARENT, CHILD, AND THERAPIST CHARACTERISTICS ON INTERVENTION POINTS OF ENTRY

Theoretical preferences often influence the selection of intervention points of entry. The success of interventions can be empirically tested through rigorous execution of intervention protocols and evaluation of the outcomes to be modified. Intervention evaluators ask two questions: (1) Does the intervention modify the outcomes targeted by the therapist? (2) Which intervention points of entry are targeted most effectively for which parents and children? As discussed earlier, attachment-based early intervention programs usually target maternal sensitivity and infant attachment security as variables to be modified. More recent intervention strategies focus on maternal reflective functioning and maternal mental representations of the relationship with the child (Slade, Sadler, and Mayes, 2005).

Attachment-based intervention programs with the prepubertal child, however, need to emphasize other outcomes such as the regulation of severely dysregulated affects (found notably in aggression and depression reviewed earlier), frustration tolerance and self-inhibition, autonomy, social competence, self-esteem, intellectual functioning, and academic achievement. Erikson (1950) identified industry versus inferiority as the prevailing psychosocial crisis of the prepubertal developmental period, with competence as the successful outcome and inferiority as the failed outcome. Thus, I am proposing that intervention strategies need to target psychological domains that enhance competencies particular to a psychosocial developmental period.

The intervention points of entry to be selected and outcomes to be modified also depend on the psychological characteristics of the parents and child as well as the therapist. The effectiveness of an attachment-based intervention program depends on the extent to which these psychological characteristics either facilitate or interfere with the implementation of the intervention. The intellectual functioning of both the parents and child should influence the selection of the intervention points of entry as well as outcomes to be targeted for modification. For example, some psychoanalysts (e.g., Clarkin, Yeomans, and Kernberg, 1999; Kernberg, Selzer, Koenigsberg, Carr, and Appelbaum, 1989) recommend insight-oriented therapy only to patients assessed as having average or higher intellectual functioning, while referring the rest to cognitive-behavioral therapy such as dialectical behavior therapy (Linehan, 1993). It is believed that patients assessed as having higher intellectual functioning are more likely than others to have the capacity to engage in the kind of abstract reasoning and symbolic thinking required of insight-oriented clinical work.

Reflecting on the effectiveness of their intervention program that targets the improvement of reflective functioning in low-income, high-risk, first-time mothers, Slade and her colleagues (Slade, Sadler, and Mayes, 2005) commented that reflective functioning "is linked to executive capacities such as planning and reasoning that are part and parcel of higher cortical functioning" (p. 171). In mothers assessed as having intellectual functioning in the borderline range, "we have at times had so much difficulty just getting them to hold onto an idea, let alone link it to other mental or objective phenomena, that we have had to lower our goals and expectations significantly" (p. 171). Considering my thesis that intervention points of entry need to vary with parental characteristics, I question whether the authors' selection of mothers' reflective functioning as the primary intervention point of entry was appropriate for everyone, given the serious intellectual limitations of some of the mothers. The same caution applies to the intellectually limited prepubertal child. A more behavioral intervention approach might therefore be indicated.

I am similarly proposing that the severity of psychopathology present in the parents and child should also influence the selection of the intervention points of entry as well as outcomes to be targeted. For example, Slade and her colleagues (Slade, Sadler, and Mayes, 2005) identified severe psychopathology (notably, posttraumatic stress disorder [PTSD] and borderline personality disorder) among at least 40 percent of the mothers enrolled in their attachment-based early intervention program. Because of the underlying personality disorganization, these mothers experienced particular difficulty in acquiring reflective functioning. The therapist working with such mothers must tend to both the daily chaos and upheaval in these mothers' lives as well as "the mothers' awareness of their babies' needs and intentions" (p. 172). Poverty, social deprivation, community violence, and the resultant sense of powerlessness might also be barriers to the acquisition of reflective functioning. It appears that severe psychopathology, like low intellectual functioning, might pose formidable obstacles to the exploration of mental representations or the acquisition of reflective functioning in both parents and prepubertal children. Thus, a more behavioral approach might be indicated for this population.

Yet others believe that a more intensive, psychodynamic intervention approach in which mental representations are explored and modified is especially indicated, while behavioral interventions are contraindicated. For example, in a discussion of the four principles that underlie their attachment-based early intervention program, Cooper and his colleagues (Cooper et al., 2005) suggested that

> teaching parents concrete behavior management techniques may be limited by a parent's problematic history and the resulting tendency to experience strong negative emotion (which may evoke defensive behavior) in response to particular signals from her or his child. Although a parent may *cognitively* learn about more sensitive responses, there may in fact be no increased likelihood of the parent applying those new responses when emotionally aroused by the child's signals. Our assumption is that applying these changes in a lasting manner requires changes in the parent's internal working models [mental representations], which are partially regulated by emotional reactions. (pp. 131, 132)

In parents who experience "strong negative emotion" or acute emotional arousal—*DSM-IV* (APA, 2000) criteria of borderline personality disorder and PTSD, respectively—perhaps the *only* interventions that have any likelihood of modifying the prepubertal child's socioemotional outcomes target those points of entry that focus on parent and child mental representations or reflective functioning (A–C, E, F). Several studies (Egeland et al., 2000; Olds, 2005; Spieker et al., 2005) concur that intensive attachment-based early intervention programs can be more effective with more psychiatrically compromised mothers than with those less compromised. Spieker and her colleagues (Spieker et al., 2005) speculated that the fragility of their clinically depressed mothers elicited more caregiving responses from their therapists, while self-sufficient mothers were more frustrating to work with.

Research demonstrates that the prepubertal child diagnosed with serious emotional disturbance is more likely to benefit from an intensive, relationship-focused intervention approach than a less intensive (fewer weekly sessions) approach (Fonagy and Target, 1996; Target and Fonagy, 1994a, 1994b). These children seem to respond less favorably to a less intensive approach, while less emotionally disturbed children respond equally well regardless of intervention intensity (frequency and duration of intervention). In fact, in a retrospective study of 763 child cases, less intensive approaches resulted in negative outcomes for almost 60 percent of the children with serious emotional disturbance, but positive outcomes for over 80 percent of the less emotionally disturbed children. These findings suggest that the selection of intervention point of entry might be more consequential for parents and children with serious emotional disturbance than for parents and children simply at risk for serious emotional disturbance. I am suggesting that intervention strategies must take into account (1) developmental period, (2) parental and child intellectual functioning, and (3) parental and child socioemotional functioning. Higher intellectual and socioemotional functioning increases one's intervention options with both parent and child. Conversely, lower intellectual functioning limits the therapist to behavioral strategies, while lower socioemotional functioning limits the therapist to relationship-focused strategies that identify underlying mental representations.

Parent and Child Mental Representations

The quality of the mental representations of both parents and prepubertal children influences the selection of the intervention points of entry as well as outcomes to be targeted for modification. Insecure and disorganized mental representations of relationships with parents or children produce general vulnerabilities to psychopathology, the manifestations of which depend on ego resources, support systems, and later life circumstances (Bowlby, 1980, 1988, 1989; Rutter, 1985, 1987; Sroufe, 1988; Sroufe and Rutter, 1984). A large body of evidence now supports the hypothesis that the levels of security and disorganization of these mental representations carry varying levels of risk for later psychopathology across the lifespan (e.g., Carlson, 1998; Greenberg, 1999; Lyons-Ruth, Easterbrooks, and Cibelli, 1997; Lyons-Ruth and Jacobvitz, 1999; Solomon and George, 1999a; van IJzendoorn, Schuengel, and Bakermans-Kranenburg, 1999; Weinfield et al., 1999). Thus, attachment-based intervention programs need to take into account the quality of these mental representations as a design feature to maximize their effectiveness. The assessment of attachment disorganization would necessitate an intensive relationship-based approach in which the fears associated with the secure base of the primary caregiver/therapist can be adequately worked through. On the other hand, children assessed as having an organized attachment might benefit from less intensive treatment approaches such as learning social skills (Greenberg, Speltz, DeKlyen, and Endriga, 1991).

The effectiveness of attachment-based intervention programs depends on formulating strategies that focus on the specific vulnerabilities associated with specific patterns of mental representation. For example, Cooper and his colleagues (Cooper et al., 2005; see also Dozier and Sepulveda, 2004) hypothesized that parents with insecure mental representations of their relationships with their own parents can feel either (1) less comfortable with their child's need for exploration, independence, and autonomy, or (2) less comfortable with their child's need for closeness, protection, and comfort. Parents in the first category might feel that their child is too independent and does not need them. The child, acting in accordance with the parents' fears, might miscue parents by acting needy or distressed at the prospect of moving away to explore, even when he or she might be interested in doing so. Conversely, parents in the second category might feel that their child is too clingy and dependent. The child, also acting in accordance with parents' fears, might miscue parents by acting self-sufficient or precociously autonomous, even when he or she might be experiencing a need for comfort. Such compromises enable both parents and child to gratify the attachment needs of the child while simultaneously protecting both parties against mutual discomfort elicited by closeness or separation.

A third category of parents have mental representations that make them prone to engaging in frightening or frightened behaviors during moments when the child's attachment system is activated, creating an approach/avoidance conflict in which the child must protect himself or herself from the presumed source of protection, the caregiver (Main and Hesse, 1990). The child responds by acting confused, disoriented, frightened, or listless. By age six, however, the child organizes these responses into controlling-punitive (in which the child seeks to humiliate the parent) or controlling-overbright/caregiving (in which the child seeks to take care of the parent) behavioral patterns (Main and Cassidy, 1988). This apparent reversal of parent-child roles serves to protect both parties from unspeakable dread while simultaneously providing some pretense of a secure base for the child. Underneath this façade of control, however, lie primitive fears of annihilation and cosmic calamity

(Solomon et al., 1995) that the therapist, through transference, inevitably inherits in the therapeutic relationship (see below).

These three parent categories can then be used to design intervention strategies suited to parents' individual needs based on the quality of mental representations. For example, an attachment-based intervention program targeting point of entry C might use videotaped feedback of parent-child interaction to focus on a moment when the child needed comfort based on the situation but has miscued by moving away—in accordance with what the child perceives to be the parent's expectation. Helping the parent to interpret the miscue (defensive process), interpret the underlying need that the child is disguising with the miscue, and respond to the underlying need rather than the miscue will ultimately modify the parents' mental representations of their relationship with the child and resultant behavior toward the child (Cooper et al., 2005). Similarly, the therapist can use videotaped feedback to focus on a moment when the child needed to express autonomy based on the situation but has miscued by seeking proximity, or when the child needed to feel safe but became listless because of a frightening parental behavior. Exploring the complex web of parent-child interactions, based on prior knowledge of the parent's pattern of mental representation, can deepen the parent's understanding of the child and result in a modified mental representation of the relationship with him or her.

Considering the phase-specific psychological tasks that the prepubertal child must accomplish (Erikson, 1950), therapists need to consider children's inevitable transition from the world of home to the world of school and peers. This transition places increased stress on the attachment system and produces changes in the goal-corrected partnership with parents (Bowlby, 1982). Mayseless (2005) referred to this transition as a "shift in responsibility between child and parent for monitoring and maintaining the availability and accessibility of the caregiver" (p. 10). I am therefore proposing that these phase-specific tasks could differentially affect parent-child dyads, depending on the nature of the compromises both parties reached in infancy and toddlerhood. For example, parents who expressed discomfort during the earlier developmental period with the child's need for security and closeness tended to have children who learned to miscue their parents by refraining from signaling for comfort when they needed it. These parents and children will traverse the developmental period of prepubescence with greater upheaval than those parents and children who have a history of acknowledging needs for closeness, comfort, and protection. These children as adolescents will stay away from home with peers for longer periods than their securely attached counterparts will and thus be exposed to greater risks. Attachment-based intervention programs that serve the needs of prepubertal children and parents need to consider the nature of the psychological stresses stimulated by this developmental period.

An apparent absence of psychological stresses during this developmental period, however, does not mean that children of parents who tend to avoid or dismiss their needs for comfort and security present with a low risk for future psychopathology. Perhaps these children will encounter emotional difficulties during a later developmental period such as young adulthood, when the developmental crisis to be overcome is intimacy versus isolation (Erikson, 1950). These children might appear relatively well-adjusted during prepubescence because they separate easily from parents, make acquaintances easily, and demonstrate an eagerness to explore their environment. Difficulties might arise during young adulthood, however, because such children fear making an intimate emotional connection with another person in a love relationship. This failure could result in a retreat into isolation or a pattern of indiscriminate superficiality in relationships (Goodman, 2002). Attachment-based intervention programs need to adjust their intervention protocols to accommodate the specific vulnerabilities of parents and children in consideration of their defensive processes and current developmental tasks.

Intervention outcome studies (Bakermans-Kranenburg, Juffer, and van IJzendoorn, 1998; Bosquet and Egeland, 2001; Korfmacher, Adam, Ogawa, and Egeland, 1997; Routh, Hill, Steele, Elliott, and Dewey, 1995) suggest that the quality of parents' mental representations of relationships with their own parents not only influences intervention strategies but also predicts outcome success. In a high-risk sample, mothers with preoccupied mental representations (discomfort with separation and exploration) who received the attachment-based intervention demonstrated greater improvement than their counterparts in the control group, while mothers with other patterns of mental representation did not seem to benefit (Bosquet and Egeland, 2001). In a low-risk sample, preoccupied mothers benefited more than mothers with dismissing mental representations (discomfort with closeness and connection) when the intervention included both video feedback and discussions about childhood attachment experiences, while dismissing mothers benefited more than preoccupied mothers when the intervention included only video feedback (Bakermans-Kranenburg et al., 1998). Considering various intervention strategies with parents, therapists need to consider the quality of parents' underlying mental representations and their differential responsiveness to these strategies.

Two other empirical studies further illustrate this point. In a high-risk sample, mothers with unresolved mental representations (frightening or frightened responses to attachment needs) were more likely to use intervention to seek relief from crisis than other mothers, while dismissing mothers had a more disengaged involvement with intervention than other mothers did (Korfmacher et al., 1997). In the only study to predict the differential impact of a parent management-training course on the child from the quality of the mothers' mental representations (Routh et al., 1995), children of mothers with unresolved mental representations demonstrated less behavior change than children of other mothers. As a whole, this small but formidable body of research challenges intervention designers to take into account parents' individual mental representations and their differential impact on intervention participation and outcome when selecting an intervention point of entry to target and a set of outcomes to modify.

For example, the Bakermans-Kranenburg et al. (1998) study suggests that intervention point of entry A (parents' mental representations of their relationships with their own parents) might prove more successful at producing parental sensitivity for preoccupied parents than for parents with other patterns of mental representation, while intervention point of entry D (parents' behavior toward the child) might prove more successful for dismissing parents than for other parents. Clearly, more research needs to be conducted to account for the differential impact of various attachment-based intervention programs on parent and child socioemotional outcomes based on this representational information. Specifically, individual intervention points of entry need to be systematically tested on parents with varying patterns of mental representation to determine which points of entry are most effective at modifying which outcomes for which patterns of mental representation.

Research could also assess the differential impact of prepubertal children's mental representations on intervention effectiveness. This research, in combination with research investigating the differential impact of parents' mental representations on child outcomes (Bosquet and Egeland, 2001; Routh et al., 1995), could provide a more comprehensive assessment of the selection of intervention points of entry as well as modifiable outcomes for both parent and child. Research might indicate that parents and children with mental representations that produce discomfort with exploration and autonomy might require intervention at points of entry A and E (see figure 7.1), whereas parents and children with mental representations that produce discomfort with closeness and connection might require intervention at points of entry D and G.

My own data (Goodman, Sapp, Stroh, and Valdez, 2007) suggest that a prepubertal child's chaotic, confused mental representation mediates the influence of the mother's performance impairment (one factor of depression) on the child's aggression. If the child's aggression is targeted as the outcome to be modified, then the intervention needs to focus on the mother's depression but especially the child's mental representation. In another study, the quality of infant attachment mediated methadone-maintained mothers' quality of communication with their toddlers (Goodman, Hans, and Bernstein, 2005). Again, the therapist needs to target the mother's quality of communication as well as the toddler's use of the mother/therapist as a secure base. A transactional model of development (Sameroff, 1975) predicts that modifications in the child will produce modifications in the mother, which in turn will produce further modifications in the child. Modifications in a child's attachment security might produce a favorable modification in the parents' mental representations and in turn greater emotional responsiveness from the parents (van IJzendoorn et al., 1995; van IJzendoorn et al., 2005).

Therapist Mental Representations

A clear understanding of each therapist's mental representation of the relationships with his or her own parents should influence the selection of parent-child dyads to which the therapist is assigned. Research has shown that the therapist's expertise and professional credentials positively influence mother and infant outcomes because of the greater therapeutic competency associated with expertise (Olds, 2005). I am therefore proposing that the therapist's mental representations can also influence an intervention program's effectiveness. Dozier and her colleagues (Dozier, 2003; Dozier et al., 1994; Tyrrell et al., 1999) are the only group of researchers to have explored this issue in depth. According to their findings, the quality of the therapist's mental representation, and the correspondence between the therapist's mental representation and the adult patient's mental representation (no work has been published with child patients), partially determine the therapist's competence and intervention's effectiveness.

Specifically, I am suggesting that therapists with more secure mental representations of parental relationships are more likely to attend and respond to patients' underlying needs better than therapists with more insecure mental representations (discomfort with autonomy or closeness; Dozier et al., 1994). Therapists with mental representations that reflected discomfort with closeness, paired with patients with mental representations that reflected discomfort with autonomy, tended to have a better working alliance than therapists and patients with matching mental representations. Conversely, therapists with mental representations that reflected discomfort with autonomy, paired with patients with mental representations that reflected discomfort with closeness, also tended to have a better working alliance than therapists and patients with matching mental representations (Tyrrell et al., 1999). In other words, complementary or mismatched mental representations seem to work better in the service of establishing and maintaining the working alliance than matching mental representations (see Goodman, in press, chapters 2, 3, and 6).

Dozier (2003) suggested that based on these results, intervention is most effective when the therapist provides a "gentle challenge" (p. 254) to the patient. According to Dozier, therapists with more secure mental representations tend to provide more challenging interventions than therapists with more insecure mental representations. These therapists' interventions also seemed individualized to the patient's particular discomfort. Specifically, these therapists provided more psychologically oriented interventions to patients with mental representations that reflected discomfort with closeness and more independence-promoting interventions to patients with mental representations that reflected discomfort with autonomy. Applying Dozier's hypothesis to prepubertal intervention, therapists with more secure mental representations are more likely to provide a gentle challenge to their patients, a key ingredient to intervention program effectiveness. Dozier further suggested that therapists whose mental representations do not match their patients' mental representations also tend to provide a gentle challenge as a function of the representational differences that naturally exist between them.

Although therapeutic confrontation is an enduring staple of some forms of psychodynamic psychotherapy (e.g., Clarkin et al., 1999; Kernberg et al., 1989), Dozier's findings amplify the justification often given for its use—integrating split-off mental representations. This amplification originates in an understanding of attachment theory as a theory of affect regulation (Kobak and Sceery, 1988). Patients need both affect containment—the metabolization and organization of chaotic, overwhelming affects (Bion, 1962, 1967)—and affect tolerance—permission to experience and express unpleasant, repressed affects (Fraiberg et al., 1975).

I am suggesting that some patients—generally those who experience discomfort with autonomy and exploration—need assistance with affect containment, while other patients—generally those who experience discomfort with closeness and connection—need assistance with affect tolerance. Therapist-patient mismatches might be particularly effective because the therapist, by virtue of his or her own pattern of affect regulation, is providing an intervention needed by the patient. When the therapist-patient mental representations match, however, the therapist is providing either affect containment for the patient whose affects are already overcontrolled, or affect tolerance for the patient whose affects are already undercontrolled.

The quality of the therapist's mental representations could therefore be used to enhance the effectiveness of an attachment-based intervention program by systematically mismatching therapists and parents prior to the beginning of the intervention. Therapist-parent mismatches are probably most important to arrange with attachment-based intervention programs that have selected the parents' or child's mental representations as the points of entry

(A, C, E). Modification at these points of entry relies on working through affects associated with the discussion of significant others in attachment situations. Representational matching also needs to be considered between the therapist and prepubertal child, although no research is available that suggests its potential to improve intervention effectiveness.

The groundbreaking work of Dozier and her colleagues, however, offers no insight into the third category of parents mentioned earlier: those whose mental representations make them prone to engaging in frightening or frightened behaviors during moments when the child's attachment system is activated, creating an approach/avoidance conflict in which the child must protect himself or herself from the presumed source of protection—the caregiver. Which therapist mental representation would be most effective with this kind of parent? A high degree of overlap has been demonstrated between persons whose mental representations reflect discomfort with autonomy and exploration and persons whose mental representations make them prone to engaging in frightening or frightened behaviors (Adam, Sheldon-Keller, and West, 1996; Fonagy et al., 1996; Pianta, Egeland, and Adam, 1996). Thus, a therapist whose mental representation makes him or her skilled at containing affect might be most effective with this kind of parent.

A prepubertal child whose attachment system is disorganized poses specific challenges to any attachment-based intervention program. Owing to the disorganized nature of their mental representations, these children could become increasingly frightened by potential attachment figures (Solomon, George, and De Jong, 1995) such as the therapist, who is offering them the opportunity to experience a secure, trusting relationship. In a doll-story task, disorganized children demonstrated "frightened" behavior in their doll play: "Catastrophe, sometimes multiple catastrophes, often arise without warning; dangerous people or events are vanquished, only to surface again and again. Objects float and have magical, malignant powers; punishments are abusive and unrelenting" (p. 454). Cognitive-behavioral intervention with these children that focuses on point of entry G has been suggested (Green and Goldwyn, 2002), yet there is no empirical evidence to support it.

Attachment-based intervention programs that focus on relationships—either with the parents themselves or with the therapist as a symbolic representative of them—can work toward resolving the underlying affect dysregulation and conflict related to parental dread, mortal vulnerability, utter helplessness, rage, and despondency. This intensive and challenging work needs to occur to establish a sense of internal and external security and thus remove some of the precipitants of these children's aggression and depression, which have been interpreted as desperate attempts at engaging an emotionally unresponsive or unprotective parent (Adam, 1994; Goodman,

2002; Goodman, Gerstadt, Pfeffer, Stroh, and Valdez, 2008; Goodman and Pfeffer, 1998).

As prepubertal children with disorganized mental representations enter adolescence—a developmental period that coincides with an increased opportunity to carry out these symptoms' lethal forms—it is critical that they have had the opportunity to experience a trusting relationship with an attachment figure that has the potential to modify their frightening representations of relationships with others. I believe that those therapists most highly qualified to conduct an attachment-based intervention with such parents and children have already engaged in their own process of self-exploration with a senior therapist—a secure base. This therapy process has the potential to facilitate reflective functioning and aid in restoring an integrated, coherent set of mental representations that can then serve as a reliable guide in the chaotic cauldron of these therapeutic relationships. Indeed, Freud's (1912) prescription that would-be analysts undergo their own personal analysis to increase their understanding of their own mental lives, and thus the mental lives of their patients, seems as relevant to therapists in the twenty-first century as it was in 1912.

In summary, attachment-based intervention with prepubertal children needs to take into account the points of entry where the therapist can most effectively improve their well-being. The selection of an appropriate intervention point of entry within the complex parent-child family system depends on a knowledge of the child's current psychosocial developmental tasks as well as the attachment histories of the key players—parents, child, and therapist. Other factors, such as the intellectual functioning and severity of psychopathology of the parents and child, also require consideration in how and where to intervene. Children classified with disorganized mental representations tend to be experiencing primitive anxieties that predispose them to severe forms of psychopathology that require intensive, relationship-focused therapy to modify the underlying fragmentation. Children classified with organized mental representations tend to be experiencing less severe forms of psychopathology that could remit with less intensive (briefer, less frequent) therapy conducted psychodynamically or cognitive-behaviorally. Finally, matching therapists and children according to the differences in their respective patterns of mental representations along the closeness-autonomy continuum can facilitate the establishment and maintenance of the working alliance and increase the likelihood of a desired outcome for the prepubertal child.

Chapter Eight

The Internal World Meets External Reality: Entering the Mind of Victims of Political Torture

This is the story of two adolescent brothers who live in New York City. Except for their accents, they seem ordinary in every way. They play basketball and tennis, hang out with friends, and attend high school. Yet the journey that these two boys have taken is anything but ordinary. Their story left me to wonder: Is the concealment of human misery sometimes so absolute that current therapeutic methods are incapable of challenging it?

Earlier in my career, as a graduate student and postdoctoral fellow, I gratified my altruistic needs by performing volunteer work. Now, as an established psychologist, I let my quest for tenure, a viable private practice, and a psychoanalytic certificate lure me away from helping people with no money. I have always been politically active but had never used my clinical psychology training in this arena. I decided to contact Doctors of the World (www.dowusa.org) to find out how they could put me to work. I learned that they needed licensed clinical psychologists to provide assessment of psychological sequelae of torture for their clients seeking political asylum. After completing the training, I was assigned two adolescent brothers to interview—Issa and Mohammed (I have changed names, locations, and certain details in this account). Issa and Mohammed were born in the small African country of Cote d'Ivoire in the city of Daloa. Their father was a local businessman in telecommunications. He had two sons by two different wives—Issa and Mohammed. The family of five lived an upper-middle-class lifestyle in this poor African country. Where most people in Daloa eat one meal a day, Issa and Mohammed's family ate three. As the brothers described it, life in Daloa for them was idyllic.

There was one small problem, however. The boys' father was involved in political activities considered subversive to the ruling party. Any political activity not sanctioned by the government was routinely dismantled. The father's political activities were no exception. The father never talked about his political activities because any knowledge of these activities would make his sons accomplices. The brothers knew that their father was involved in something dangerous. The secrecy surrounding his comings and goings made them suspicious; he was often away from home at night or on trips for days at a time. A neighbor had disappeared and never returned. He had been involved in political activities. Was their father also involved?

Doctors of the World provided me with contact information for the two attorneys also assigned to these two cases. I contacted Issa's attorney and scheduled the first of two interviews with him. Appearing relaxed and on time, Issa struck me as an ordinary adolescent boy. He was quiet and made fair eye contact. I noted a strong French accent. I escorted him into my office. After a short conversation about how he traveled to my office (car service), what he thought of his attorney ("she's nice"), and how old he was (nineteen), I then asked him to tell me his story. Issa fled his native country of Cote d'Ivoire with his younger brother three years ago because his family had decided that their lives were in danger. Their father had been arrested and taken from his home and detained in Daloa four months earlier because he had engaged in political activities that supported the opposition party in Cote d'Ivoire. Issa and his family had gone to the local police station in an attempt to secure the father's release, but the police did not provide them with any information about his whereabouts. Issa recalled fearing for his father's safety, not knowing whether he was dead or alive. In his words, which I recorded verbatim, "I thought my life would change forever when my father was taken. It was like someone shot me in my heart—crazy." He remembered coming home from school earlier that day and seeing neighbors and family friends gathered inside the house. Noticing that his mother was crying, he twice asked her what was wrong. Finally, she told Issa that the police had ransacked his father's bedroom and taken him away. Issa rushed into his father's bedroom to find the bed overturned, desk drawers flung to the floor, and clothes strewn all over.

After failing to secure the father's release at the local police station, Issa's family held a meeting with a group of the father's friends at which both Issa and Mohammed were present. At this meeting, which took place three months after the father's disappearance, one of the men stated that if the father refused to disclose information regarding his political activities, his two oldest sons, Issa and Mohammed, would be killed in retribution. The men at the meeting decided that both sons should flee the country for their own safety as quickly as possible. Issa, then sixteen, and Mohammed, then fifteen, obtained counterfeit passports and visas and traveled with one of their father's business associates, who dropped them off at an undisclosed location in New York City, gave them $500, and left.

Issa describes this period of his life as frightening. He did not know where he was, did not know English, and did not know anyone. He also felt responsible for his younger brother. The people living in the house where his father's friend had dropped off the brothers informed Issa that they would have to pay rent to stay there. Issa knew that the money they were given would run out soon. Issa met a man from Cote d'Ivoire who referred him to a Mauritanian taxi driver who had a three-bedroom apartment in the Bronx. Two bedrooms are rented out to other tenants. Issa informed me that he and Mohammed sleep in this man's bed at night while he drives his taxi. The man uses the same bed to sleep on during the day. Both Issa and his brother have been living in this apartment since they came to New York City three years ago.

Issa described this period of his odyssey as filled with profound feelings of loneliness and worry about his father. He felt completely isolated, exacerbated by his inability to speak English, and unable to contact his family. The taxi driver managed to enroll Issa and his brother in Malcolm X High School in the Bronx by declaring himself their legal guardian. Issa graduated from Malcolm X last year, while his brother was completing eleventh grade. School provided Issa with structure, friends, and a mentor—his French teacher, Miss Pierre. Issa had already known French in addition to his native language of Dioula; therefore, Miss Pierre became someone with whom Issa could communicate. He quickly learned English and made some friends. Miss Pierre also sometimes gave Issa money, paid for lunch, or aided him with translating English. Although he was able to make friends at school, it was not safe to disclose his circumstances. Whenever he tried, they would tell him "it's a joke—like a bad movie." After that point, he stopped confiding in others because their responses "made me feel different." Issa enjoyed relative stability as he finished high school. He was able to find odd jobs such as cleaning windows and lifting heavy objects to help pay the rent. He used some of these earnings to purchase calling cards to contact his family in Cote d'Ivoire. Two years ago, he learned that his father was released from detention. He always suspected, but never knew for certain, that his father had been tortured in detention until a recent telephone conversation with his father confirmed it.

Issa shared that as his high school graduation drew near, he became frustrated and resentful toward some of his friends who were completing college applications. Issa's father had always emphasized the attainment of education as a top priority for Issa and his brother. The father had never received an education and wanted both boys to experience that privilege; thus, he had sent both of them to private schools in Cote d'Coitre. Issa wanted to continue his education because "I loved school." He could have qualified to attend college with an overall academic average of 88—higher than many of his friends who were applying—but his financial and legal status blocked him from pursuing his dream. Issa felt left behind.

Issa's solid academic performance is remarkable, considering the conditions under which he was living. At the time of his enrollment, he knew no English at all, and no one at the school knew his native language of Dioula, so communication with anyone other than Miss Pierre was impossible. He was financially supporting himself and Mohammed, living in a cramped bedroom he shared with Mohammed and the taxi driver. Issa also stated that he had "no concentration in school" because he would be worrying about "how my family would survive." It is interesting to speculate what Issa could have accomplished in high school or college had his circumstances been more favorable. If he had the opportunity and the money, Issa emphatically stated, "I would want to go to college any time."

After graduation, the supportive environment that high school had provided Issa was gone: "I felt like my life ended after high school." He found a job distributing flyers in midtown Manhattan, but that job ended when his employer no longer needed him. He quickly learned that he could not find legitimate employment without a social security number. Issa confided that he struggles to support himself and his brother, who is still completing his high school education, as well as his family back in Cote d'Ivoire, because his father can no longer conduct business and provide for the family. After his graduation, Issa kept to himself because he feared that telling others his story might result in deportation. Convinced by members of the Bronx African community that he could not apply for political asylum until he turned twenty-one, he waited until he turned eighteen to seek assistance with his application—after realizing that he was given misinformation.

Issa reminisced about his childhood days that seem so far away. Prior to his arrest and torture, Issa's father had been a businessman, selling telecommunications. By the standards of his community, Issa lived a privileged lifestyle. The family owned a computer, a cell phone, and a VCR and ate three meals a day, while other families in their community had no electronic equipment and struggled to eat even one meal a day. Issa longed for not only his loved ones but also the comforts of home—a standard of living that far exceeded his current existence. The logical question to ask was "Why not return to Cote d'Ivoire, where you can once again enjoy a comfortable lifestyle and be reunited with your family?" Without hesitation, Issa answered that he would either go to prison or get killed by the government to punish his father for his father's political activities. To Issa, the poverty, loneliness, and aimlessness he was experiencing in the Bronx were a small price to pay in comparison to the likely loss of life he would face in his native country.

When I asked him where he sees himself in five years, Issa replied that he wants to become a legal resident, go to college, and provide for a family. After he found his attorney, Issa stated that he started "feeling better" because she provided hope for him and his brother. In spite of his father's horrid experiences, Issa said he also wants to become like his father—"a very devout Muslim trying to make the world a better place." Regarding religious observance, Issa said he attends Islamic services regularly and does not drink alcohol or take drugs, as Islamic law prohibits ingestion of these substances.

After my first interview with Issa, I contacted Mohammed's attorney and scheduled the first of two interviews with him. Mohammed also struck me as an ordinary adolescent boy; however, he was much quieter and made less eye contact. The silences between us were uncomfortable. He did not seem to be struggling with English or with formulating answers to my questions. Mohammed just seemed uninterested in the process even though he knew that his answers would partially determine whether the U.S. government would be placing him on the path to citizenship or the path to deportation and the horrors that would likely await him at home.

The details that Mohammed gave me of his father's detention closely matched those of his brother. I noticed, however, that the reactions of the boys' mothers differed. (As mentioned earlier, Issa and Mohammed were actually half-brothers because their father had two wives.) Whereas Issa's mother, though upset, told her son about his father's disappearance, Mohammed's mother locked herself in her bedroom and refused to come out. The contrasting behavioral responses of these two mothers reflect important differences in their characteristic response to stressful situations, which could imply a differential ability to contain a child's distressing affects and to mentalize distressing experiences on a child's behalf. Instead of feeling scared for himself, Mohammed recalls fearing for his father's safety. Mohammed remembers that he felt sad that his mother appeared so upset and angry that his father had been taken away. Not once did he mention feeling sad or scared because of his own loss.

Regarding his travel to the United States, Mohammed stated that he does not recall much from that time because he "didn't know what was going on." The overall picture that unfolded of Mohammed's state of mind at the time is that he was confused about his father's abduction and the adults' reactions to it. According to him, he was not really aware of the implications of his father's abduction until after he had boarded the plane to come to the United States: "My mother and a friend of the family decided [that my brother and I should come to the United States]. . . . I was not happy. . . . I worried who would take care of my family." Mohammed learned only on the day of his departure when he and Issa would be leaving Cote d'Ivoire. At the time, he did not realize that it might be the last time that he would see his mother and the rest of his family.

I asked Mohammed to outline the difficulties adjusting to his new life in the United States. Curiously, he noted the differences in food and climate as the most difficult aspects of his adjustment. The language barrier also made it difficult to communicate with anyone except his brother.

Academically, Mohammed was maintaining an 89 academic average—a remarkably solid performance, considering the conditions under which he was living. At the time of his enrollment, he knew no English at all, and no one at the school knew his native language of Dioula. He told me his favorite subject was math, but "I like all subjects." When asked what he would wish for if he were granted three wishes, he replied that his first wish was "to go to college." If given the opportunity to attend college, Mohammed stated that he would want to study engineering or medicine. Like his brother, Mohammed mentioned his father's emphasis on acquiring an education. In spite of his father's release from detention two years earlier, Mohammed remained concerned about his father's physical health. Mohammed explained that his father was "sick" at the time of his release, but his health had since improved. His family's situation makes him feel "confused" because his family was telling him that everyone has enough food, but he was also aware that food costs money, and without his father's income, he did not know how the family was adjusting. According to him, Mohammed and Issa never talk about their father or their family.

When asked why he wants to stay in this country, Mohammed explained that his father told him that the government of Cote d'Ivoire believed that his father had given Mohammed and Issa secret documents that would expose the government's "corruption and how it is run." According to Mohammed, the government of Cote d'Ivoire wanted to punish Mohammed and Issa for treason. I asked Mohammed how he knows that his government is capable of doing such things. He replied, "Some people disappear." I asked him to provide me with an example. Mohammed replied that prior to his father's abduction, a neighbor involved in political activities disappeared and was never heard from again. Mohammed wondered whether the same fate could befall his brother and him if they were sent back. He denied knowing much about the political activities that resulted in his father's abduction and detention because "our father did not want us to ask any questions." In the only display of emotion in this first interview, Mohammed said that if he were sent back home, he would flee to another country. "Why?" He responded softly, "May be killed, right?"

In my second interview, conducted separately with both boys, I asked them about their childhoods and their feelings about their parents, other loved ones, and their new life here in the United States. Whereas Mohammed claimed that he did not know what a psychologist was while offering me emotionally barren responses, Issa risked telling me how he felt about coming to speak with me. When his attorney informed him that he would have to speak to a psychologist, Issa initially refused because "it means I'm crazy." He explained that in Cote d'Ivoire, the government puts the mentally ill in a prison, "and that's it"; they get out only "if they stop acting crazy." Overall, Issa displayed a wider range of affect than his brother did. Several times, Issa rubbed his reddened eyes as though he had something in them. These moments occurred when he was discussing his father's arrest and his ongoing worries about his father's health and safety. Although half a world away, Issa "always" worries for his father's safety. Issa never once, however, expressed worries about his own safety or well-being.

Issa did express sadness, however, in recounting how his academically inferior peers were heading off to college in the fall, while he was heading off to distribute flyers in midtown Manhattan. During this period, he came to the realization that "it's all up to me"—that he would not be living with his mother and father anymore and would have to "grow up quickly." Issa, a good-looking boy, confided in me that he refused to go on dates because he lacked the money to pay for food, let alone two movie tickets. He sent home what little money he had left over after paying the rent and Mohammed's and his expenses. A dream that he reported illustrates the additional emotional burden he carried as the responsible guardian of his younger brother: Issa dreamed that his brother was killed, and he was responsible for it. Mohammed's mother accused Issa of killing her son—then he woke up. Issa's willingness to share this dream, and his relative emotional openness and treatment of me as a confidant, made me feel closer to him and more willing to lend him a hand than I felt toward his brother. Perhaps my being an older brother myself also contributed to my feeling closer to Issa.

In contrast to his current dire circumstances, Issa provided a general memory of an idyllic childhood full of love and caring, where others were concerned for his well-being: "I never felt depressed in Cote d'Ivoire." Many doting caregivers were involved in Issa's upbringing. In spite of this overtly bland portrayal, Issa did psychologically differentiate his parents. He described his father as emotionally distant and having high standards and his mother as more understanding and compassionate. He demonstrated reflective functioning in suggesting that, at times, "My mother might have been angry, but she didn't show it to me." He limited his description of his father's demonstration of love for him to the provision of food and clothing. Issa inevitably excused his father's emotional distance, and with it, any potential feelings of resentment: "He just comes home tired, he eats and goes to sleep, but I understand it because that's his job." The father conveyed his caring of Issa and his brother because "he wanted us to succeed." Beatings with a belt were an expected consequence of misbehavior. Issa normalized this behavior: "Everybody do it over there." Whenever he wanted to know something about his father, Issa would ask his mother because "something stopped me from asking him." As a young child, Issa remembered being occasionally separated from his mother for a week at a time when she would travel to another city to take care of family business. When asked how he felt about it, Issa minimized his feelings: "It's a part of life, it's nothing. She'll come back, I know that." "Fear" did not seem to be in Issa's vocabulary.

Mohammed's restricted affect and fearlessness were even more extreme than his brother's. Mohammed appeared to attempt to avoid discussing emotionally difficult content at all costs—even though he knew that his emotional candor would partially determine his fate. For example, he stated that he did not know the extent of his father's torture although the intake report clearly states the nature of this torture. Mohammed provided exceptionally brief answers to questions regarding his father's abduction and torture and his own feelings about these events. He made extremely poor eye contact and appeared to be distracting himself from the emotional content of these questions. In my report to Doctors of the World, I wrote, "In my fourteen years of experience as a licensed clinical psychologist, I have never interviewed an adolescent so avoidant of his thoughts and feelings."

In fact, for the entire three hours that I spent interviewing him, Mohammed's range of affect almost never changed. I attempted to use humor at times to disrupt the atmosphere, which to me felt tense, but he barely cracked a smile at anything I said. Typically, an adolescent boy will show some range of emotional expression that includes happiness, sadness, anxiety, embarrassment, anger, and pride. Mohammed's emotional restrictiveness, however, was severe, which suggests that he was engaged in a massive denial of feelings associated with his father's abduction and torture and his own traumatic departure from his family and arrival in a new country with a strange language, climate, and food. At times, his denial was dramatic. When asked how things are for him now, Mohammed replied, "Everything is good."

Like his brother, Mohammed characterized his childhood as idyllic. He also psychologically differentiated his parents. His father was the disciplinarian, while his mother was more compassionate. Mohammed described his father as working to get money for food, clothing, and education. Also like his brother, Mohammed minimized his description of the beatings he received on his back with bamboo: "Everybody got it if you did something wrong." Even his teachers beat him and the other students because "it makes you work hard, have respect for other people, help other people." His parents and teachers "wanted me to be a good person. . . . All those things were for my own good—beating me, giving me food, putting me through [private] school. Not for [my father], for me." When asked directly, both boys categorically denied that they had ever been physically abused. I asked Mohammed what he would do as a child if he were ever upset. He replied, "Just cried, that's it."

Mohammed described his mother as someone who would give him "money to buy things." She would also perform perfunctory domestic tasks—cook his food and serve it to him. He also characterized her as "friendly" and "helpful." She was helpful because when he approached her for help with homework, she "could ask another [person] to help me." Mohammed claimed that his mother cared about him but could not recall a specific moment during his childhood to support this claim. Interestingly, Mohammed spontaneously mentioned that Issa's mother would look after him while his own mother was away, while Issa never mentioned the same reciprocal caring from Mohammed's mother. Astonishingly, when asked what was the one thing he learned from his childhood, Mohammed replied, "I learned how to play [soccer]." In spite of his generally casual responses to the interview, turmoil seemed to lurk beneath the surface. Mohammed shared having vague dreams in which he saw "weapons and blood and I hear gunfire—that's it."

Issa and Mohammed are two brothers who experienced two different childhoods with two different mothers and who responded differently to a family tragedy that resulted in what could be a permanent separation from their parents. Although I did not administer the AAI (George et al., 1996) to either boy, I nevertheless drew the conclusion that both boys tended to dismiss their attachment experiences and deactivate their attachment systems in the face of serious external dangers. Neither boy expressed anxiety or fear about his own predicament—only fear for the safety of their family back home. Both boys also seemed to express the fact that they were on their own now. Any other adolescent boy might have killed himself under the same circumstances. Are the two brothers constitutionally resilient, well-defended against overwhelming feelings of loss and helplessness, or some combination of the two?

Based on my limited experiences with them and on my knowledge of attachment theory, and at the risk of appearing to propagate cultural insensitivity, I would answer this question by saying that Issa and Mohammed both grew up in an emotionally oppressive environment. The caregivers did not contain—or even respect—feelings of vulnerability or distress. Perhaps the parents' responses to the emotional life of these boys reflect a broader approach to parenting predominant in the culture of Cote d'Ivoire. I cannot comment on this wider context. I know only what I heard from these boys' mouths. Beginning with Mary Ainsworth's first study of the relation between parenting and infant attachment in Uganda (Ainsworth, 1967) and replicated in dozens of other countries and cultures (van IJzendoorn and Sagi, 1999), the tripartite classification system of A, B, and C attachments with their caregiving correlates transcends cultural context. In my nonscientific view, both boys seemed to experience their parents as caring for their physical needs but not their emotional needs. These boys' pretraumatic childhood experiences facilitated the development of an attachment strategy in which all distressing affect states are tightly regulated through defensive exclusion, John Bowlby's (1989) term for the massive denial of attachment needs. Defensive exclusion acts like a coat of armor that protects a person from experiencing the most painful human emotions—rejection, loss, and helplessness. Issa and Mohammed might be constitutionally resilient, but there is plenty of evidence in their childhood histories to suggest that they were both well-defended against overwhelming feelings of loss and helplessness.

In spite of the obvious similarities in their childhood histories, these two brothers nevertheless responded differently to the traumatic events that had occurred to both of them three years earlier. While Issa was forthcoming with information about these events and candid about how he felt coming to speak to me, Mohammed seemed disaffected, removed, and closed off from me as well as his own internal world. Issa shared a dream that clearly communicated the emotional burden he feels having to take care of his brother. Mohammed reported a nebulous dream about violence. In the countertransference, I could feel Issa's pain. After three hours of trying, I could not feel Mohammed's pain. Instead, I felt my own pain caused by my inability to feel Mohammed's pain. It is easy to see the similarities between the two brothers, but how do we understand the differences?

Buried within my copious notes, I found what I believe to be the answer: Issa and Mohammed shared the same authoritarian father but not the same mother. In fact, I inadvertently collected information on the differential responses of both mothers to their husband's abduction. Whereas Issa's mother put her own distress aside to communicate with her son about what had happened to his father, Mohammed's mother locked herself in her bedroom and refused to come out, no doubt leaving Mohammed confused and helpless. What he remembers feeling, however, is sad for his mother. If you multiply this experience a million times over the course of a person's childhood, it makes sense that the human mind can deactivate the emotional impact of these experiences. If the caregiver were to fail to keep the child's mind in mind, then the child would be in danger of losing his own mind. As I mentioned earlier, the contrasting behavioral responses of these two mothers reflect important differences in their characteristic response to stressful situations, which could imply a differential ability to contain a child's distressing affects and to mentalize distressing experiences on a child's behalf. This ability to mentalize on behalf of a child apparently reaches beyond the scope of one's own child. Mohammed specifically recalled the caring he received from Issa's mother, while Issa did not specifically recall any caring from Mohammed's mother. The differences in emotional availability could account for the differences observed in the impenetrability of the boys' respective coats of armor.

How these parents responded to their sons in times of fright, injury, illness, and impending separation—while the internal world was still in formation—largely determines the structure of this internal world and the expectations derived from it. The anticipatory anxiety associated with the expectation of ungratified attachment needs calls for a system of defenses—another layer of structure woven into this internal world. It is only a small step to connect these experiences of the parent-child relationship to these sons' vastly different emotional responses to the trauma as evidenced by their interview responses. Just as Mohammed's mother dismissed him from her thoughts and locked herself in her bedroom, thus depriving him of physical access to her during a crisis, so too Mohammed seemed to dismiss his own inner turmoil, replacing it with a position of invincibility—his own detention facility of denial. By contrast, Issa's mother kept him safely in her mind by maintaining physical access and communicating to him in spite of her own traumatic response. This abiding sense of safety, therefore, permitted Issa to express his inner turmoil more openly than his brother did.

In the intervening years, I have often wondered how a trial of psychotherapy could have helped Issa and Mohammed. Waiting for Issa to show up for his first interview appointment, I wondered how he would respond to my questions about his family tragedy and what could be a permanent separation from his family. I had expected that he would be an emotional mess. I could only project how I thought I would respond to these traumatic events. But both boys contradicted my expectations at every turn. Outwardly, they appeared to be holding it together amazingly well, both before and after their court hearings (both boys were granted political asylum). In the end, the answer to my wondering is that psychotherapy would not be helpful to Issa or Mohammed because neither one would see any need for it. Ultimately, the concealment of human misery is sometimes so absolute that current therapeutic methods are incapable of challenging it. As therapists, we need to keep in mind that with the limitations of our craft comes the cold realization that not every internal world, not every attachment, can be transformed or desires to be transformed. Defensive processes are available to us for reasons that have insured our physical and emotional survival through the ages. Perhaps the best we can do in some circumstances is to listen, focus on the feelings, and carry the burden of pain that the patient temporarily hands over to us. For if we can hold onto it and not drop it, we stand a chance of transforming it and, ultimately, returning it to the patient in a tolerable form.

References

Ablon, J. S., & Jones, E. E. (1998). How expert clinicians' prototypes of an ideal treatment correlate with outcome in psychodynamic and cognitive-behavioral therapy. *Psychotherapy Research, 8*, 71–83.

Adam, K. S. (1994). Suicidal behavior and attachment: A developmental model. In M. B. Sperling and W. H. Berman (Eds.), *Attachment in adults: Clinical and developmental perspectives* (pp. 275–98). New York: Guilford Press.

Adam, K. S., Sheldon-Keller, A. E., & West, M. (1996). Attachment organization and history of suicidal behavior in clinical adolescents. *Journal of Consulting and Clinical Psychology, 64*, 264–72.

Ainsworth, M. D. S. (1967). *Infancy in Uganda: Infant care and the growth of love.* Baltimore: Johns Hopkins University Press.

Ainsworth, M. D. S., Blehar, M. C., Waters, E., & Wall, S. (1978). *Patterns of attachment: A psychological study of the strange situation.* Hillsdale, NJ: Erlbaum.

Altman, N., Briggs, R., Frankel, J., Gensler, D., & Pantone, P. (2002). *Relational child psychotherapy.* New York: Other Press.

American Psychiatric Association. (1994). *Diagnostic and statistical manual of mental disorders* (Fourth ed.). Washington, DC: Author.

———. (2000). *Diagnostic and statistical manual of mental disorders* (Fourth ed., text revision). Washington, DC: Author.

———. (2002a). Ethical principles of psychologists and code of conduct. *American Psychologist, 57*, 1060–73.

American Psychological Association, Committee on Accreditation. (2002b). *Guidelines and principles for accreditation of programs in professional psychology.* Washington, DC: Author.

Anisfeld, E., Casper, V., Nozyce, M., & Cunningham, N. (1990). Does infant carrying promote attachment? An experimental study of the effects of increased physical contact on the development of attachment. *Child Development, 61*, 1617–27.

Baker, R. (1989). Sam: An adolescent with necrophilic fantasies. In M. Laufer and M. E. Laufer (Eds.), *Developmental breakdown and psychoanalytic treatment in adolescence* (pp. 29–42). New Haven, CT: Yale University Press.

Bakermans-Kranenburg, M. J., Juffer, F., & van IJzendoorn, M. H. (1998). Interventions with video feedback and attachment discussions: Does type of maternal insecurity make a difference? *Infant Mental Health Journal, 19*, 202–19.

Bakermans-Kranenburg, M. J., van IJzendoorn, M. H., & Juffer, F. (2003). Less is more: Meta-analysis of sensitivity and attachment interventions in early childhood. *Psychological Bulletin, 129*, 195–215.

Barnett, B., Blignault, I., Holmes, S., Payne, A., & Parker, G. (1987). Quality of attachment in a sample of 1-year-old Australian children. *Journal of the American Academy of Child and Adolescent Psychiatry, 26*, 303–7.

Bateman, A. W., & Fonagy, P. (2004). *Psychotherapy for borderline personality disorder: Mentalization-based treatment*. Oxford: Oxford University Press.

Beck, R., & McDonald, A. (2004). Attachment to God: The Attachment to God Inventory, tests of working model correspondence, and an exploration of faith group differences. *Journal of Psychology and Theology, 32*, 92–103.

Benoit, D., Madigan, S., Lecce, S., Shea, B., & Goldberg, S. (2001). Atypical maternal behavior toward feeding-disordered infants before and after intervention. *Infant Mental Health Journal, 22*, 611–26.

Berlin, L. J. (2005). Interventions to enhance early attachments: The state of the field today. In L. J. Berlin, Y. Ziv, L. Amaya-Jackson, and M. T. Greenberg (Eds.), *Enhancing early attachments: Theory, research, intervention, and policy* (pp. 3–33). New York: Guilford Press.

Berlin, L. J., Ziv, Y., Amaya-Jackson, L., & Greenberg, M. T. (Eds.). (2005). *Enhancing early attachments: Theory, research, intervention, and policy*. New York: Guilford Press.

Bernier, A., & Dozier, M. (2002). The client-counselor match and the corrective emotional experience: Evidence from interpersonal and attachment research. *Psychotherapy: Theory/Research/Practice/Training, 39*, 32–43.

Betan, E., Heim, A. K., Conklin, C. Z., & Westen, D. (2005). Countertransference phenomena and personality pathology in clinical practice: An empirical investigation. *American Journal of Psychiatry, 162*, 890–98.

Bion, W. R. (1959). Attacks on linking. *International Journal of Psycho-Analysis, 40*, 308–15.

——. (1962). *Learning from experience*. London: Heinemann.

——. (1967). *Second thoughts*. London: Heinemann.

Blatt, S. J., Chevron, E. S., Quinlan, D. M., Schaffer, C. E., & Wein, S. (1992). *The assessment of qualitative and structural dimensions of object representations* (Rev. ed.). Unpublished manuscript, Yale University, New Haven, Connecticut.

Block, J. (1978). *The Q-sort method in personality assessment and psychiatric research*. Palo Alto, CA: Consulting Psychologists. (Original work published 1961.)

Bosquet, M., & Egeland, B. (2001). Associations among maternal depressive symptomatology, state of mind and parent and child behaviors: Implications for attachment-based interventions. *Attachment and Human Development, 3*, 173–99.

Bowlby, J. (1958). The nature of the child's tie to his mother. *International Journal of Psycho-Analysis, 39*, 350–73.

——. (1973). *Attachment and loss: Vol. 2. Separation: Anxiety and anger.* New York: Basic Books.

——. (1977). The making and breaking of affectional bonds. I. Aetiology and psychopathology in the light of attachment theory. *British Journal of Psychiatry, 130*, 201–10.

——. (1980). *Attachment and loss: Vol. 3. Loss, sadness and depression.* New York: Basic Books.

——. (1982). *Attachment and loss: Vol. 1. Attachment* (Second ed.). New York: Basic Books.

——. (1988). *A secure base: Parent-child attachment and healthy human development.* New York: Basic Books.

——. (1989). The role of attachment in personality development and psychopathology. In S. I. Greenspan and G. H. Pollock (Eds.), *The course of life: Vol. 1. Infancy* (pp. 229–70). Madison, CT: International University Press.

Brent, D. A., Oquendo, M., Birmaher, B., Greenhill, L., Kolko, D., Stanley, B., Zelazny, J., Brodsky, B., Bridge, J., Ellis, S., Salazar, J. O., & Mann, J. J. (2002). Familial pathways to early-onset suicide attempt: Risk for suicidal behavior in offspring of mood-disordered suicide attempters. *Archives of General Psychiatry, 59*, 801–7.

Bretherton, I. (1985). Attachment theory: Retrospect and prospect. In I. Bretherton and E. Waters (Eds.), *Growing points in attachment theory and research. Monographs of the Society for Research in Child Development, 50* (1-2, Serial No. 209), 3–35.

Bretherton, I., Ridgeway, D., & Cassidy, J. (1990). Assessing internal working models of the attachment relationship: An attachment story completion task for 3-year-olds. In M. T. Greenberg, D. Cicchetti, and E. M. Cummings (Eds.), *Attachment in the preschool years: Theory, research, and intervention* (pp. 273–308). University of Chicago Press: Chicago.

Carlson, E. A. (1998). A prospective longitudinal study of attachment disorganization/disorientation. *Child Development, 69*, 1107–28.

Carter, S. L., Osofsky, J. D., & Hann, D. M. (1991). Speaking for the baby: A therapeutic intervention with adolescent mothers and their infants. *Infant Mental Health Journal, 12*, 291–301.

Cassidy, J., Woodhouse, S. S., Cooper, G., Hoffman, K., Powell, B., & Rodenberg, M. (2005). Examination of the precursors of infant attachment security: Implications for early intervention and intervention research. In L. J. Berlin, Y. Ziv, L. Amaya-Jackson, and M. T. Greenberg (Eds.), *Enhancing early attachments: Theory, research, intervention, and policy* (pp. 34–60). New York: Guilford Press.

Cicchetti, D., Toth, S. L., & Rogosch, F. A. (1999). The efficacy of toddler-parent psychotherapy to increase attachment security in offspring of depressed mothers. *Attachment and Human Development, 1*, 34–66.

Clarkin, J. F., Yeomans, F. E., & Kernberg, O. F. (1999). *Psychotherapy for borderline personality.* New York: Wiley.

——. (2006). *Psychotherapy for borderline personality: Focusing on object relations*. Washington, DC: American Psychiatric Publishing.

Cohen, N. J., Muir, E., Parker, C. J., Brown, M., Lojkasek, M., Muir, R., & Barwick, M. (1999). Watch, wait, and wonder: Testing the effectiveness of a new approach to mother-infant psychotherapy. *Infant Mental Health Journal, 20*, 429–51.

Cooper, G., Hoffman, K., Powell, B., & Marvin, R. (2005). The Circle of Security intervention: Differential diagnosis and differential treatment. In L. J. Berlin, Y. Ziv, L. Amaya-Jackson, and M. T. Greenberg (Eds.), *Enhancing early attachments: Theory, research, intervention, and policy* (pp. 127–51). New York: Guilford Press.

Cooper, P. J., & Murray, L. (1997). The impact of psychological treatments of postpartum depression on maternal mood and infant development. In L. Murray and P. J. Cooper (Eds.), *Postpartum depression and child development* (pp. 201–20). New York: Guilford Press.

Cramer, B., Robert-Tissot, C., Stern, D. N., Serpa-Rusconi, S., De Muralt, M., Besson, G., Palacio-Espasa, F., Bachmann, J., Knauer, D., Berney, C., & D'Arcis, U. (1990). Outcome evaluation in brief mother-infant psychotherapy: A preliminary report. *Infant Mental Health Journal, 11*, 278–300.

Cummings, N. A. (2008, July/August). Are graduate students being deceived? *The National Psychologist, 17*, 14.

Derogatis, L. (1983). *SCL-90-R: Administration, scoring and procedures manual II*. Towson, MD: Clinical Psychometric Research.

De Wolff, M., & van IJzendoorn, M. H. (1997). Sensitivity and attachment: A meta-analysis on parental antecedents of infant attachment. *Child Development, 68*, 571–91.

Diamond, D., Clarkin, J., Levine, H., Levy, K., Foelsch, P., & Yeomans, F. (1999). Borderline conditions and attachment: A preliminary report. *Psychoanalytic Inquiry, 19*, 831–84.

Diamond, D., Stovall-McClough, C., Clarkin, J. F., & Levy, K. N. (2003). Patient-therapist attachment in the treatment of borderline personality disorder. *Bulletin of the Menninger Clinic, 67*, 227–59.

Dozier, M. (1990). Attachment organization and treatment use for adults with serious psychopathological disorders. *Development and Psychopathology, 2*, 47–60.

——. (2003). Attachment-based treatment for vulnerable children. *Attachment and Human Development, 5*, 253–57.

Dozier, M., Cue, K. L., & Barnett, L. (1994). Clinicians as caregivers: Role of attachment organization in treatment. *Journal of Consulting and Clinical Psychology, 62*, 793–800.

Dozier, M., Dozier, D., & Manni, M. (2002). Attachment and biobehavioral catch-up: The ABC's of helping infants in foster care cope with early adversity. *Zero to Three Bulletin, 22*, 7–13.

Dozier, M., Lindhiem, O., & Ackerman, J. P. (2005). Attachment and biobehavioral catch-up: An intervention targeting empirically identified needs of foster infants. In L. J. Berlin, Y. Ziv, L. Amaya-Jackson, and M. T. Greenberg (Eds.), *Enhancing early attachments: Theory, research, intervention, and policy* (pp. 178–94). New York: Guilford Press.

Dozier, M., & Sepulveda, S. (2004). Foster mother state of mind and treatment use: Different challenges for different people. *Infant Mental Health Journal, 25*, 368–78.

Dozier, M., Stevenson, A. L., Lee, S. W., & Velligan, D. I. (1991). Attachment organization and familial overinvolvement for adults with serious psychopathological disorders. *Development and Psychopathology, 3*, 475–89.

Egeland, B., & Erickson, M. (1993). Implications of attachment theory for prevention and intervention. In S. Kramer and H. Parens (Eds.), *Prevention in mental health: Now, tomorrow, ever?* (pp. 21–50). Northvale, NJ: Jason Aronson.

Egeland, B., Weinfield, N. S., Bosquet, M., & Cheng, V. K. (2000). Remembering, repeating, and working through: Lessons from attachment-based interventions. In J. D. Osofsky and H. E. Fitzgerald (Eds.), *Handbook of infant mental health/World Association for Infant Mental Health: Vol. 4 Infant mental health in groups at high risk* (pp. 35–89). New York: Wiley.

Ellis, M. V., Ladany, N., Krengel, M., & Schult, D. (1996). Clinical supervision research from 1981 to 1993: A methodological critique. *Journal of Counseling Psychology, 43*, 35–50.

Erickson, M. F., Korfmacher, J., & Egeland, B. R. (1992). Attachments past and present: Implications for therapeutic intervention with mother-infant dyads. *Development and Psychopathology, 4*, 495–507.

Erikson, E. H. (1950). Childhood and society. New York: W. W. Norton.

Fehrenbach, P., & Coffman, S. (2001). Private practitioners in clinical trials: Supervision issues. *Behavior Therapist, 24*, 147, 148.

Feldman, M. (1997). The dynamics of reassurance. In R. Schafer (Ed.), *The contemporary Kleinians of London* (pp. 321–43). Madison, CT: International Universities Press.

Finley, K. (1990). *Shock treatment*. San Francisco: City Lights Books.

Fintzy, R. T. (1971). Vicissitudes of the transitional object in a borderline child. *International Journal of Psycho-Analysis, 52*, 107–14.

First, E. (1999). Getting worse for their sake. In D. Bassin (Ed.), *Female sexuality: Contemporary engagements* (pp. 209–19). Northvale, NJ: Jason Aronson.

Flavell, J. H., Green, F. L., & Flavell, E. R. (1986). Development of knowledge about the appearance-reality distinction. *Monographs of the Society for Research in Child Development, 51*(Serial No. 212), 1–68.

Fonagy, P., Gergely, G., Jurist, E. L., & Target, M. (2002). *Affect regulation, mentalization, and the development of the self.* New York: Other Press.

Fonagy, P., Leigh, T., Steele, M., Steele, H., Kennedy, R., Mattoon, G., Target, M., & Gerber, A. (1996). The relation of attachment status, psychiatric classification, and response to psychotherapy. *Journal of Consulting and Clinical Psychology, 64*, 22–31.

Fonagy, P., Steele, M., Steele, H., Moran, G. S., & Higgitt, A. C. (1991). The capacity for understanding mental states: The reflective self in parent and child and its significance for security of attachment. *Infant Mental Health Journal, 12*, 201–18.

Fonagy, P., & Target, M. (1996). Predictors of outcome in child psychoanalysis: A retrospective study of 763 cases at the Anna Freud Centre. *Journal of the American Psychoanalytic Association, 44*, 27–77.

——. (1997). Attachment and reflective function: Their role in self-organization. *Development and Psychopathology, 9*, 679–700.

——. (2000). Mentalization and personality disorder in children: A current perspective from the Anna Freud Centre. In T. Lubbe (Ed.), *The borderline psychotic child: A selective integration* (pp. 69–89). London: Routledge.

Fonagy, P., Target, M., Steele, H., & Steele, M. (1998). *Reflective-functioning manual, version 5: For application to Adult Attachment Interviews*, University College, London.

Fraiberg, S., Adelson, E., & Shapiro, V. (1975). Ghosts in the nursery: A psychoanalytic approach to impaired infant-mother relationships. *Journal of the American Academy of Child Psychiatry, 14*, 1387–1422.

Freud, S. (1912). Recommendations to physicians practising psycho-analysis. In J. Strachey (Ed. and Trans.), *The standard edition of the complete psychological works of Sigmund Freud* (Vol. 12, pp. 109–20). London: Hogarth Press, 1961.

——. (1914). Remembering, repeating and working-through (Further recommendations on the technique of psycho-analysis II). In J. Strachey (Ed. and Trans.), *The standard edition of the complete psychological works of Sigmund Freud* (Vol. 12, pp. 147–56). London: Hogarth Press, 1958.

——. (1933). New introductory lectures on psycho-analysis: Lecture XXXI: The dissection of the psychical personality. In J. Strachey (Ed. and Trans.), *The standard edition of the complete psychological works of Sigmund Freud* (Vol. 22, pp. 57–80). London: Hogarth Press, 1964.

Gallagher, R. E., Manierre, A., & Castelli, C. (1994). From the valley of the shadow of death: A group model for borderline patients. *The Journal of Pastoral Care, 48*, 45–53.

Gazelle, H., & Ladd, G. W. (2003). Anxious solitude and peer exclusion: A diathesis-stress model of internalizing trajectories in childhood. *Child Development, 74*, 257–78.

George, C., Kaplan, N., & Main, M. (1996). *Adult Attachment Interview* (Third ed.). Unpublished manuscript, University of California, Berkeley.

Gonsalvez, C. J., Oades, L. G., & Freestone, J. (2002). The objectives approach to clinical supervision: Towards integration and empirical evaluation. *Australian Psychologist, 37*, 68–77.

Goodman, G. (2002). *The internal world and attachment*. Hillsdale, NJ: The Analytic Press.

——. (2005a). Empirical evidence supporting the conceptual relatedness of object representations and internal working models. *Journal of the American Psychoanalytic Association, 53*, 597–617.

——. (2005b). "I feel stupid and contagious": Countertransference reactions of fledgling clinicians to patients who have negative therapeutic reactions. *American Journal of Psychotherapy, 59*, 149–68.

——. (2007a). Attachment-based intervention with prepubertal children: The impact of parent, child, and therapist mental representations on intervention points of entry. *Journal of Psychiatry and Psychology, 1*, 1–20, www.scientificjournals.org /journals2007/articles/1065.htm.

——. (2007b). Quantitatively-based methods of assessing competence in clinical supervision. *The Psychologist-Psychoanalyst, 27*, 16–23.

——. (in press). *Therapeutic attachment relationships: Interaction structures and the processes of therapeutic change*. Lanham, MD: Jason Aronson.

Goodman, G., Gerstadt, C., Pfeffer, C. R., Stroh, M., & Valdez, A. (2008). ADHD and aggression as correlates of suicidal behavior in assaultive prepubertal psychiatric inpatients. *Suicide and Life-Threatening Behavior, 38*, 46–59.

Goodman, G., Hans, S. L., & Bernstein, V. J. (2005). Mother expectation of bother and infant attachment behaviors as predictors of mother and child communication at 24 months in children of methadone-maintained women. *Infant Mental Health Journal, 26*, 549–69.

Goodman, G., & Manierre, A. (2008). Representations of God uncovered in a spirituality group of borderline inpatients. *International Journal of Group Psychotherapy, 58*, 1–15.

Goodman, G., & Pfeffer, C. R. (1998). Attachment disorganization in prepubertal children with severe emotional disturbance. *Bulletin of the Menninger Clinic, 62*, 490–525.

Goodman, G., Sapp, M. S., Stroh, M., & Valdez, A. (2007). Maternal depression, prepubertal children's representations of attachment disorganization, and the development of aggression and depression: A mediational model. In C. Yoon (Ed.), *Focus on family relations in the 21st century* (pp. 43–68). New York: Nova Science.

Graham, P. J. (Ed.). (1998). *Cognitive-behaviour therapy for children and families*. New York: Cambridge University.

Green, J., & Goldwyn, R. (2002). Annotation: Attachment disorganisation and psychopathology: New findings in attachment research and their potential implications for developmental psychopathology in childhood. *Journal of Child Psychology and Psychiatry, 43*, 835–46.

Greenberg, M. T. (1999). Attachment and psychopathology in childhood. In J. Cassidy and P. R. Shaver (Eds.), *Handbook of attachment: Theory, research, and clinical applications* (pp. 469–96). New York: Guilford Press.

Greenberg, M. T., Speltz, M. L., DeKlyen, M., & Endriga, M. C. (1991). Attachment security in preschoolers with and without externalizing behavior problems: A replication. *Development & Psychopathology, 3*, 413–30.

Greene, R. W. (1998). *The explosive child: A new approach for understanding and parenting easily frustrated, "chronically inflexible" children*. New York: HarperCollins.

Grienenberger, J., Kelly, K., & Slade, A. (2005). Maternal reflective functioning, mother-infant affective communication, and infant attachment: Exploring the link between mental states and observed caregiving behavior in the intergenerational transmission of attachment. *Attachment and Human Development, 7*, 299–311.

Grotstein, J., & Mason, A. (1995, April). *Contemporary Kleinian theory and practice.* Symposium conducted at the meeting of the Division of Psychoanalysis 39 of the American Psychological Association, Santa Monica, California.

Heimann, P. (1950). On counter-transference. *International Journal of Psycho-Analysis, 31*, 81–84.

Heinicke, C. M., Fineman, N. R., Ponce, V. A., & Guthrie, D. (2001). Relation-based intervention with at-risk mothers: Outcome in the second year of life. *Infant Mental Health Journal, 22*, 431–62.

Heinicke, C. M., Fineman, N. R., Ruth, G., Recchia, S. L., Guthrie, D., & Rodning, C. (1999). Relationship-based intervention with at-risk mothers: Outcome in the first year of life. *Infant Mental Health Journal, 20*, 349–74.

Heinicke, C. M., Goorsky, M., Moscov, S., Dudley, K., Gordon, J., Schneider, C., & Guthrie, D. (2000). Relationship-based intervention with at-risk mothers: Factors affecting variations in outcome. *Infant Mental Health Journal, 21*, 133–55.

Hesse, E. (1996). Discourse, memory, and the Adult Attachment Interview: A note with emphasis on the emerging cannot classify category. *Infant Mental Health Journal, 17*, 4–11.

Horowitz, L. M., Rosenberg, S. E., & Bartholomew, K. (1996). Interpersonal problems, attachment styles, and outcome in brief dynamic psychotherapy. *Journal of Consulting and Clinical Psychology, 61*, 549–60.

International Bible Society (1984). *The holy Bible, new international version.* Grand Rapids, MI: Zondervan.

Jones, E. E. (2000). *Therapeutic action: A guide to psychoanalytic therapy.* Northvale, NJ: Jason Aronson.

Jones, E. E., & Pulos, S. M. (1993). Comparing the process in psychodynamic and cognitive-behavioral therapies. *Journal of Consulting and Clinical Psychology, 61*, 306–16.

Joseph, B. (1987). Projective identification: Clinical aspects. In J. Sandler (Ed.), *Projection, identification, projective identification* (pp. 65–76). Madison, CT: International Universities Press.

Josephs, L., Anderson, E., Bernard, A., Fatzer, K., & Streich, J. (2004). Assessing progress in analysis interminable. *Journal of the American Psychoanalytic Association, 52*, 1185–1214.

Josephs, L., & Fatzer, K. (2006). *Therapeutic interaction with a schizoid patient.* Manuscript submitted for publication, Adelphi University, Garden City, New York.

Katsurada, E., & Sugawara, A. I. (2000). Moderating effects of mothers' attribution on the relationships between their affect and parenting behaviors and children's aggressive behaviors. *Journal of Child and Family Studies, 9*, 39–50.

Katzenstein, T. (2005, June). *Validating change: Empirical methods and clinical work.* Paper presented at the annual meeting of the American Psychoanalytic Association, Seattle, Washington.

Kernberg, O. (1975). *Borderline conditions and pathological narcissism.* New York: Jason Aronson.

———. (1980). *Internal world and external reality: Object relations theory applied.* New York: Jason Aronson.

——. (1984). *Severe personality disorders: Psychotherapeutic strategies.* New Haven, CT: Yale University Press.

——. (1986a). Borderline personality organization. In M. Stone (Ed.), *Essential papers on borderline disorders: One hundred years at the border* (pp. 279–319). New York: New York University Press.

——. (1986b). Further contributions to the treatment of narcissistic personalities. In A. Morrison (Ed.), *Essential papers on narcissism* (pp. 245–92). New York: New York University Press.

——. (1987). Discussion of Betty Joseph's paper. In J. Sandler (Ed.), *Projection, identification, projective identification* (pp. 77–91). Madison, CT: International Universities Press.

——. (1996). A psychoanalytic theory of personality disorders. In J. F. Clarkin and M. F. Lenzenweger (Eds.), *Major theories of personality disorder* (pp. 106–40). New York: Guilford Press.

——. (2003). Reply to panel follow-up questions. *Psychoanalytic Dialogues, 13,* 443, 444.

Kernberg, O. F., Selzer, M. A., Koenigsberg, H. W., Carr, A. C., & Appelbaum, A. H. (1989). *Psychodynamic psychotherapy of borderline patients.* New York: Basic Books.

Kerns, K. A., & Richardson, R. A. (Eds.). (2005). *Attachment in middle childhood.* New York: Guilford Press.

Kirkpatrick, L. A. (1999). Attachment and religious representations and behavior. In J. Cassidy and P. R. Shaver (Eds.), *Handbook of attachment: Theory, research, and clinical applications* (pp. 803–22). New York: Guilford Press.

Kirkpatrick, L. A., & Shaver, P. R. (1990). Attachment theory and religion: Childhood attachments, religious beliefs, and conversion. *Journal for the Scientific Study of Religion, 29,* 315–34.

Klein, M. (1946). Notes on some schizoid mechanisms. In R. E. Money-Kyrle (Ed.), *Envy and gratitude and other works 1946–1963* (pp. 1–24). New York: Delacorte Press, 1975.

Kobak, R. R., & Sceery, A. (1988). Attachment in late adolescence: Working models, affect regulation, and representations of self and others. *Child Development, 59,* 135–46.

Kohut, H. (1971). *The analysis of the self: A systematic approach to the psychoanalytic treatment of narcissistic personality disorders.* New York: International Universities Press.

——. (1977). *The restoration of the self.* New York: International Universities Press.

Korfmacher, J., Adam, E., Ogawa, J., & Egeland, B. (1997). Adult attachment: Implications for the therapeutic process in a home visitation intervention. *Applied Developmental Science, 1,* 43–52.

Ladany, N., & Muse-Burke, J. L. (2001). Understanding and conducting supervision research. In L. J. Bradley and N. Ladany (Eds.), *Counselor supervision: Principles, process, and practice* (Third ed., pp. 304–29). New York: Brunner-Routledge.

Lanyado, M., & Horne, A. (Eds.). (1999). *The handbook of child and adolescent psychotherapy: Psychoanalytic approaches*. Florence, KY: Routledge.

Lieberman, A. F., Weston, D. R., & Pawl, J. H. (1991). Preventive intervention and outcome with anxiously attached dyads. *Child Development, 62*, 199–209.

Lieberman, A. F., & Zeanah, C. H. (1999). Contributions of attachment theory to infant-parent psychotherapy and other interventions with infants and young children. In J. Cassidy and P. R. Shaver (Eds.), *Handbook of attachment: Theory, research, and clinical applications* (pp. 555–74). New York: Guilford Press.

Linehan, M. M. (1993). *Cognitive-behavioral treatment of borderline personality disorder*. New York: Guilford Press.

Luborsky, L., & Crits-Christoph, P. (1998). *Understanding transference: The core conflictual relationship theme method* (Second ed.). Washington, DC: American Psychological Association.

Lyons-Ruth, K., Connell, D. B., Grunebaum, H., & Botein, S. (1990). Infants at social risk: Maternal depression and family support services as mediators of infant development and security of attachment. *Child Development, 61*, 85–98.

Lyons-Ruth, K., Easterbrooks, M. A., & Cibelli, C. D. (1997). Infant attachment strategies, infant mental lag, and maternal depressive symptoms: Predictors of internalizing and externalizing problems at age 7. *Developmental Psychology, 33*, 681–92.

Lyons-Ruth, K., & Jacobvitz, D. (1999). Attachment disorganization: Unresolved loss, relational violence, and lapses in behavioral and attentional strategies. In J. Cassidy and P. R. Shaver (Eds.), *Handbook of attachment: Theory, research, and clinical applications* (pp. 520–54). New York: Guilford Press.

Main, M., & Cassidy, J. (1988). Categories of response to reunion with the parent at age 6: Predictable from infant attachment classifications and stable over a 1-month period. *Developmental Psychology, 24*, 415–26.

Main, M., & Goldwyn, R. (1994). *Adult attachment scoring and classification systems* (Sixth ed.). Unpublished manuscript, University College, London.

Main, M., & Hesse, E. (1990). Parents' unresolved traumatic experiences are related to infant disorganized attachment status: Is frightened and/or frightening parental behavior the linking mechanism? In M. T. Greenberg, D. Cicchetti, and E. M. Cummings (Eds.), *Attachment in the preschool years: Theory, research, and intervention* (pp. 161–82). Chicago: University of Chicago Press.

Main, M., Kaplan, N., & Cassidy, J. (1985). Security in infancy, childhood, and adulthood: A move to the level of representation. In I. Bretherton and E. Waters (Eds.), *Growing points in attachment theory and research. Monographs of the Society for Research in Child Development, 50*(1-2, Serial No. 209), 66–104.

Main, M., & Weston, D. R. (1981). The quality of the toddler's relationship to mother and to father: Related to conflict behavior and the readiness to establish new relationships. *Child Development, 52*, 932–40.

Mayseless, O. (2005). Ontogeny of attachment in middle childhood: Conceptualization of normative changes. In K. A. Kerns and R. A. Richardson (Eds.), *Attachment in middle childhood* (pp. 1–23). New York: Guilford Press.

McDonald, A., Beck, R., Allison, S., & Norsworthy, L. (2005). Attachment to God and parents: Testing the correspondence vs. compensation hypotheses. *Journal of Psychology and Christianity, 24*, 21–28.

McWilliams, N. (1999). *Psychoanalytic case formulation*. New York: Guilford Press.

Michels, R. (2000). The case history. *Journal of the American Psychoanalytic Association, 48*, 355–75.

Milne, D. (2006). Developing clinical supervision research through reasoned analogies with therapy. *Clinical Psychology and Psychotherapy, 13*, 215–22.

Modell, A. H. (1961). Denial and the sense of separateness. *Journal of the American Psychoanalytic Association, 9*, 533–47.

———. (1975). A narcissistic defence against affects and the illusion of self-sufficiency. *International Journal of Psycho-Analysis, 56*, 275–82.

National Institute of Mental Health (2000). *Depression in children and adolescents: A fact sheet for physicians*. Available from National Institute of Mental Health, www.nimh.nih.gov/publicat/depchildresfact.cfm.

Olds, D. L. (2005). The nurse-family partnership: Foundations in attachment theory and epidemiology. In L. J. Berlin, Y. Ziv, L. Amaya-Jackson, and M. T. Greenberg (Eds.), *Enhancing early attachments: Theory, research, intervention, and policy* (pp. 217–49). New York: Guilford Press.

Pfeffer, C. R., Conte, H. R., Plutchik, R., & Jerrett, I. (1979). Suicidal behavior in latency-age children: An empirical study. *Journal of the American Academy of Child Psychiatry, 18*, 679–92.

Pianta, R. C., Egeland, B., & Adam, E. K. (1996). Adult attachment classification and self-reported psychiatric symptomatology as assessed by the Minnesota Multiphasic Personality Inventory-2. *Journal of Consulting and Clinical Psychology, 64*, 273–81.

Pine, F. (1985). *Developmental theory and clinical process*. New Haven, CT: Yale University Press.

Racker, H. (1968). *Transference and countertransference*. New York: International Universities Press.

Reid, J. B., Patterson, G. R., & Snyder, J. (Eds.). (2002). *Antisocial behavior in children and adolescents: A developmental analysis and model for intervention*. Washington, DC: American Psychological Association.

Rivieré, J. (1936). A contribution to the analysis of the negative therapeutic reaction. *International Journal of Psycho-Analysis, 17*, 304–20.

Rizzuto, A.-M. (1979). *The birth of the living God: A psychoanalytic study*. Chicago: The University of Chicago Press.

Rosenfeld, H. (1952). Notes on the psycho-analysis of the superego conflict in an acute catatonic schizophrenic. *International Journal of Psycho-Analysis, 33*, 111–31.

Rosenzweig, S. (1936). Some implicit common factors in diverse methods of psychotherapy. *American Journal of Orthopsychiatry, 6*, 412–15.

Routh, C. P., Hill, J. H., Steele, H., Elliot, C. E., & Dewey, M. E. (1995). Maternal attachment status, psychosocial stressors, and problem behavior: Follow-up after parent training courses for conduct disorder. *Journal of Child Psychology and Psychiatry, 36*, 1179–98.

Russell, R. K., Crimmings, A. M., & Lent, R. W. (1984). Counselor training and supervision: Theory and research. In S. D. Brown and R. W. Lent (Eds.), *Handbook of counseling psychology* (pp. 625–81). New York: John Wiley.

Rutter, M. (1985). Resilience in the face of adversity: Protective factors and resistance to psychiatric disorders. *British Journal of Psychiatry, 147*, 598–611.

———. (1987). Psychosocial resilience and protective mechanisms. *American Journal of Orthopsychiatry, 57*, 316–31.

Sameroff, A. J. (1975). Transactional models in early social relations. *Human Development, 18*, 65–79.

Schafer, R. (1983). *The analytic attitude*. New York: Basic Books.

Schneider, C. (2004). The development of the child psychotherapy Q-set. (Doctoral dissertation, University of California, Berkeley, 2004). *Dissertation Abstracts International, 65*(2-B), 1039.

Schneider, C., & Jones, E. E. (2004). *Child Psychotherapy Q-Set coding manual.* Unpublished manuscript, University of California, Berkeley.

Schneider, C., Pruetzel-Thomas, A., & Midgley, N. (in press). Discovering new ways of seeing and speaking about psychotherapy process: The Child Psychotherapy Q-Set. In N. Midgley, J. Anderson, E. Grainger, T. Nesic-Vuckovic, and C. Urwin (Eds.), *Child psychotherapy and research: New approaches, emerging findings.* New York: Routledge.

Seligman, S. (1991). Conceptual and methodological issues in the study of internal representation: A commentary on *Infant Mental Health Journal*, volume 10.3. *Infant Mental Health Journal, 12*, 126–29.

Silverman, D. K. (2001). Sexuality and attachment: A passionate relationship or a marriage of convenience? *Psychoanalytic Quarterly, 70*, 325–58.

Slade, A. (1999). Attachment theory and research: Implications for the theory and practice of individual psychotherapy with adults. In J. Cassidy and P. R. Shaver (Eds.), *Handbook of attachment: Theory, research, and clinical applications* (pp. 575–94). New York: Guilford Press.

Slade, A., Grienenberger, J., Bernbach, E., Levy, D., & Locker, A. (2005). Maternal reflective functioning, attachment, and the transmission gap: A preliminary study. *Attachment and Human Development, 7*, 283–98.

Slade, A., Sadler, L. S., & Mayes, L. C. (2005). Minding the baby: Enhancing parental reflective functioning in a nursing/mental health home visiting program. In L. J. Berlin, Y. Ziv, L. Amaya-Jackson, and M. T. Greenberg (Eds.), *Enhancing early attachments: Theory, research, intervention, and policy* (pp. 152–77). New York: Guilford Press.

Solomon, J., & George, C. (Eds.). (1999a). *Attachment disorganization*. New York: Guilford Press.

———. (1999b). The measurement of attachment security in infancy and childhood. In J. Cassidy and P. R. Shaver (Eds.), *Handbook of attachment: Theory, research, and clinical applications* (pp. 287–316). New York: Guilford Press.

———. (1999c). The place of disorganization in attachment theory: Linking classic observations with contemporary findings. In J. Solomon and C. George (Eds.), *Attachment disorganization* (pp. 3–32). New York: Guilford Press.

Solomon, J., George, C., & De Jong, A. (1995). Children classified as controlling at age six: Evidence of disorganized representational strategies and aggression at home and at school. *Development and Psychopathology, 7*, 447–63.

Spiegel, S. (1989). *An interpersonal approach to child therapy: The treatment of children and adolescents from an interpersonal point of view*. New York: Columbia University Press.

Spieker, S., Nelson, D., DeKlyen, M., & Staerkel, F. (2005). Enhancing early attachments in the context of Early Head Start: Can programs emphasizing family support improve rates of secure infant-mother attachments in low-income families? In L. J. Berlin, Y. Ziv, L. Amaya-Jackson, and M. T. Greenberg (Eds.), *Enhancing early attachments: Theory, research, intervention, and policy* (pp. 250–75). New York: Guilford Press.

Sroufe, L. A. (1985). Attachment classification from the perspective of infant-caregiver relationships and infant temperament. *Child Development, 56*, 1–14.

———. (1988). The role of infant-caregiver attachment in development. In J. Belsky and T. Nezworski (Eds.), *Clinical implications of attachment* (pp. 18–38). Hillsdale, NJ: Erlbaum.

Sroufe, L. A., & Rutter, M. (1984). The domain of developmental psychopathology. *Child Development, 55*, 17–29.

Stern, D. N. (1985). *The interpersonal world of the infant: A view from psychoanalysis and developmental psychology*. New York: Basic Books.

———. (1995). *The motherhood constellation: A unified view of parent-infant psychotherapy*. New York: Basic Books.

Stern-Bruschweiler, N., & Stern, D. N. (1989). A model for conceptualizing the role of the mother's representational world in various mother-infant therapies. *Infant Mental Health Journal, 10*, 142–56.

Tansey, M. J., & Burke, W. F. (1989). *Understanding countertransference: From projective identification to empathy*. Hillsdale, NJ: The Analytic Press.

Target, M., & Fonagy, P. (1994a). The efficacy of psychoanalysis for children: Developmental considerations. *Journal of the American Academy of Child and Adolescent Psychiatry, 33*, 1134–44.

———. (1994b). The efficacy of psychoanalysis for children with emotional disorders. *Journal of the American Academy of Child and Adolescent Psychiatry, 33*, 361–71.

Truman, S., Levy, D., & Mayes, L. (in press). Reflective functioning as mediator between drug use, parenting stress, and child behavior. *Attachment and Human Development*.

Tsui, M. (1997). Empirical research on social work supervision: The state of the art (1970–1995). *Journal of Social Service Research, 23*, 39–54.

Tyrrell, C. L., Dozier, M., Teague, G. B., & Fallot, R. D. (1999). Effective treatment relationships for persons with serious psychiatric disorders: The importance of attachment states of mind. *Journal of Consulting and Clinical Psychology, 67*, 725–33.

van den Boom, D. C. (1994). The influence of temperament and mothering on attachment and exploration: An experimental manipulation of sensitive responsiveness among lower-class mothers with irritable infants. *Child Development, 65*, 1457–77.

——. (1995). Do first-year intervention effects endure? Follow-up during toddlerhood of a sample of Dutch irritable infants. *Child Development, 66*, 1798–1816.

van IJzendoorn, M. H. (1995). Adult attachment representations, parental responsiveness, and infant attachment: A meta-analysis on the predictive validity of the Adult Attachment Interview. *Psychological Bulletin, 117*, 387–403.

van IJzendoorn, M., Bakermans-Kranenburg, M. J., & Juffer, F. (2005). Why less is more: From the dodo bird verdict to evidence-based interventions on sensitivity and early attachments. In L. J. Berlin, Y. Ziv, L. Amaya-Jackson, and M. T. Greenberg (Eds.), *Enhancing early attachments: Theory, research, intervention, and policy* (pp. 297–312). New York: Guilford Press.

van IJzendoorn, M. H., Juffer, F., & Duyvesteyn, M. G. C. (1995). Breaking the intergenerational cycle of insecure attachment: A review of the effects of attachment-based interventions on maternal sensitivity and infant security. *Journal of Child Psychology and Psychiatry, 36*, 225–48.

van IJzendoorn, M. H., & Sagi, A. (1999). Cross-cultural patterns of attachment: Universal and contextual dimensions. In J. Cassidy and P. R. Shaver (Eds.), *Handbook of attachment: Theory, research, and clinical applications* (pp. 713–34). New York: Guilford Press.

van IJzendoorn, M. H., Schuengel, C., & Bakermans-Kranenburg, M. J. (1999). Disorganized attachment in early childhood: Meta-Analysis of precursors, concomitants, and sequelae. *Development and Psychopathology, 11*, 225–49.

Volkan, V. D. (1973). Transitional fantasies in the analysis of a narcissistic personality. *Journal of the American Psychoanalytic Association, 21*, 351–76.

Vygotsky, L. (1978). *Mind in society: The development of higher psychological processes*. Cambridge, MA: Harvard University Press.

Wampold, B. E. (2001). *The great psychotherapy debate: Models, methods, and findings*. Mahwah, NJ: Erlbaum.

Warrick-Swansen, S. A. (1999). Risk factors of comorbidity between aggressive behaviors and depressive disorders in school-aged children. *Dissertation Abstracts International, 59* (7-B), 3742.

Waters, E., & Cummings, E. M. (2000). A secure base from which to explore close relationships. *Child Development, 71*, 164–72.

Waters, E., & Deane, K. E. (1985). Defining and assessing individual differences in attachment relationships: Q-methodology and the organization of behavior in infancy and early childhood. In I. Bretherton and E. Waters (Eds.), *Growing points in attachment theory and research. Monographs of the Society for Research in Child Development, 50* (1-2, Serial No. 209), 41–65.

Watkins, C. E., Jr. (Ed.). (1997). *Handbook of psychotherapy supervision*. Hoboken, NJ: John Wiley.

Watson, T. S., & Gresham, F. M. (Eds.). (1998). *Handbook of child behavior therapy*. New York: Plenum.

Weinfield, N. S., Sroufe, L. A., Egeland, B., & Carlson, E. A. (1999). The nature of individual differences in infant-caregiver attachment. In J. Cassidy and P. R. Shaver (Eds.), *Handbook of attachment: Theory, research, and clinical applications* (pp. 68–88). New York: Guilford Press.

Westen, D. (1993). *Social cognition and object relations scale: Q-sort and TAT data (SCORS-Q)* (Rev. ed.). Unpublished manuscript, Harvard University Medical School, Cambridge, Massachusetts.

——. (1995). *Social Cognition and Object Relations Scale—Global Ratings (SCORS-G)*. Unpublished manuscript, Harvard University Medical School, Cambridge, Massachusetts.

Westen, D., Nakash, O., Thomas, C., & Bradley, R. (2006). Clinical assessment of attachment patterns and personality disorder in adolescents and adults. *Journal of Consulting and Clinical Psychology, 74*, 1065–85.

Westen, D., Novotny, C. M., & Thompson-Brenner, H. (2004). The empirical status of empirically supported psychotherapies: Assumptions, findings, and reporting in controlled clinical trials. *Psychological Bulletin, 130*, 631–63.

Williams, S., & Harper, J. (1979). Depression in childhood: I. Clinical correlates of depressed children admitted for treatment to a residential program. *Australian and New Zealand Journal of Psychiatry, 13*, 248–54.

Winnicott, D. W. (1950). Hate in the counter-transference. *International Journal of Psycho-Analysis, 30*, 69–74.

——. (1953). Transitional objects and transitional phenomena. *International Journal of Psycho-Analysis, 34*, 89–97.

——. (1971). *Playing and reality*. New York: Basic Books.

Author Index

Subject Index

About the Author

Geoff Goodman, PhD, is associate professor of psychology at Long Island University. He is also a licensed clinical and school psychologist with a private practice in Manhattan and New City and is certified by the American Board of Professional Psychology (ABPP). Goodman earned a PhD in clinical psychology from Northwestern University, and he completed a child clinical psychology internship at Babies Hospital, Columbia-Presbyterian Medical Center, a two-year postdoctoral fellowship in developmental research at Columbia University under Larry Aber, and a two-year postdoctoral fellowship in the research and treatment of borderline personality disorder under Frank Yeomans and Otto Kernberg.

Goodman was instructor of psychology in psychiatry at Cornell University Medical College from 1995 to 1998 and was assistant unit chief of the children's psychiatric inpatient unit. He also holds adjunct faculty positions at Columbia University and Weill Medical College of Cornell University, and he is an advanced candidate in the child and adult programs at the Psychoanalytic Training Institute of the New York Freudian Society. Goodman is the author of over a dozen articles on the development of psychopathology in high-risk infants, children, and adults and of *The Internal World and Attachment* (2002).

www.ingramcontent.com/pod-product-compliance
Lightning Source LLC
Chambersburg PA
CBHW051252200926
51612CB00001B/17
9780765707093